# **FREE** Test Taking Tips DVD Offer

To help us better serve you, we have developed a Test Taking Tips DVD that we would like to give you for FREE. **This DVD covers world-class test taking tips that you can use to be even more successful when you are taking your test.**

All that we ask is that you email us your feedback about your study guide. Please let us know what you thought about it – whether that is good, bad or indifferent.

To get your **FREE Test Taking Tips DVD**, email freedvd@studyguideteam.com with "FREE DVD" in the subject line and the following information in the body of the email:

a. The title of your study guide.

b. Your product rating on a scale of 1-5, with 5 being the highest rating.

c. Your feedback about the study guide. What did you think of it?

d. Your full name and shipping address to send your free DVD.

If you have any questions or concerns, please don't hesitate to contact us at freedvd@studyguideteam.com.

Thanks again!

# FTCE General Knowledge Test Prep 2015-2016

## Table of Contents

## *Quick Overview*

As you draw closer to taking your exam, preparing becomes more and more important. Thankfully, you have this study guide to help you get ready. Use this guide to help keep your studying on track and refer to it often.

This study guide contains several key sections that will help you be successful on your exam. The guide contains tips for what you should do the night before and the day of the test. Also included are test-taking tips. Knowing the right information is not always enough. Many well-prepared test takers struggle with exams. These tips will help equip you to accurately read, assess, and answer test questions.

A large part of the guide is devoted to showing you what content to expect on the exam and to helping you better understand that content. Near the end of this guide is a practice test so that you can see how well you have grasped the content. Then, answers explanations are provided so that you can understand why you missed certain questions.

Don't try to cram the night before you take your exam. This is not a wise strategy for a few reasons. First, your retention of the information will be low. Your time would be better used by reviewing information you already know rather than trying to learn lots of new information. Second, you will likely become stressed as you try to gain large amount of knowledge in a short amount of time. Third, you will be depriving yourself of sleep. So be sure to go to bed at a reasonable time the night before. Being well-rested helps you focus and remain calm.

Be sure to eat a substantial breakfast the morning of the exam. If you are taking the exam in the afternoon, be sure to have a good lunch as well. Being hungry is distracting and can make it difficult to focus. You have hopefully spent lots of time preparing for the exam. Don't let an empty stomach get in the way of success!

When travelling to the testing center, leave earlier than needed. That way, you have a buffer in case you experience any delays. This will help you remain calm and will keep you from missing your appointment time at the testing center.

Be sure to pace yourself during the exam. Don't try to rush through the exam. There is no need to risk performing poorly on the exam just so you can leave the testing center early. Allow yourself to use all of the allotted time if needed.

Remain positive while taking the exam even if you feel like you are performing poorly. Thinking about the content you should have mastered will not help you perform better on the exam.

Once the exam is complete, take some time to relax. Even if you feel that you need to take the exam again, you will be well served by some down time before you begin studying again. It's often easier to convince yourself to study if you know that it will come with a reward!

# *Test-Taking Strategies*

### 1. Predicting the Answer

When you feel confident in your preparation for a multiple-choice test, try predicting the answer before reading the answer choices. This is especially useful on questions that test objective factual knowledge or that ask you to fill in a blank. By predicting the answer before reading the available choices, you eliminate the possibility that you will be distracted or led astray by an incorrect answer choice. You will feel much more confident in your selection if you read the question, predict the answer, and then find your prediction among the answer choices. After using this strategy, be sure to still read all of the answer choices carefully and completely. If you feel unprepared, you should not attempt to predict the answers. This would be a waste of time and an opportunity for your mind to wander in the wrong direction.

### 2. Reading the Whole Question

Too often, test takers scan a multiple-choice question, recognize a few familiar words, and immediately jump to the answer choices. Test authors are aware of this common impatience, and they will sometimes prey upon it. For instance, a test author might subtly turn the question into a negative, or he or she might redirect the focus of the question right at the end. The only way to avoid falling into these traps is to read the entirety of the question carefully before reading the answer choices.

### 3. Looking for Wrong Answers

Long and complicated multiple-choice questions can be intimidating. One way to simplify a difficult multiple-choice question is to eliminate all of the answer choices that are clearly wrong. In most sets of answers, there will be at least one selection that can be dismissed right away. If the test is administered on paper, the test taker could draw a line through it to indicate that it may be ignored; otherwise, the test taker will have to perform this operation mentally or on scratch paper. In either case, once the obviously incorrect answers have been eliminated, the remaining choices may be considered. Sometimes identifying the clearly wrong answers will give the test taker some information about the correct answer. For instance, if one of the remaining answer choices is a direct opposite of one of the eliminated answer choices, it may well be the correct answer. The opposite of obviously wrong is obviously right! Of course, this is not always the case. Some answers are obviously incorrect simply because they are irrelevant to the question being asked. Still, identifying and eliminating some incorrect answer choices is a good way to simplify a multiple-choice question.

### 4. Don't Overanalyze

Anxious test takers often overanalyze questions. When you are nervous, your brain will often run wild causing you to make associations and discover clues that don't actually exist. If you feel that this may be a problem for you, do whatever you can to slow down during the test. Try taking a deep breath or counting to ten. As you read and consider the question, restrict yourself to the particular words used by the author. Avoid thought tangents about what the author *really* meant, or what he or she was *trying* to say. The only things that matter on a multiple-choice test are the words that are actually in the question. You must avoid reading too much into a multiple-choice question, or supposing that the writer meant something other than what he or she wrote.

### 5. No Need for Panic

It is wise to learn as many strategies as possible before taking a multiple-choice test, but it is likely that you will come across a few questions for which you simply don't know the answer. In this situation, avoid panicking. Because most multiple-choice tests include dozens of questions, the relative value of a single wrong answer is small. Moreover, your failure on one question has no effect on your success elsewhere on the test. As much as possible, you should compartmentalize each question on a multiple-choice test. In other words, you should not allow your feelings about one question to affect your success on the others. When you find a question that you either don't understand or don't know how to answer, just take a deep breath and do your best. Read the entire question slowly and carefully. Try rephrasing the question a couple of different ways. Then, read all of the answer choices carefully. After eliminating obviously wrong answers, make a selection and move on to the next question.

### 6. Confusing Answer Choices

When working on a difficult multiple-choice question, there may be a tendency to focus on the answer choices that are the easiest to understand. Many people, whether consciously or not, gravitate to the answer choices that require the least concentration, knowledge, and memory. This is a mistake. When you come across an answer choice that is confusing, you need to give it extra attention. A question might be confusing because you do not know the subject matter to which it refers. If this is the case, don't eliminate the answer before you have affirmatively settled on another. When you come across an answer choice of this type, set it aside as you look at the remaining choices. If you can confidently assert that one of the other choices is correct, you can leave the confusing answer aside. Otherwise, you will need to take a moment to try to better understand the confusing answer choice. Rephrasing is one way to tease out the sense of a confusing answer choice.

### 7. Your First Instinct

Many people struggle with multiple-choice tests because they overthink the questions. If you have studied sufficiently for the test, you should be prepared to trust your first instinct once you have carefully and completely read the question and all of the answer choices. There is a great deal of research to suggest that the mind can come to the correct conclusion very quickly once it has obtained all of the relevant information. At times, it may seem to you as if your intuition is working faster even than your reasoning mind. This may in fact be true. The knowledge you obtain while studying may be retrieved from your subconscious before you have a chance to work out the associations that support it. Verify your instinct by working out the reasons that it should be trusted.

### 8. Key Words

Many test takers struggle with multiple-choice questions because they have poor reading comprehension skills. Quickly reading and understanding a multiple-choice question requires a mixture of skill and experience. To help with this, try jotting down a few key words and phrases on a piece of scrap paper. Doing this concentrates the process of reading and forces the mind to weigh the relative importance of the question's parts. In selecting words and phrases to write down, the test taker thinks about the question more deeply and carefully. This is especially true for multiple-choice questions that are preceded by a long prompt.

**9. Subtle Negatives**

One of the oldest tricks in the multiple-choice test writer's book is to subtly reverse the meaning of a question with a word like *not* or *except.* If you are not paying attention to each word in the question, you can easily be led astray by this trick. For instance, a common question format is, "Which of the following is...?" Obviously, if the question instead is, "Which of the following is not....?," then the answer will be quite different. Even worse, the test makers are aware of the potential for this mistake and will include one answer choice that would be correct if the question were not negated or reversed. A test taker who misses the reversal will find what he or she believes to be a correct answer and will be so confident that he or she will fail to reread the question and discover the original error. The only way to avoid this is to practice a wide variety of multiple-choice questions and to pay close attention to each and every word.

**10. Reading Every Answer Choice**

It may seem obvious, but you should always read every one of the answer choices! Too many test takers fall into the habit of scanning the question and assuming that they understand the question because they recognize a few key words. From there, they pick the first answer choice that answers the question they believe they have read. Test takers who read all of the answer choices might discover that one of the latter answer choices is actually *more* correct. Moreover, reading all of the answer choices can remind you of facts related to the question that can help you arrive at the correct answer. Sometimes, a misstatement or incorrect detail in one of the latter answer choices will trigger your memory of the subject and will enable you to find the right answer. Failing to read all of the answer choices is like not reading all of the items on a restaurant menu. You might miss out on the perfect choice.

**11. Spot the Hedges**

One of the keys to success on multiple-choice tests is paying close attention to every word. This is never more true than with words like *almost*, *most*, *some*, and *sometimes*. These words are called "hedges", because they indicate that a statement is not totally true or not true in every place and time. An absolute statement will contain no hedges, but in many subjects, like literature and history, the answers are not always straightforward. There are always exceptions to the rules in these subjects. For this reason, you should favor those multiple-choice questions that contain hedging language. The presence of qualifying words indicates that the author is taking special care with his or her words, which is certainly important when composing the right answer. After all, there are many ways to be wrong, but there is only one way to be right! For this reason, it is wise when taking a multiple-choice test to avoid answers that are absolute. An absolute answer is one that says things are either all one way or all another. They often include words like *every*, *always*, *best*, and *never.* If you are taking a multiple-choice test in a subject that doesn't lend itself to absolute answers, be on your guard if you see any of these words.

**12. Long Answers**

In many subject areas, the answers are not simple. As already mentioned, the right answer often requires hedges. Another common feature of the answers to a complex or subjective question are qualifying clauses, which are groups of words that subtly modify the meaning of the sentence. If the question or answer choice describes a rule to which there are exceptions or the subject matter is complicated, ambiguous, or confusing, the correct answer will require many words in order to be expressed clearly and accurately. In essence, you should not be deterred by answer choices that seem excessively long. Oftentimes, the author of the text will not be able to write the correct answer without offering some qualifications and modifications. As a test taker, your job is to read the answer choices thoroughly and completely and to select the one that most accurately and precisely answers the question.

**13. Restating to Understand**

Sometimes, a question on a multiple-choice test is difficult not because of what it asks but because of how it is written. If this is the case, restate the question or answer choice in different words. This process serves a couple of important purposes. First, it forces you to concentrate on the core of the question. In order to rephrase the question accurately, you have to understand it well. Rephrasing the question will concentrate your mind on the key words and ideas. Second, it will present the information to your mind in a fresh way. This process may trigger your memory of some useful scrap of information picked up while studying.

**14. True Statements**

Sometimes an answer choice will be true in itself, but it does not answer the question. This is one of the main reasons why it is essential to read the question carefully and completely before proceeding to the answer choices. Too often, test takers skip ahead to the answer choices and look for true statements. Having found one of these, they are content to select it without reference to the question above. Obviously, this provides an easy way for test makers to play tricks. The savvy test taker will always read the entire question before turning to the answer choices. Then, having settled on a correct answer choice, he or she will refer to the original question and ensure that the selected answer is relevant. The mistake of choosing a correct-but-irrelevant answer choice is especially common on questions related to specific pieces of objective knowledge, like historical or scientific facts. A prepared test taker will have a wealth of factual knowledge at his or her disposal, but may be careless in its application.

**15. No Patterns**

One of the more dangerous ideas that circulate about multiple-choice tests is that the correct answers tend to fall into patterns. These erroneous ideas range from a belief that B and C are the most common right answers, to the idea that an unprepared test-taker should answer "A-B-A-C-A-D-A-B-A." It cannot be emphasized enough that pattern-seeking of this type is exactly the WRONG way to approach a multiple-choice test. To begin with, it is highly unlikely that the test maker will plot the correct answers according to some predetermined pattern. The questions are scrambled and delivered in a random order. Furthermore, even if the test maker was following a pattern in the assignation of correct answers, there is no reason why the test maker would know which pattern he or she was using. Any attempt to discern a pattern in the answer choices is a waste of time and a distraction from the real work of taking the test. A test taker would be much better served by extra preparation before the test than by reliance on a pattern in the answers.

# Essays and Reading

## Understanding literature

Reading literature is a different experience than reading non-fiction works. Our imagination is more active as we review what we have read, imagine ourselves as characters in the novel, and try to guess what will happen next. Suspense, surprise, fantasy, fear, anxiety, compassion, and a host of other emotions and feelings may be stirred by a provocative novel.

Reading longer works of fiction is a cumulative process. Some elements of a novel have a great impact, while others may go virtually unnoticed. Therefore, as novels are read with a critical eye to language, it is helpful to perceive and identify larger patterns and movements in the work as a whole. This will benefit the reader by placing characters and events in perspective, and will enrich the reading experience greatly. Novels should be savored rather than gulped. Careful reading and thoughtful analysis of the major themes of the novel are essential to a clear understanding of the work.

One of the most important skills in reading comprehension is the identification of **topics** and **main ideas.** There is a subtle difference between these two features. The topic is the subject of a text, or what the text is about. The main idea, on the other hand, is the most important point being made by the author. The topic is usually expressed in a few words at the most, while the main idea often needs a full sentence to be completely defined. As an example, a short passage might have the topic of penguins and the main idea *Penguins are different from other birds in many ways.* In most nonfiction writing, the topic and the main idea will be stated directly, often in a sentence at the very beginning or end of the text. When being tested on an understanding of the author's topic, the reader can quickly *skim* the passage for the general idea, stopping to read only the first sentence of each paragraph. A paragraph's first sentence is often (but not always) the main topic sentence, and it gives you a summary of the content of the paragraph. However, there are cases in which the reader must figure out an unstated topic or main idea. In these instances, the student must read every sentence of the text, and try to come up with an overarching idea that is supported by each of those sentences.

While the main idea is the overall premise of a story, **supporting details** provide evidence and backing for the main point. In order to show that a main idea is correct, or valid, the author needs to add details that prove their point. All texts contain details, but they are only classified as supporting details when they serve to reinforce some larger point. Supporting details are most commonly found in informative and persuasive texts. In some cases, they will be clearly indicated with words like *for example* or *for instance*, or they will be enumerated with words like *first, second*, and *last*. However, they may not be indicated with special words. As a reader, it is important to consider whether the author's supporting details really back up his or her main point. Supporting details can be factual and correct but still not relevant to the author's point. Conversely, supporting details can seem pertinent but be ineffective because they are based on opinion or assertions that cannot be proven.

An example of a main idea is: “Giraffes live in the Serengeti of Africa.” A supporting detail about giraffes could be: “A giraffe uses its long neck to reach twigs and leaves on trees.” The main idea gives the general idea that the text is about giraffes. The supporting detail gives a specific fact about how the giraffes eat.

As opposed to a main idea, themes are seldom expressed directly in a text, so they can be difficult to identify. A **theme** is an issue, an idea, or a question raised by the text. For instance, a theme of William Shakespeare's *Hamlet* is indecision, as the title character explores his own psyche and the results of his failure to make bold choices. A great work of literature may have many themes, and the reader is justified in identifying any for which he or she can find support.

One common characteristic of themes is that they raise more questions than they answer. In a good piece of fiction, the author is not always trying to convince the reader, but is instead trying to elevate the reader's perspective and encourage him to consider the themes more deeply. When reading, one can identify themes by constantly asking what general issues the text is addressing. A good way to evaluate an author's approach to a theme is to begin reading with a question in mind (for example, how does this text approach the theme of love?) and then look for evidence in the text that addresses that question.

**Purposes for writing**

In order to be an effective reader, one must pay attention to the author's **position** and purpose. Even those texts that seem objective and impartial, like textbooks, have some sort of position and bias. Readers need to take these positions into account when considering the author's message. When an author uses emotional language or clearly favors one side of an argument, his position is clear. However, the author's position may be evident not only in what he writes, but in what he doesn't write. For this reason, it is sometimes necessary to review some other texts on the same topic in order to develop a view of the author's position. If this is not possible, then it may be useful to acquire a little background personal information about the author. When the only source of information is the text, however, the reader should look for language and argumentation that seems to indicate a particular stance on the subject.

Identifying the **purpose** of an author is usually easier than identifying her position. In most cases, the author has no interest in hiding his or her purpose. A text that is meant to entertain, for instance, should be obviously written to please the reader. Most narratives, or stories, are written to entertain, though they may also inform or persuade. Informative texts are easy to identify as well. The most difficult purpose of a text to identify is persuasion, because the author has an interest in making this purpose hard to detect. When a person knows that the author is trying to convince him, he is automatically more wary and skeptical of the argument. For this reason persuasive texts often try to establish an entertaining tone, hoping to amuse the reader into agreement, or an informative tone, hoping to create an appearance of authority and objectivity.

An author's purpose is often evident in the organization of the text. For instance, if the text has headings and subheadings, if key terms are in bold, and if the author makes his main idea clear from the beginning, then the likely purpose of the text is to inform. If the author begins by making a claim and then makes various arguments to support that claim, the purpose is probably to persuade. If the author is telling a story, or is more interested in holding the attention of the reader than in making a particular point or delivering information, then his purpose is most likely to entertain. As a reader, it is best to judge an author on how well he accomplishes his purpose. In other words, it is not entirely fair to complain that a textbook is boring: if the text is clear and easy to understand, then the author has done his job. Similarly, a storyteller should not be judged too harshly for getting some facts wrong, so long as he is able to give pleasure to the reader.

The author's purpose for writing will affect his writing style and the response of the reader. In a **persuasive essay**, the author is attempting to change the reader's mind or convince him of something he did not believe previously. There are several identifying characteristics of persuasive writing. One is opinion presented as fact. When an author attempts to persuade the reader, he often presents his or her opinions as if they were fact. A reader must be on guard for statements that sound factual but which cannot be subjected to research, observation, or experiment. Another characteristic of persuasive writing is emotional language. An author will often try to play on the reader's emotion by appealing to his sympathy or sense of morality. When an author uses colorful or evocative language with the intent of arousing the reader's passions, it is likely that he is attempting to persuade. Finally, in many cases a persuasive text will give an unfair explanation of opposing positions, if these positions are mentioned at all.

An **informative text** is written to educate and enlighten the reader. Informative texts are almost always nonfiction, and are rarely structured as a story. The intention of an informative text is to deliver information in the most comprehensible way possible, so the structure of the text is likely to be very clear. In an informative text, the thesis statement is often in the first sentence. The author may use some colorful language, but is likely to put more emphasis on clarity and precision. Informative essays do not typically appeal to the emotions. They often contain facts and figures, and rarely include the opinion of the author. Sometimes a persuasive essay can resemble an informative essay, especially if the author maintains an even tone and presents his or her views as if they were established fact.

The success or failure of an author's intent to **entertain** is determined by those who read the author's work. Entertaining texts may be either fiction or nonfiction, and they may describe real or imagined people, places, and events. Entertaining texts are often narratives, or stories. A text that is written to entertain is likely to contain colorful language that engages the imagination and the emotions. Such writing often features a great deal of figurative language, which typically enlivens its subject matter with images and analogies. Though an entertaining text is not usually written to persuade or inform, it may accomplish both of these tasks. An entertaining text may appeal to the reader's emotions and cause him or her to think differently about a particular subject. In any case, entertaining texts tend to showcase the personality of the author more so than do other types of writing.

When an author intends to **express feelings,** she may use colorful and evocative language. An author may write emotionally for any number of reasons. Sometimes, the author will do so because she is describing a personal situation of great pain or happiness. Sometimes an author is attempting to persuade the reader, and so will use emotion to stir up the passions. It can be easy to identify this kind of expression when the writer uses phrases like *I felt* and *I sense*. However, sometimes the author will simply describe feelings without introducing them. As a reader, it is important to recognize when an author is expressing emotion, and not to become overwhelmed by sympathy or passion. A reader should maintain some detachment so that he or she can still evaluate the strength of the author's argument or the quality of the writing.

In a sense, almost all writing is descriptive, insofar as it seeks to describe events, ideas, or people to the reader. Some texts, however, are primarily concerned with **description**. A descriptive text focuses on a particular subject, and attempts to depict it in a way that will be clear to the reader. Descriptive texts contain many adjectives and adverbs, words that give shades of meaning and create a more detailed mental picture for the reader. A descriptive text fails when it is unclear or vague to the reader. On the other hand, however, a descriptive text that compiles too much detail can be boring and overwhelming to the reader. A descriptive text will certainly be informative, and it may be persuasive and entertaining as well. Descriptive writing is a challenge for the author, but when it is done well, it can be fun to read.

**Writing devices**

Authors will use different stylistic and writing devices to make their meaning more clearly understood. One of those devices is comparison and contrast. When an author describes the ways in which two things are alike, he or she is **comparing** them. When the author describes the ways in which two things are different, he or she is **contrasting** them. The "compare and contrast" essay is one of the most common forms in nonfiction. It is often signaled with certain words: a comparison may be indicated with such words as *both*, *same*, *like*, *too*, and *as well*; while a contrast may be indicated by words like *but*, *however*, *on the other hand*, *instead*, and *yet*. Of course, comparisons and contrasts may be implicit without using any such signaling language. A single sentence may both compare and contrast. Consider the sentence *Brian and Sheila love* *ice cream, but Brian prefers vanilla and Sheila prefers strawberry*. In one sentence, the author has described both a similarity (love of ice cream) and a difference (favorite flavor).

One of the most common text structures is **cause and effect**. A cause is an act or event that makes something happen, and an effect is the thing that happens as a result of that cause. A cause-and-effect relationship is not always explicit, but there are some words in English that signal causality, such as *since*, *because*, and *as a result*. As an example, consider the sentence *Because the sky was clear, Ron did not bring an umbrella*. The cause is the clear sky, and the effect is that Ron did not bring an umbrella. However, sometimes the cause-and-effect relationship will not be clearly noted. For instance, the sentence *He was late and missed the meeting* does not contain any signaling words, but it still contains a cause (he was late) and an effect (he missed the meeting). It is possible for a single cause to have multiple effects, or for a single effect to have multiple causes. Also, an effect can in turn be the cause of another effect, in what is known as a cause-and-effect chain.

Authors often use analogies to add meaning to the text. An **analogy** is a comparison of two things. The words in the analogy are connected by a certain, often undetermined relationship. Look at this analogy: moo is to cow as quack is to duck. This analogy compares the sound that a cow makes with the sound that a duck makes. Even if the word 'quack' was not given, one could figure out it is the correct word to complete the analogy based on the relationship between the words 'moo' and 'cow'. Some common relationships for analogies include synonyms, antonyms, part to whole, definition, and actor to action.

Another element that impacts a text is the author's point of view. The **point of view** of a text is the perspective from which it is told. The author will always have a point of view about a story before he draws up a plot line. The author will know what events they want to take place, how they want the characters to interact, and how the story will resolve. An author will also have an opinion on the topic, or series of events, which is presented in the story, based on their own prior experience and beliefs. The two main points of view that authors use are first person and third person. If the narrator of the story is also the main character, or *protagonist*, the text is written in first-person point of view. In first person, the author writes with the word *I*. Third-person point of view is probably the most common point of view that authors use. Using third person, authors refer to each character using the words *he* or *she*. In third-person omniscient, the narrator is not a character in the story and tells the story of all of the characters at the same time.

A good writer will use **transitional words** and phrases to guide the reader through the text. You are no doubt familiar with the common transitions, though you may never have considered how they operate. Some transitional phrases (*after, before, during, in the middle of*) give information about time. Some indicate that an example is about to be given (*for example, in fact, for instance*). Writers use them to compare (*also, likewise*) and contrast (*however, but, yet*). Transitional words and phrases can suggest addition (*and, also, furthermore, moreover*) and logical relationships (*if, then, therefore, as a result, since*). Finally, transitional words and phrases can demarcate the steps in a process (*first, second, last*). You should incorporate transitional words and phrases where they will orient your reader and illuminate the structure of your composition.

**Types of passages**

A **narrative** passage is a story. Narratives can be fiction or nonfiction. However, there are a few elements that a text must have in order to be classified as a narrative. To begin with, the text must have a plot. That is, it must describe a series of events. If it is a good narrative, these events will be interesting and emotionally engaging to the reader. A narrative also has characters. These could be people, animals, or even inanimate objects, so long as they participate in the plot. A narrative passage often contains figurative language, which is meant to stimulate the imagination of the reader by making comparisons and observations. A metaphor, which is a description of one thing in terms of another, is a common piece of figurative language. *The moon was a frosty snowball* is an example of a metaphor: it is obviously untrue in the literal sense, but it suggests a certain mood for the reader. Narratives often proceed in a clear sequence, but they do not need to do so.

An **expository** passage aims to inform and enlighten the reader. It is nonfiction and usually centers around a simple, easily defined topic. Since the goal of exposition is to teach, such a passage should be as clear as possible. It is common for an expository passage to contain helpful organizing words, like *first*, *next*, *for example*, and *therefore*. These words keep the reader oriented in the text. Although expository passages do not need to feature colorful language and artful writing, they are often more effective when they do. For a reader, the challenge of expository passages is to maintain steady attention. Expository passages are not always about subjects in which a reader will naturally be interested, and the writer is often more concerned with clarity and comprehensibility than with engaging the reader. For this reason, many expository passages are dull. Making notes is a good way to maintain focus when reading an expository passage.

A **technical** passage is written to describe a complex object or process. Technical writing is common in medical and technological fields, in which complicated mathematical, scientific, and engineering ideas need to be explained simply and clearly. To ease comprehension, a technical passage usually proceeds in a very logical order. Technical passages often have clear headings and subheadings, which are used to keep the reader oriented in the text. It is also common for these passages to break sections up with numbers or letters. Many technical passages look more like an outline than a piece of prose. The amount of jargon or difficult vocabulary will vary in a technical passage depending on the intended audience. As much as possible, technical passages try to avoid language that the reader will have to research in order to understand the message. Of course, it is not always possible to avoid jargon.

A **persuasive** passage is meant to change the reader's mind or lead her into agreement with the author. The persuasive intent may be obvious, or it may be quite difficult to discern. In some cases, a persuasive passage will be indistinguishable from an informative passage: it will make an assertion and offer supporting details. However, a persuasive passage is more likely to make claims based on opinion and to appeal to the reader's emotions. Persuasive passages may not describe alternate positions and, when they do, they often display significant bias. It may be clear that a persuasive passage is giving the author's viewpoint, or the passage may adopt a seemingly objective tone. A persuasive passage is successful if it can make a convincing argument and win the trust of the reader.

A persuasive essay will likely focus on one central argument, but it may make many smaller claims along the way. These are subordinate arguments with which the reader must agree if he or she is going to agree with the central argument. The central argument will only be as strong as the subordinate claims. These claims should be rooted in fact and observation, rather than subjective judgment. The best persuasive essays provide enough supporting detail to justify claims without overwhelming the reader. Remember that a fact must be susceptible to independent verification: that is, it must be something the reader could confirm. Also, statistics are only effective when they take into account possible objections. For instance, a statistic on the number of foreclosed houses would only be useful if it was taken over a defined interval and in a defined area. Most readers are wary of statistics, because they are so often misleading. If possible, a persuasive essay should always include references so that the reader can obtain more information. Of course, this means that the writer's accuracy and fairness may be judged by the inquiring reader.

Opinions are formed by emotion as well as reason, and persuasive writers often appeal to the feelings of the reader. Although readers should always be skeptical of this technique, it is often used in a proper and ethical manner. For instance, there are many subjects that have an obvious emotional component, and therefore cannot be completely treated without an appeal to the emotions. Consider an article on drunk driving: it makes sense to include some specific examples that will alarm or sadden the reader. After all, drunk driving often has serious and tragic consequences. Emotional appeals are not appropriate, however, when they attempt to mislead the reader. For instance, in political advertisements it is common to emphasize the patriotism of the preferred candidate, because this will encourage the audience to link their own positive feelings about the country with their opinion of the candidate. However, these ads often imply that the other candidate is unpatriotic, which in most cases is far from the truth. Another common and improper emotional appeal is the use of loaded language, as for instance referring to an avidly religious person as a "fanatic" or a passionate environmentalist as a "tree hugger." These terms introduce an emotional component that detracts from the argument.

**History and culture**

Historical context has a profound influence on literature: the events, knowledge base, and assumptions of an author's time color every aspect of his or her work. Sometimes, authors hold opinions and use language that would be considered inappropriate or immoral in a modern setting, but that was acceptable in the author's time. As a reader, one should consider how the historical context influenced a work and also how today's opinions and ideas shape the way modern readers read the works of the past. For instance, in most societies of the past, women were treated as second-class citizens. An author who wrote in 18th-century England might sound sexist to modern readers, even if that author was relatively feminist in his time. Readers should not have to excuse the faulty assumptions and prejudices of the past, but they should appreciate that a person's thoughts and words are, in part, a result of the time and culture in which they live or lived, and it is perhaps unfair to expect writers to avoid all of the errors of their times.

Even a brief study of world literature suggests that writers from vastly different cultures address similar themes. For instance, works like the *Odyssey* and *Hamlet* both tackle the individual's battle for self-control and independence. In every culture, authors address themes of personal growth and the struggle for maturity. Another universal theme is the conflict between the individual and society. In works as culturally disparate as *Native Son*, the *Aeneid*, and *1984*, authors dramatize how people struggle to maintain their personalities and dignity in large, sometimes oppressive groups. Finally, many cultures have versions of the hero's (or heroine's) journey, in which an adventurous person must overcome many obstacles in order to gain greater knowledge, power, and perspective. Some famous works that treat this theme are the *Epic of Gilgamesh*, Dante's *Divine Comedy*, and *Don Quixote.*

Authors from different genres (for instance poetry, drama, novel, short story) and cultures may address similar themes, but they often do so quite differently. For instance, poets are likely to address subject matter obliquely, through the use of images and allusions. In a play, on the other hand, the author is more likely to dramatize themes by using characters to express opposing viewpoints. This disparity is known as a dialectical approach. In a novel, the author does not need to express themes directly; rather, they can be illustrated through events and actions. In some regional literatures, like those of Greece or England, authors use more irony: their works have characters that express views and make decisions that are clearly disapproved of by the author. In Latin America, there is a great tradition of using supernatural events to illustrate themes about real life. In China and Japan, authors frequently use well-established regional forms (haiku, for instance) to organize their treatment of universal themes.

**Responding to literature**

When reading good literature, the reader is moved to engage actively in the text. One part of being an active reader involves making predictions. A **prediction** is a guess about what will happen next. Readers are constantly making predictions based on what they have read and what they already know. Consider the following sentence: *Staring at the computer screen in shock,*

*Kim blindly reached over for the brimming glass of water on the shelf to her side.* The sentence suggests that Kim is agitated and that she is not looking at the glass she is going to pick up, so a reader might predict that she is going to knock the glass over. Of course, not every prediction will be accurate: perhaps Kim will pick the glass up cleanly. Nevertheless, the author has certainly created the expectation that the water might be spilled. Predictions are always subject to revision as the reader acquires more information.

***Test-taking tip***: To respond to questions requiring future predictions, the student's answers should be based on evidence of past or present behavior.

Readers are often required to understand text that claims and suggests ideas without stating them directly. An **inference** is a piece of information that is implied but not written outright by the author. For instance, consider the following sentence: *Mark made more money that week than he had in the previous year.* From this sentence, the reader can infer that Mark either has not made much money in the previous year or made a great deal of money that week. Often, a reader can use information he or she already knows to make inferences. Take as an example the sentence *When his coffee arrived, he looked around the table for the silver cup.* Many people know that cream is typically served in a silver cup, so using their own base of knowledge they can infer that the subject of this sentence takes his coffee with cream. Making inferences requires concentration, attention, and practice.

***Test-taking tip***: While being tested on his ability to make correct inferences, the student must look for contextual clues. An answer can be *true* but not *correct.* The contextual clues will help you find the answer that is the best answer out of the given choices. Understand the context in which a phrase is stated. When asked for the implied meaning of a statement made in the passage, the student should immediately locate the statement and read the context in which it was made. Also, look for an answer choice that has a similar phrase to the statement in question.

A reader must be able to identify a text's **sequence**, or the order in which things happen. Often, and especially when the sequence is very important to the author, it is indicated with signal words like *first*, *then*, *next*, and *last*. However, sometimes a sequence is merely implied and must be noted by the reader. Consider the sentence *He walked in the front door and switched on the hall lamp.* Clearly, the man did not turn the lamp on before he walked in the door, so the implied sequence is that he first walked in the door and then turned on the lamp. Texts do not always proceed in an orderly sequence from first to last: sometimes, they begin at the end and then start over at the beginning. As a reader, it can be useful to make brief notes to clarify the sequence.

In addition to inferring and predicting things about the text, the reader must often **draw conclusions** about the information he has read. When asked for a *conclusion* that may be drawn, look for critical "hedge" phrases, such as *likely*, *may*, *can*, *will often*, among many others. When you are being tested on this knowledge, remember that question writers insert these hedge phrases to cover every possibility. Often an answer will be wrong simply because it leaves no room for exception. Extreme positive or negative answers (such as always, never, etc.) are usually not correct. The reader should not use any outside knowledge that is not gathered from the reading passage to answer the related questions. Correct answers can be derived straight from the reading passage.

### Literary genres

Literary genres refer to the basic generic types of poetry, drama, fiction, and nonfiction. Literary genre is a method of classifying and analyzing literature. There are numerous subdivisions within genre, including such categories as novels, novellas, and short stories in fiction. Drama may also be subdivided into comedy, tragedy, and many other categories. Poetry and nonfiction have their own distinct divisions.

Genres often overlap, and the distinctions among them are blurred, such as that between the nonfiction novel and docudrama, as well as many others. However, the use of genres is helpful to the reader as a set of understandings that guide our responses to a work. The generic norm sets expectations and forms the framework within which we read and evaluate a work. This framework will guide both our understanding and interpretation of the work. It is a useful tool for both literary criticism and analysis.

**Fiction** is a general term for any form of literary narrative that is invented or imagined rather than being factual. For those individuals who equate fact with truth, the imagined or invented character of fiction tends to render it relatively unimportant or trivial among the genres. Defenders of fiction are quick to point out that the fictional mode is an essential part of being. The ability to imagine or discuss what-if plots, characters, and events is clearly part of the human experience.

*Prose* is derived from the Latin and means "straightforward discourse." Prose fiction, although having many categories, may be divided into three main groups:

- **Short stories**: a fictional narrative, the length of which varies, usually under 20,000 words. Short stories usually have only a few characters and generally describe one major event or insight. The short story began in magazines in the late 1800s and has flourished ever since.
- **Novels**: a longer work of fiction, often containing a large cast of characters and extensive plotting. The emphasis may be on an event, action, social problems, or any experience. There is now a genre of nonfiction novels pioneered by Truman Capote's *In Cold Blood* in the 1960s. Novels may also be written in verse.
- **Novellas**: a work of narrative fiction longer than a short story but shorter than a novel. Novellas may also be called short novels or novelettes. They originated from the German tradition and have become common forms in all of the world's literature.

Many elements influence a work of prose fiction. Some important ones are:

- Speech and dialogue: Characters may speak for themselves or through the narrator. Dialogue may be realistic or fantastic, depending on the author's aim.
- Thoughts and mental processes: There may be internal dialogue used as a device for plot development or character understanding.
- Dramatic involvement: Some narrators encourage readers to become involved in the events of the story, whereas others attempt to distance readers through literary devices.
- Action: This is any information that advances the plot or involves new interactions between the characters.
- Duration: The time frame of the work may be long or short, and the relationship between described time and narrative time may vary.
- Setting and description: Is the setting critical to the plot or characters? How are the action scenes described?
- Themes: This is any point of view or topic given sustained attention.
- Symbolism: Authors often veil meanings through imagery and other literary constructions.

Fiction is much wider than simply prose fiction. Songs, ballads, epics, and narrative poems are examples of non-prose fiction. A full definition of fiction must include not only the work itself but also the framework in which it is read. Literary fiction can also be defined as not true rather than nonexistent, as many works of historical fiction refer to real people, places, and events that are treated imaginatively as if they were true. These imaginary elements enrich and broaden literary expression.

When analyzing fiction, it is important for the reader to look carefully at the work being studied. The plot or action of a narrative can become so entertaining that the language of the work is ignored. The language of fiction should not simply be a way to relate a plot—it should also yield many insights to the judicious reader. Some prose fiction is based on the reader's engagement with the language rather than the story. A studious reader will analyze the mode of expression as well as the narrative. Part of the reward of reading in this manner is to discover how the author uses different language to describe familiar objects, events, or emotions. Some works focus the reader on an author's unorthodox use of language, whereas others may emphasize characters or storylines. What happens in a story is not always the critical element in the work. This type of reading may be difficult at first but yields great rewards.

The **narrator** is a central part of any work of fiction, and can give insight about the purpose of the work and its main themes and ideas. The following are important questions to address to better understand the voice and role of the narrator and incorporate that voice into an overall understanding of the novel:

- Who is the narrator of the novel? What is the narrator's perspective, first person or third person? What is the role of the narrator in the plot? Are there changes in narrators or the perspective of narrators?
- Does the narrator explain things in the novel, or does meaning emerge from the plot and events? The personality of the narrator is important. She may have a vested interest in a character or event described. Some narratives follow the time sequence of the plot, whereas others do not. A narrator may express approval or disapproval about a character or events in the work.
- Tone is an important aspect of the narration. Who is actually being addressed by the narrator? Is the tone familiar or formal, intimate or impersonal? Does the vocabulary suggest clues about the narrator?

A **character** is a person intimately involved with the plot and development of the novel. Development of the novel's characters not only moves the story along but will also tell the reader a lot about the novel itself. There is usually a physical description of the character, but this is often omitted in modern and postmodern novels. These works may focus on the psychological state or motivation of the character. The choice of a character's name may give valuable clues to his role in the work.

Characters are said to be flat or round. Flat characters tend to be minor figures in the story, changing little or not at all. Round characters (those understood from a well-rounded view) are more central to the story and tend to change as the plot unfolds. Stock characters are similar to flat characters, filling out the story without influencing it.

Modern literature has been greatly affected by Freudian psychology, giving rise to such devices as the interior monologue and magical realism as methods of understanding characters in a work. These give the reader a more complex understanding of the inner lives of the characters and enrich the understanding of relationships between characters.

Another important genre is that of **drama**: a play written to be spoken aloud. The drama is in many ways inseparable from performance. Reading drama ideally involves using imagination to visualize and re-create the play with characters and settings. The reader stages the play in his imagination, watching characters interact and developments unfold. Sometimes this involves simulating a theatrical presentation; other times it involves imagining the events. In either case, the reader is imagining the unwritten to re-create the dramatic experience. Novels present some of the same problems, but a narrator will provide much more information about the setting, characters, inner dialogues, and many other supporting details. In drama, much of this is missing, and we are required to use our powers of projection and imagination to taste the full flavor of the dramatic work. There are many empty spaces in dramatic texts that must be filled by the reader to fully appreciate the work.

When reading drama in this way, there are some advantages over watching the play performed (though there is much criticism in this regard):

- Freedom of point of view and perspective: Text is free of interpretations of actors, directors, producers, and technical staging.
- Additional information: The text of a drama may be accompanied by notes or prefaces placing the work in a social or historical context. Stage directions may also provide relevant information about the author's purpose. None of this is typically available at live or filmed performances.
- Study and understanding: Difficult or obscure passages may be studied at leisure and supplemented by explanatory works. This is particularly true of older plays with unfamiliar language, which cannot be fully understood without an opportunity to study the material.

Critical elements of drama, especially when it is being read aloud or performed, include dialect, speech, and dialogue. Analysis of speech and dialogue is important in the critical study of drama. Some playwrights use speech to develop their characters. Speeches may be long or short, and written in as normal prose or blank verse. Some characters have a unique way of speaking which illuminates aspects of the drama. Emphasis and tone are both important, as well. Does the author make clear the tone in which lines are to be spoken, or is this open to interpretation? Sometimes there are various possibilities in tone with regard to delivering lines.

**Dialect** is any distinct variety of a language, especially one spoken in a region or part of a country. The criterion for distinguishing dialects from languages is that of mutual understanding. For example, people who speak Dutch cannot understand English unless they have learned it. But a speaker from Amsterdam can understand one from Antwerp; therefore, they speak different dialects of the same language. This is, however, a matter of degree; there are languages in which different dialects are unintelligible.

Dialect mixtures are the presence in one form of speech with elements from different neighboring dialects. The study of speech differences from one geographical area to another is called dialect geography. A dialect atlas is a map showing distribution of dialects in a given area. A dialect continuum shows a progressive shift in dialects across a territory, such that adjacent dialects are understandable, but those at the extremes are not.

Dramatic dialogue can be difficult to interpret and changes depending upon the tone used and which words are emphasized. Where the stresses, or meters, of dramatic dialogue fall can determine meaning. Variations in emphasis are only one factor in the manipulability of dramatic speech. Tone is of equal or greater importance and expresses a range of possible emotions and feelings that cannot be readily discerned from the script of a play. The reader must add tone to the words to understand the full meaning of a passage. Recognizing tone is a cumulative process as the reader begins to understand the characters and situations in the play. Other elements that influence the interpretation of dialogue include the setting, possible reactions of the characters to the speech, and possible gestures or facial expressions of the actor. There are no firm rules to guide the interpretation of dramatic speech. An open and flexible attitude is essential in interpreting dramatic dialogue.

**Action** is a crucial element in the production of a dramatic work. Many dramas contain little dialogue and much action. In these cases, it is essential for the reader to carefully study stage directions and visualize the action on the stage. Benefits of understanding stage directions include knowing which characters are on the stage at all times, who is speaking to whom, and following these patterns through changes of scene.

**Stage directions** also provide additional information, some of which is not available to a live audience. The nature of the physical space where the action occurs is vital, and stage directions help with this. The historical context of the period is important in understanding what the playwright was working with in terms of theaters and physical space. The type of staging possible for the author is a good guide to the spatial elements of a production.

Asides and soliloquies are devices that authors use in plot and character development. **Asides** indicate that not all characters are privy to the lines. This may be a method of advancing or explaining the plot in a subtle manner. **Soliloquies** are opportunities for character development, plot enhancement, and to give insight to characters motives, feelings, and emotions. Careful study of these elements provides a reader with an abundance of clues to the major themes and plot of the work.

Art, music, and literature all interact in ways that contain many opportunities for the enrichment of all of the arts. Students could apply their knowledge of art and music by creating illustrations for a work or creating a musical score for a text. Students could discuss the meanings of texts and decide on their illustrations, or a score could amplify the meaning of the text.

Understanding the art and music of a period can make the experience of literature a richer, more rewarding experience. Students should be encouraged to use the knowledge of art and music to illuminate the text. Examining examples of dress, architecture, music, and dance of a period may be helpful in a fuller engagement of the text. Much of period literature lends itself to the analysis of the prevailing taste in art and music of an era, which helps place the literary work in a more meaningful context.

**Opinions, facts, and fallacies**

Critical thinking skills are mastered through understanding various types of writing and the different purposes that authors have for writing the way they do. Every author writes for a purpose. Understanding that purpose, and how they accomplish their goal, will allow you to critique the writing and determine whether or not you agree with their conclusions.

Readers must always be conscious of the distinction between fact and opinion. A **fact** can be subjected to analysis and can be either proved or disproved. An **opinion**, on the other hand, is the author's personal feeling, which may not be alterable by research, evidence, or argument. If the author writes that the distance from New York to Boston is about two hundred miles, he is stating a fact. But if he writes that New York is too crowded, then he is giving an opinion, because there is no objective standard for overpopulation. An opinion may be indicated by words like *believe*, *think*, or *feel.* Also, an opinion may be supported by facts: for instance, the author might give the population density of New York as a reason for why it is overcrowded. An opinion supported by fact tends to be more convincing. When authors support their opinions with other opinions, the reader is unlikely to be moved.

Facts should be presented to the reader from reliable sources. An opinion is what the author thinks about a given topic. An opinion is not common knowledge or proven by expert sources, but it is information that the author believes and wants the reader to consider. To distinguish between fact and opinion, a reader needs to look at the type of source that is presenting information, what information backs-up a claim, and whether or not the author may be motivated to have a certain point of view on a given topic. For example, if a panel of scientists has conducted multiple studies on the effectiveness of taking a certain vitamin, the results are more likely to be factual than if a company selling a vitamin claims that taking the vitamin can produce positive effects. The company is motivated to sell its product, while the scientists are using the scientific method to prove a theory. If the author uses words such as "I think...", the statement is an opinion.

In their attempt to persuade, writers often make mistakes in their thinking patterns and writing choices. It's important to understand these so you can make an informed decision. Every author has a point of view, but when an author ignores reasonable counterarguments or distorts opposing viewpoints, she is demonstrating a **bias**. A bias is evident whenever the author is unfair or inaccurate in his or her presentation. Bias may be intentional or unintentional, but it should always alert the reader to be skeptical of the argument being made. It should be noted that a biased author may still be correct. However, the author will be correct in spite of her bias, not because of it. A **stereotype** is like a bias, except that it is specifically applied to a group or place. Stereotyping is considered to be particularly abhorrent because it promotes negative generalizations about people. Many people are familiar with some of the hateful stereotypes of certain ethnic, religious, and cultural groups. Readers should be very wary of authors who stereotype. These faulty assumptions typically reveal the author's ignorance and lack of curiosity.

Sometimes, authors will **appeal to the reader's emotion** in an attempt to persuade or to distract the reader from the weakness of the argument. For instance, the author may try to inspire the pity of the reader by delivering a heart-rending story. An author also might use the bandwagon approach, in which he suggests that his opinion is correct because it is held by the majority. Some authors resort to name-calling, in which insults and harsh words are delivered to the opponent in an attempt to distract. In advertising, a common appeal is the testimonial, in which a famous person endorses a product. Of course, the fact that a celebrity likes something should not really mean anything to the reader. These and other emotional appeals are usually evidence of poor reasoning and a weak argument.

Certain *logical fallacies* are frequent in writing. A logical fallacy is a failure of reasoning. As a reader, it is important to recognize logical fallacies, because they diminish the value of the author's message. The four most common logical fallacies in writing are the false analogy, circular reasoning, false dichotomy, and overgeneralization. In a **false analogy**, the author suggests that two things are similar, when in fact they are different. This fallacy is often committed when the author is attempting to convince the reader that something unknown is like something relatively familiar. The author takes advantage of the reader's ignorance to make this false comparison. One example might be the following statement: *Failing to tip a waitress is like stealing money out of somebody's wallet.* Of course, failing to tip is very rude, especially when the service has been good, but people are not arrested for failing to tip as they would for stealing money from a wallet. To compare stingy diners with thieves is a false analogy.

**Circular reasoning** is one of the more difficult logical fallacies to identify, because it is typically hidden behind dense language and complicated sentences. Reasoning is described as circular when it offers no support for assertions other than restating them in different words. Put another way, a circular argument refers to itself as evidence of truth. A simple example of circular argument is when a person uses a word to define itself, such as saying *Niceness is the state of being nice.* If the reader does not know what *nice* means, then this definition will not be very useful. In a text, circular reasoning is usually more complex. For instance, an author might say *Poverty is a problem for society because it creates trouble for people throughout the community.* It is redundant to say that poverty is a problem because it creates trouble. When an author engages in circular reasoning, it is often because he or she has not fully thought out the argument, or cannot come up with any legitimate justifications.

One of the most common logical fallacies is the **false dichotomy**, in which the author creates an artificial sense that there are only two possible alternatives in a situation. This fallacy is common when the author has an agenda and wants to give the impression that his view is the only sensible one. A false dichotomy has the effect of limiting the reader's options and imagination. An example of a false dichotomy is the statement *You need to go to the party with me, otherwise you'll just be bored at home.* The speaker suggests that the only other possibility besides being at the party is being bored at home. But this is not true, as it is perfectly possible to be entertained at home, or even to go somewhere other than the party. Readers should always be wary of the false dichotomy: when an author limits alternatives, it is always wise to ask whether he is being valid.

**Overgeneralization** is a logical fallacy in which the author makes a claim that is so broad it cannot be proved or disproved. In most cases, overgeneralization occurs when the author wants to create an illusion of authority, or when he is using sensational language to sway the opinion of the reader. For instance, in the sentence *Everybody knows that she is a terrible teacher*, the author makes an assumption that cannot really be believed. This kind of statement is made when the author wants to create the illusion of consensus when none actually exists: it may be that most people have a negative view of the teacher, but to say that *everybody* feels that way is an exaggeration. When a reader spots overgeneralization, she should become skeptical about the argument that is being made, because an author will often try to hide a weak or unsupported assertion behind authoritative language.

Two other types of logical fallacies are **slippery slope** arguments and **hasty generalizations**. In a slippery slope argument, the author says that if something happens, it automatically means that something else will happen as a result, even though this may not be true. (i.e., just because you study hard does not mean you are going to ace the test). "Hasty generalization" is drawing a conclusion too early, without finishing analyzing the details of the argument. Writers of persuasive texts often use these techniques because they are very effective. In order to **identify logical fallacies**, readers need to read carefully and ask questions as they read. Thinking critically means not taking everything at face value. Readers need to critically evaluate an author's argument to make sure that the logic used is sound.

**Organization of the text**

The way a text is organized can help the reader to understand more clearly the author's intent and his conclusions. There are various ways to organize a text, and each one has its own purposes and uses. Some nonfiction texts are organized to **present a problem** followed by a solution. In this type of text, it is common for the problem to be explained before the solution is offered. In some cases, as when the problem is well known, the solution may be briefly introduced at the beginning. The entire passage may focus on the solution, and the problem will be referenced only occasionally. Some texts will outline multiple solutions to a problem, leaving the reader to choose among them. If the author has an interest or an allegiance to one solution, he may fail to mention or may describe inaccurately some of the other solutions. Readers should be careful of the author's agenda when reading a problem-solution text. Only by understanding the author's point of view and interests can one develop a proper judgment of the proposed solution.

Authors need to organize information logically so the reader can follow it and locate information within the text. Two common organizational structures are cause and effect and chronological order. When using **chronological order**, the author presents information in the order that it happened. For example, biographies are written in chronological order; the subject's birth and childhood are presented first, followed by their adult life, and lastly by the events leading up to the person's death.

In **cause and effect**, an author presents one thing that makes something else happen. For example, if one were to go to bed very late, they would be tired. The cause is going to bed late, with the effect of being tired the next day. It can be tricky to identify the cause-and-effect relationships in a text, but there are a few ways to approach this task. To begin with, these relationships are often signaled with certain terms. When an author uses words like *because*, *since*, *in order*, and *so*, she is likely describing a cause-and-effect relationship. Consider the sentence, "He called her because he needed the homework." This is a simple causal relationship, in which the cause was his need for the homework and the effect was his phone call. Not all cause-and-effect relationships are marked in this way, however. Consider the sentences, "He called her. He needed the homework." When the cause-and-effect relationship is not indicated with a keyword, it can be discovered by asking why something happened. He called her: why? The answer is in the next sentence: He needed the homework.

Persuasive essays, in which an author tries to make a convincing argument and change the reader's mind, usually include cause-and-effect relationships. However, these relationships should not always be taken at face value. An author frequently will assume a cause or take an effect for granted. To read a persuasive essay effectively, one needs to judge the cause-and-effect relationships the author is presenting. For instance, imagine an author wrote the following: "The parking deck has been unprofitable because people would prefer to ride their bikes." The relationship is clear: the cause is that people prefer to ride their bikes, and the effect is that the parking deck has been unprofitable. However, a reader should consider whether this argument is conclusive. Perhaps there are other reasons for the failure of the parking deck: a down economy, excessive fees, etc. Too often, authors present causal relationships as if they are fact rather than opinion. Readers should be on the alert for these dubious claims.

Thinking critically about ideas and conclusions can seem like a daunting task. One way to make it easier is to understand the basic elements of ideas and writing techniques. Looking at the way different ideas relate to each other can be a good way for the reader to begin his analysis. For instance, sometimes writers will write about two different ideas that are in opposition to each other. The analysis of these opposing ideas is known as **contrast**. Contrast is often marred by the author's obvious partiality to one of the ideas. A discerning reader will be put off by an author who does not engage in a fair fight. In an analysis of opposing ideas, both ideas should be presented in their clearest and most reasonable terms. If the author does prefer a side, he should avoid indicating this preference with pejorative language. An analysis of opposing ideas should proceed through the major differences point by point, with a full explanation of each side's view. For instance, in an analysis of capitalism and communism, it would be important to outline each side's view on labor, markets, prices, personal responsibility, etc. It would be less effective to describe the theory of communism and then explain how capitalism has thrived in the West. An analysis of opposing views should present each side in the same manner.

Many texts follow the **compare-and-contrast** model, in which the similarities and differences between two ideas or things are explored. Analysis of the similarities between ideas is called comparison. In order for a comparison to work, the author must place the ideas or things in an equivalent structure. That is, the author must present the ideas in the same way. Imagine an author wanted to show the similarities between cricket and baseball. The correct way to do so would be to summarize the equipment and rules for each game. It would be incorrect to summarize the equipment of cricket and then lay out the history of baseball, since this would make it impossible for the reader to see the similarities. It is perhaps too obvious to say that an analysis of similar ideas should emphasize the similarities. Of course, the author should take care to include any differences that must be mentioned. Often, these small differences will only reinforce the more general similarity.

**Drawing conclusions**

Authors should have a clear purpose in mind while writing. Especially when reading informational texts, it is important to understand the logical conclusion of the author's ideas. **Identifying this logical conclusion** can help the reader understand whether he agrees with the writer or not. Identifying a logical conclusion is much like making an inference: it requires the reader to combine the information given by the text with what he already knows to make a supportable assertion. If a passage is written well, then the conclusion should be obvious even when it is unstated. If the author intends the reader to draw a certain conclusion, then all of his argumentation and detail should be leading toward it. One way to approach the task of drawing conclusions is to make brief notes of all the points made by the author. When these are arranged on paper, they may clarify the logical conclusion. Another way to approach conclusions is to consider whether the reasoning of the author raises any pertinent questions. Sometimes it will be possible to draw several conclusions from a passage, and on occasion these will be conclusions that were never imagined by the author. It is essential, however, that these conclusions be supported directly by the text.

The term **text evidence** refers to information that supports a main point or points in a story, and can help lead the reader to a conclusion. Information used as *text evidence* is precise, descriptive, and factual. A main point is often followed by supporting details that provide evidence to back-up a claim. For example, a story may include the claim that winter occurs during opposite months in the Northern and Southern hemispheres. *Text evidence* based on this claim may include countries where winter occurs in opposite months, along with reasons that winter occurs at different times of the year in separate hemispheres (due to the tilt of the Earth as it rotates around the sun).

Readers interpret text and respond to it in a number of ways. Using textual support helps defend your response or interpretation because it roots your thinking in the text. You are interpreting based on information in the text and not simply your own ideas. When crafting a response, look for important quotes and details from the text to help bolster your argument. If you are writing about a character's personality trait, for example, use details from the text to show that the character acted in such a way. You can also include statistics and facts from a nonfiction text to strengthen your response. For example, instead of writing, "A lot of people use cell phones," use statistics to provide the exact number. This strengthens your argument because it is more precise.

The text used to support an argument can be the argument's downfall if it is not credible. A text is **credible**, or believable, when the author is knowledgeable and objective, or unbiased. The author's motivations for writing the text play a critical role in determining the credibility of the text and must be evaluated when assessing that credibility. The author's motives should be for the dissemination of information. The purpose of the text should be to inform or describe, not to persuade. When an author writes a persuasive text, he has the motivation that the reader will do what they want. The extent of the author's knowledge of the topic and their motivation must be evaluated when assessing the credibility of a text. Reports written about the Ozone layer by an environmental scientist and a hairdresser will have a different level of credibility.

After determining your own opinion and evaluating the credibility of your supporting text, it is sometimes necessary to communicate your ideas and findings to others. When **writing a response to a text**, it is important to use elements of the text to support your assertion or defend your position. Using supporting evidence from the text strengthens the argument because the reader can see how in depth the writer read the original piece and based their response on the details and facts within that text. Elements of text that can be used in a response include: facts, details, statistics, and direct quotations from the text. When writing a response, one must make sure they indicate which information comes from the original text and then base their discussion, argument, or defense around this information.

A reader should always be drawing conclusions from the text. Sometimes conclusions are implied from written information, and other times the information is **stated directly** within the passage. It is always more comfortable to draw conclusions from information stated within a passage, rather than to draw them from mere implications. At times an author may provide some information and then describe a counterargument. The reader should be alert for direct statements that are subsequently rejected or weakened by the author. The reader should always read the entire passage before drawing conclusions. Many readers are trained to expect the author's conclusions at either the beginning or the end of the passage, but many texts do not adhere to this format.

Drawing conclusions from information implied within a passage requires confidence on the part of the reader. **Implications** are things the author does not state directly, but which can be assumed based on what the author does say. For instance, consider the following simple passage: "I stepped outside and opened my umbrella. By the time I got to work, the cuffs of my pants were soaked." The author never states that it is raining, but this fact is clearly implied. Conclusions based on implication must be well supported by the text. In order to draw a solid conclusion, a reader should have multiple pieces of evidence, or, if he only has one, must be assured that there is no other possible explanation than his conclusion. A good reader will be able to draw many conclusions from information implied by the text, which enriches the reading experience considerably.

As an aid to drawing conclusions, the reader should be adept at **outlining** the information contained in the passage; an effective outline will reveal the structure of the passage, and will lead to solid conclusions. An effective outline will have a title that refers to the basic subject of the text, though it need not recapitulate the main idea. In most outlines, the main idea will be the first major section. It will have each major idea of the passage established as the head of a category. For instance, the most common outline format calls for the main ideas of the passage to be indicated with Roman numerals. In an effective outline of this kind, each of the main ideas will be represented by a Roman numeral and none of the Roman numerals will designate minor details or secondary ideas. Moreover, all supporting ideas and details should be placed in the appropriate place on the outline. An outline does not need to include every detail listed in the text, but it should feature all of those that are central to the argument or message. Each of these details should be listed under the appropriate main idea.

It is also helpful to **summarize** the information you have read in a paragraph or passage format. This process is similar to creating an effective outline. To begin with, a summary should accurately define the main idea of the passage, though it does not need to explain this main idea in exhaustive detail. It should continue by laying out the most important supporting details or arguments from the passage. All of the significant supporting details should be included, and none of the details included should be irrelevant or insignificant. Also, the summary should accurately report all of these details. Too often, the desire for brevity in a summary leads to the sacrifice of clarity or veracity. Summaries are often difficult to read, because they omit all of graceful language, digressions, and asides that distinguish great writing. However, if the summary is effective, it should contain much the same message as the original text.

**Paraphrasing** is another method the reader can use to aid in comprehension. When paraphrasing, one puts what they have read into their own words, rephrasing what the author has written to make it their own, to "translate" all of what the author says to their own words, including as many details as they can.

**Informational sources**

Informational sources often come in short forms like a memo or recipe, or longer forms like books, magazines, or journals. These longer sources of information each have their own way of organizing information, but there are some similarities that the reader should be aware of.

Most books, magazines, and journals have a **table of contents** at the beginning. This helps the reader find the different parts of the book. The table of contents is usually found a page or two after the title page in a book, and on the first few pages of a magazine. However, many magazines now place the table of contents in the midst of an overabundance of advertisements, because they know readers will have to look at the ads as they search for the table. The standard orientation for a table of contents is the sections of the book listed along the left side, with the initial page number for each along the right. It is common in a book for the prefatory material (preface, introduction, etc.) to be numbered with Roman numerals. The contents are always listed in order from the beginning of the book to the end.

A nonfiction book will also typically have an **index** at the end so that the reader can easily find information about particular topics. An index lists the topics in alphabetical order. The names of people are listed with the last name first. For example, *Adams, John* would come before *Washington, George*. To the right of the entry, the relevant page numbers are listed. When a topic is mentioned over several pages, the index will often connect these pages with a dash. For instance, if the subject is mentioned from pages 35 to 42 and again on 53, then the index entry will be labeled as *35-42, 53*. Some entries will have subsets, which are listed below the main entry, indented slightly, and placed in alphabetical order. This is common for subjects that are discussed frequently in the book. For instance, in a book about Elizabethan drama, William Shakespeare will likely be an important topic. Beneath Shakespeare's name in the index, there might be listings for *death of*, *dramatic works of*, *life of*, etc. These more specific entries help the reader refine his search.

Many informative texts, especially textbooks, use **headings** and **subheadings** for organization. Headings and subheadings are typically printed in larger and bolder fonts, and are often in a different color than the main body of the text. Headings may be larger than subheadings. Also, headings and subheadings are not always complete sentences. A heading announces the topic that will be addressed in the text below. Headings are meant to alert the reader to what is about to come. Subheadings announce the topics of smaller sections within the entire section indicated by the heading. For instance, the heading of a section in a science textbook might be *AMPHIBIANS*, and within that section might be subheadings for *Frogs*, *Salamanders*, and *Newts*. Readers should always pay close attention to headings and subheadings, because they prime the brain for the information that is about to be delivered, and because they make it easy to go back and find particular details in a long text.

**Reference materials**

Knowledge of reference materials such as dictionaries, encyclopedias, and manuals are vital for any reader. **Dictionaries** contain information about words. A standard dictionary entry begins with a pronunciation guide for the word. The entry will also give the word's part of speech: that is, whether it is a noun, verb, adjective, etc. A good dictionary will also include the word's origins, including the language from which it is derived and its meaning in that language. This information is known as the word's etymology. Dictionary entries are in alphabetical order. Many words have more than one definition, in which case the definitions will be numbered. Also, if a word can be used as different parts of speech, its various definitions in those different capacities may be separated. A sample entry might look like this:

- WELL: (adverb) 1. in a good way (noun) 1. a hole drilled into the earth

The correct definition of a word will vary depending on how it is used in a sentence. When looking up a word found while reading, the best way to determine the relevant definition is to substitute the dictionary's definitions for the word in the text, and select the definition that seems most appropriate.

**Encyclopedias** used to be the best source for general information on a range of common subjects. Many people took pride in owning a set of encyclopedias, which were often written by top researchers. Now, encyclopedias largely exist online. Although they no longer have a preeminent place in general scholarship, these digital encyclopedias now often feature audio and video clips. A good encyclopedia remains the best place to obtain basic information about a well-known topic. There are also specialty encyclopedias that cover more obscure or expert information. For instance, there are many medical encyclopedias that contain the detail and sophistication required by doctors. For a regular person researching a subject like ostriches, Pennsylvania, or the Crimean War, an encyclopedia is a good source.

A **thesaurus** is a reference book that gives synonyms of words. It is different from a dictionary because a thesaurus does not give definitions, only lists of synonyms. A thesaurus can be helpful in finding the meaning of an unfamiliar word when reading. If the meaning of a synonym is known, then the meaning of the unfamiliar word will be known. The other time a thesaurus is helpful is when writing. Using a thesaurus helps authors to vary their word choice.

A **database** is an informational source that has a different format than a publication or a memo. They are systems for storing and organizing large amounts of information. As personal computers have become more common and accessible, databases have become ever more present. The standard layout of a database is as a grid, with labels along the left side and the top. The horizontal rows and vertical columns that make up the grid are usually numbered or lettered, so that a particular square within the database might have a name like A3 or G5. Databases are good for storing information that can be expressed succinctly. They are most commonly used to store numerical data, but they also can be used to store the answers to yes-no questions and other brief data points. Information that is ambiguous (that is, has multiple possible meanings) or difficult to express in a few words is not appropriate for a database.

Often, a reader will come across a word that he does not recognize. The reader needs to know how to identify the definition of a word from its context. This means defining a word based on the words around it and the way it is used in a sentence. For instance, consider the following sentence: *The elderly scholar spent his evenings hunched over arcane texts that few other people even knew existed.* The adjective *arcane* is uncommon, but the reader can obtain significant information about it based on its use here. Based on the fact that few other people know of their existence, the reader can assume that arcane texts must be rare and only of interest to a few people. And, because they are being read by an elderly scholar, the reader can assume that they focus on difficult academic subjects. Sometimes, words can even be defined by what they are not. For instance, consider the following sentence: *Ron's fealty to his parents was not shared by Karen, who disobeyed their every command.* Because someone who disobeys is not demonstrating *fealty*, the word can be inferred to mean something like obedience or respect.

When conducting research, it is important to depend on reputable **primary sources**. A primary source is the documentary evidence closest to the subject being studied. For instance, the primary sources for an essay about penguins would be photographs and recordings of the birds, as well as accounts of people who have studied penguins in person. A secondary source would be a review of a movie about penguins or a book outlining the observations made by others. A primary source should be credible and, if it is on a subject that is still being explored, recent. One way to assess the credibility of a work is to see how often it is mentioned in other books and articles on the same subject. Just by reading the works cited and bibliographies of other books, one can get a sense of what are the acknowledged authorities in the field.

The Internet was once considered a poor place to find sources for an essay or article, but its credibility has improved greatly over the years. Still, students need to exercise caution when performing research online. The best sources are those affiliated with established institutions, like universities, public libraries, and think tanks. Most newspapers are available online, and many of them allow the public to browse their archives. Magazines frequently offer similar services. When obtaining information from an unknown website, however, one must exercise considerably more caution. A website can be considered trustworthy if it is referenced by other sites that are known to be reputable. Also, credible sites tend to be properly maintained and frequently updated. A site is easier to trust when the author provides some information about him or herself, including some credentials that indicate expertise in the subject matter.

## Organizing and understanding graphic information

Two of the most common ways to organize ideas from a text, paraphrasing and summarizing, are verbal ways to organize data. Ideas from a text can also be organized using **graphic organizers**. A graphic organizer is a way to simplify information and just take key points from the text. A graphic organizer such as a timeline may have an event listed for a corresponding date on the timeline, whereas an outline may have an event listed under a key point that occurs in the text. Each reader needs to create the type of graphic organizer that works the best for him or her in terms of being able to recall information from a story. Examples include a *spider-map,* which takes a main idea from the story and places it in a bubble, with supporting points branching off the main idea, an *outline,* useful for diagramming the main and supporting points of the entire story, and a *Venn diagram,* which classifies information as separate or overlapping. These graphic organizers can also be used by authors to enliven their presentation or text, but this may be counterproductive if the graphics are confusing or misleading. A graph should strip the author's message down to the essentials. It should have a clear title, and should be in the appropriate format. Authors may elect to use tables, line or bar graphs, or pie charts to illustrate their message. Each of these formats is correct for different types of data. The graphic should be large enough to read, and should be divided into appropriate categories. For instance, if the text is about the differences between federal spending on the military and on the space program, a pie chart or a bar graph would be the most effective choices. The pie chart could show each type of spending as a portion of total federal spending, while the bar graph would be better for directly comparing the amounts of money spent on these two programs.

In most cases, the work of interpreting information presented in graphs, tables, charts, and diagrams is done for the reader. The author will usually make explicit his or her reasons for presenting a certain set of data in such a way. However, an effective reader will avoid taking the author's claims for granted. Before considering the information presented in the graphic, the reader should consider whether the author has chosen the correct format for presentation, or whether the author has omitted variables or other information that might undermine his case. Interpreting the graphic itself is essentially an exercise in spotting trends. On a graph, for instance, the reader should be alert for how one variable responds to a change in the other. If education level increases, for example, does income increase as well? The same can be done for a table. Readers should be alert for values that break or exaggerate a trend; these may be meaningless outliers or indicators of a change in conditions. When a reader is required to draw conclusions from the information presented in graphs, tables, charts, or diagrams, it is important to limit these conclusions to the terms of the graphic itself. In other words, the reader should avoid extrapolating from the data to make claims that are not supportable. As an example, consider a graph that compares the price of eggs to the demand. If the price and demand rise and fall together, a reader would be justified in saying that the demand for eggs and the price are tied together. However, this simple graph does not indicate which of these variables causes the other, so the reader would not be justified in concluding that the price of eggs raises or lowers the demand. In fact, demand could be tied to all sorts of other factors not included in this chart.

## Types of tables and charts

**Tables** are presented in a standard format so that they will be easy to read and understand. At the top of the table, there will be a title. This will be a short phrase indicating the information the table or graph intends to convey. The title of a table could be something like "Average Income for Various Education Levels" or "Price of Milk Compared to Demand." A table is composed of information laid out in vertical columns and horizontal rows. Typically, each column will have a label. If "Average Income for Various Education Levels" was placed in a table format, the two columns could be labeled "Education Level" and "Average Income." Each location on the table is called a cell. Cells are defined by their column and row (e.g., second column, fifth row). The table's information is placed in these cells.

Like a table, a **graph** will typically have a title on top. This title may simply state the identities of the two axes: e.g., "Income vs. Education." However, the title may also be something more descriptive, like "A comparison of average income with level of education." In any case, bar and line graphs are laid out along two perpendicular lines, or axes. The vertical axis is called the *y*-axis, and the horizontal axis is called the *x*-axis. It is typical for the *x*-axis to be the independent variable and the *y*-axis to be the dependent variable. The independent variable is the one manipulated by the researcher or whoever put together the graph. In the above example, the independent variable would be "level of education," since the maker of the graph will define these values (high school, college, master's degree, etc.). The dependent value is not controlled by the researcher.

When selecting a graph format, it is important to consider the intention and the structure of the presentation. A bar graph, for instance, is appropriate for displaying the relations between a series of distinct quantities that are on the same scale. For instance, if one wanted to display the amount of money spent on groceries during the months of a year, a bar graph would be appropriate. The vertical axis would represent values of money, and the horizontal axis would identify the bar representing each month. A line graph also requires data expressed in common units, but it is better for demonstrating the general trend in that data. If the grocery expenses were plotted on a line graph instead of a bar graph, there would be more emphasis on whether the amount of money spent rose or fell over the course of the year. Whereas a bar graph is good for showing the relationships between the different values plotted, the line graph is good for showing whether the values tended to increase, decrease, or remain stable.

A **line graph** is a type of graph that is typically used for measuring trends over time. It is set up along a vertical and a horizontal axis. The variables being measured are listed along the left side and the bottom side of the axes. Points are then plotted along the graph, such that they correspond with their values for each variable. For instance, imagine a line graph measuring a person's income for each month of the year. If the person earned $1500 in January, there would be a point directly above January, perpendicular to the horizontal axis, and directly to the right of $1500, perpendicular to the vertical axis. Once all of the lines are plotted, they are connected with a line from left to right. This line provides a nice visual illustration of the general trends. For instance, using the earlier example, if the line sloped up, it would be clear that the person's income had increased over the course of the year.

The **bar graph** is one of the most common visual representations of information. Bar graphs are used to illustrate sets of numerical data. The graph has a vertical axis, along which numbers are listed, and a horizontal axis, along which categories, words, or some other indicators are placed. One example of a bar graph is a depiction of the respective heights of famous basketball players: the vertical axis would contain numbers ranging from five to eight feet, and the horizontal axis would contain the names of the players. The length of the bar above the player's name would illustrate his height, as the top of the bar would stop perpendicular to the height listed along the left side. In this representation, then, it would be easy to see that Yao Ming is taller than Michael Jordan, because Yao's bar would be higher.

A **pie chart**, also known as a circle graph, is useful for depicting how a single unit or category is divided. The standard pie chart is a circle within which wedges have been cut and labeled. Each of these wedges is proportional in size to its part of the whole. For instance, consider a pie chart representing a student's budget. If the student spends half her money on rent, then the pie chart will represent that amount with a line through the center of the pie. If she spends a quarter of her money on food, there will be a line extending from the edge of the circle to the center at a right angle to the line depicting rent. This illustration would make it clear that the student spends twice as much money on rent as she does on food. The pie chart is only appropriate for showing how a whole is divided.

A pie chart is effective at showing how a single entity is divided into parts. They are not effective at demonstrating the relationships between parts of different wholes. For example, it would not be as helpful to use a pie chart to compare the respective amounts of state and federal spending devoted to infrastructure, since these values are only meaningful in the context of the entire budget.

**Plot lines** are another way to visual represent information. Every plot line follows the same stages. One can identify each of these stages in every story they read. These stages are: the introduction, rising action, conflict, climax, falling action, and resolution. The introduction tells the reader what the story will be about and sets up the plot. The rising action is what happens that leads up to the conflict, which is some sort of problem that arises, with the climax at its peak. The falling action is what happens after the climax of the conflict. The resolution is the conclusion and often has the final solution to the problem in the conflict. A plot line looks like this:

### Determining word meaning

An understanding of the basics of language is helpful, and often vital, to understanding what you read. The term *structural analysis* refers to looking at the parts of a word and breaking it down into its different components to determine the word's meaning. Parts of a word include prefixes, suffixes, and the root word. By learning the meanings of prefixes, suffixes, and other word fundamentals, you can decipher the meaning of words which may not yet be in your vocabulary. Prefixes are common letter combinations at the beginning of words, while suffixes are common letter combinations at the end. The main part of the word is known as the root. Visually, it would look like this: prefix + root word + suffix. Look first at the individual meanings of the root word, prefix and/or suffix. Using knowledge of the meaning(s) of the prefix and/or suffix to see what information it adds to the root. Even if the meaning of the root is unknown, one can use knowledge of the prefix's and/or suffix's meaning(s) to determine an approximate meaning of the word. For example, if one sees the word *uninspired* and does not know what it means, they can use the knowledge that *un-* means 'not' to know that the full word means "not inspired." Understanding the common prefixes and suffixes can illuminate at least part of the meaning of an unfamiliar word.

Below is a list of common prefixes and their meanings:

| Prefix | Definition | Examples |
|---|---|---|
| a | in, on, of, up, to | abed, afoot |
| a- | without, lacking | atheist, agnostic |
| ab- | from, away, off | abdicate, abjure |
| ad- | to, toward | advance |
| am- | friend, love | amicable, amatory |
| ante- | before, previous | antecedent, antedate |
| anti- | against, opposing | antipathy, antidote |
| auto- | self | autonomy, autobiography |
| belli- | war, warlike | bellicose |
| bene- | well, good | benefit, benefactor |
| bi- | two | bisect, biennial |
| bio- | life | biology, biosphere |
| cata- | down, away, thoroughly | catastrophe, cataclysm |
| chron- | time | chronometer, synchronize |
| circum- | around | circumspect, circumference |
| com- | with, together, very | commotion, complicate |
| contra- | against, opposing | contradict, contravene |
| cred- | belief, trust | credible, credit |
| de- | from | depart |
| dem- | people | demographics, democracy |
| dia- | through, across, apart | diameter, diagnose |
| dis- | away, off, down, not | dissent, disappear |
| epi- | upon | epilogue |
| equi- | equal, equally | equivalent |
| ex- | out | extract |
| for- | away, off, from | forget, forswear |
| fore- | before, previous | foretell, forefathers |
| homo- | same, equal | homogenized |
| hyper- | excessive, over | hypercritical, hypertension |
| hypo- | under, beneath | hypodermic, hypothesis |
| in- | in, into | intrude, invade |
| in- | not, opposing | incapable, ineligible |
| inter- | among, between | intercede, interrupt |
| intra- | within | intramural, intrastate |
| magn- | large | magnitude, magnify |
| mal- | bad, poorly, not | malfunction |
| micr- | small | microbe, microscope |
| mis- | bad, poorly, not | misspell, misfire |
| mono- | one, single | monogamy, monologue |
| mor- | die, death | mortality, mortuary |
| neo- | new | neolithic, neoconservative |

| | | |
|---|---|---|
| non- | not | nonentity, nonsense |
| ob- | against, opposing | objection |
| omni- | all, everywhere | omniscient |
| ortho- | right, straight | orthogonal, orthodox |
| over- | above | overbearing |
| pan- | all, entire | panorama, pandemonium |
| para- | beside, beyond | parallel, paradox |
| per- | through | perceive, permit |
| peri- | around | periscope, perimeter |
| phil- | love, like | philosophy, philanthropic |
| poly- | many | polymorphous, polygamous |
| post- | after, following | postpone, postscript |
| pre- | before, previous | prevent, preclude |
| prim- | first, early | primitive, primary |
| pro- | forward, in place of | propel, pronoun |
| re- | back, backward, again | revoke, recur |
| retro- | back, backward | retrospect, retrograde |
| semi- | half, partly | semicircle, semicolon |
| sub- | under, beneath | subjugate, substitute |
| super- | above, extra | supersede, supernumerary |
| sym- | with, together | sympathy, symphony |
| trans- | across, beyond, over | transact, transport |
| ultra- | beyond, excessively | ultramodern, ultrasonic, ultraviolet |
| un- | not, reverse of | unhappy, unlock |
| uni- | one | uniform, unity |
| vis- | to see | visage, visible |

Below is a list of common suffixes and their meanings:

| Suffix | Definition | Examples |
|---|---|---|
| -able | able to, likely | capable, tolerable |
| -age | process, state, rank | passage, bondage |
| -ance | act, condition, fact | acceptance, vigilance |
| -arch | to rule | monarch |
| -ard | one that does excessively | drunkard, wizard |
| -ate | having, showing | separate, desolate |
| -ation | action, state, result | occupation, starvation |
| -cy | state, condition | accuracy, captaincy |
| -dom | state, rank, condition | serfdom, wisdom |
| -en | cause to be, become | deepen, strengthen |
| -er | one who does | teacher |
| -esce | become, grow, continue | convalesce, acquiesce |
| -esque | in the style of, like | picturesque, grotesque |
| -ess | feminine | waitress, lioness |
| -fic | making, causing | terrific, beatific |
| -ful | full of, marked by | thankful, zestful |
| -fy | make, cause, cause to have | glorify, fortify |
| -hood | state, condition | manhood, statehood |
| -ible | able, likely, fit | edible, possible, divisible |
| -ion | action, result, state | union, fusion |
| -ish | suggesting, like | churlish, childish |
| -ism | act, manner, doctrine | barbarism, socialism |
| -ist | doer, believer | monopolist, socialist |
| -ition | action, state, result | sedition, expedition |
| -ity | state, quality, condition | acidity, civility |
| -ize | make, cause to be, treat with | sterilize, mechanize, criticize |
| -less | lacking, without | hopeless, countless |
| -like | like, similar | childlike, dreamlike |
| -logue | type of written/spoken language | prologue |
| -ly | like, of the nature of | friendly, positively |
| -ment | means, result, action | refreshment, disappointment |
| -ness | quality, state | greatness, tallness |
| -or | doer, office, action | juror, elevator, honor |
| -ous | marked by, given to | religious, riotous |
| -ship | the art or skill of | statesmanship |
| -some | apt to, showing | tiresome, lonesome |
| -th | act, state, quality | warmth, width |
| -tude | quality, state, result | magnitude, fortitude |
| -ty | quality, state | enmity, activity |
| -ward | in the direction of | backward, homeward |

When defining words in a text, words often have a meaning that is more than the dictionary definition. The **denotative** meaning of a word is the literal meaning. The **connotative** meaning goes beyond the denotative meaning to include the emotional reaction a word may invoke. The connotative meaning often takes the denotative meaning a step further due to associations which the reader makes with the denotative meaning. The reader can differentiate between the denotative and connotative meanings by first recognizing when authors use each meaning. Most non-fiction, for example, is fact-based, the authors not using flowery, figurative language. The reader can assume that the writer is using the denotative, or literal, meaning of words. In fiction, on the other hand, the author may be using the connotative meaning. Connotation is one form of figurative language. The reader should use context clues to determine if the author is using the denotative or connotative meaning of a word.

Readers of all levels will encounter words with which they are somewhat unfamiliar. The best way to define a word in **context** is to look for nearby words that can help. For instance, unfamiliar nouns are often accompanied by examples that furnish a definition. Consider the following sentence: "Dave arrived at the party in hilarious garb: a leopard-print shirt, buckskin trousers, and high heels." If a reader was unfamiliar with the meaning of garb, he could read the examples and quickly determine that the word means "clothing." Examples will not always be this obvious. For instance, consider this sentence: "Parsley, lemon, and flowers were just a few of items he used as garnishes." Here, the possibly unfamiliar word *garnishes* is exemplified by parsley, lemon, and flowers. Readers who have eaten in a few restaurants will probably be able to identify a garnish as something used to decorate a plate.

In addition to looking at the context of a passage, readers can often use contrasts to define an unfamiliar word in context. In many sentences, the author will not describe the unfamiliar word directly, but will instead describe the opposite of the unfamiliar word. Of course, this provides information about the word the reader needs to define. Consider the following example: "Despite his intelligence, Hector's low brow and bad posture made him look obtuse." The author suggests that Hector's appearance was opposite to his actual intelligence. Therefore, *obtuse* must mean unintelligent or stupid. Here is another example: "Despite the horrible weather, we were beatific about our trip to Alaska." The word *despite* indicates that the speaker's feelings were at odds with the weather. Since the weather is described as "horrible," *beatific* must mean something good.

In some cases, there will be very few contextual clues to help a reader define the meaning of an unfamiliar word. When this happens, one strategy the reader may employ is substitution. A good reader will brainstorm some possible synonyms for the given word, and then substitute these words into the sentence. If the sentence and the surrounding passage continue to make sense, the substitution has revealed at least some information about the unfamiliar word. Consider the sentence, "Frank's admonition rang in her ears as she climbed the mountain." A reader unfamiliar with *admonition* might come up with some substitutions like "vow," "promise," "advice," "complaint," or "compliment." All of these words make general sense of the sentence, though their meanings are diverse. The process has suggested, however, that an admonition is some sort of message. The substitution strategy is rarely able to pinpoint a precise definition, but can be effective as a last resort.

It is sometimes possible to define an unfamiliar word by looking at the descriptive words in the context. Consider the following sentence: "Fred dragged the recalcitrant boy kicking and screaming up the stairs." *Dragged*, *kicking*, and *screaming* all suggest that the boy does not want to go up the stairs. The reader may assume that *recalcitrant* means something like unwilling or protesting. In that example, an unfamiliar adjective was identified. It is perhaps more typical to use description to define an unfamiliar noun, as in this sentence: "Don's wrinkled frown and constantly shaking fist identified him as a curmudgeon of the first order." Don is described as having a "wrinkled frown and constantly shaking fist," suggesting that a *curmudgeon* must be a grumpy old man. Contrasts do not always provide detailed information about the unfamiliar word, but they at least give the reader some clues.

When a word has more than one meaning, it can be tricky to determine how it is being used in a given sentence. Consider the verb *cleave*, which bizarrely can mean either "join" or "separate." When a reader comes upon this word, she will have to select the definition that makes the most sense. So, take as an example the following sentence: "The birds cleaved together as they flew from the oak tree." Immediately, the presence of the word *together* should suggest that in this sentence *cleave* is being used to mean "*join*." A slightly more difficult example would be the sentence, "Hermione's knife cleaved the bread cleanly." It doesn't make sense for a knife to join bread together, so the word must be meant to indicate separation. Discovering the meaning of a word with multiple meanings requires the same tricks as defining an unknown word: looking for contextual clues and evaluating substituted words.

**Literary devices**

Understanding how words relate to each other can often add meaning to a passage. This is explained by understanding **synonyms** (words that mean the same thing) and **antonyms** (words that mean the opposite of one another). As an example, *dry* and *arid* are synonyms, and *dry* and *wet* are antonyms. There are many pairs of words in English that can be considered synonyms, despite having slightly different definitions. For instance, the words *friendly* and *collegial* can both be used to describe a warm interpersonal relationship, so it would be correct to call them synonyms. However, *collegial* (kin to *colleague*) is more often used in reference to professional or academic relationships, while *friendly* has no such connotation. Nevertheless, it would be appropriate to call these words synonyms. If the difference between the two words is too great, however, they may not be called synonyms. *Hot* and *warm* are not synonyms, for instance, because their meanings are too distinct. A good way to determine whether two words are synonyms is to substitute one for the other and see if the sentence means the same thing. Substituting *warm* for *hot* in a sentence would convey a different meaning.

Antonyms are opposites. *Light* and *dark*, *up* and *down*, *right* and *left*, *good* and *bad*: these are all sets of antonyms. It is important to distinguish between antonyms and pairs of words that are simply different. *Black* and *gray*, for instance, are not antonyms because gray is not the opposite of black. *Black* and *white*, on the other hand, are antonyms. Not every word has an antonym. For instance, many nouns do not. What would be the antonym of *chair*, after all? On a standardized test, the questions related to antonyms are more likely to concern adjectives. Remember that adjectives are words that describe a noun. Some common adjectives include *red*, *fast*, *skinny*, and *sweet*. Of these four examples, only *red* lacks a group of obvious antonyms.

There are many types of language devices that authors use to convey their meaning in a more descriptive or interesting way. Understanding these concepts will help you understand what you read. These types of devices are called *figurative language* – language that goes beyond the literal meaning of the words. **Descriptive language** that evokes imagery in the reader's mind is one type of figurative language. **Exaggeration** is also one type of figurative language. Also, when you compare two things, you are using figurative language. **Similes** and **metaphors** are ways of comparing things, and both are types of figurative language commonly found in poetry. An example of figurative language (a simile in this case) is: "The child howled like a coyote when her mother told her to pick up the toys." In this example, the child's howling is compared to that of a coyote. Figurative language is descriptive in nature and helps the reader understand the sound being made in this sentence.

**Alliteration** is a stylistic device, or literary technique, in which successive words (more strictly, stressed syllables) begin with the same sound or letter. Alliteration is a frequent tool in poetry but it is also common in prose, particularly to highlight short phrases. Especially in poetry, it contributes to euphony of the passage, lending it a musical air. It may act to humorous effect. Alliteration draws attention to itself, which may be a good or a bad thing. Authors should be conscious of the character of the sound to be repeated. In the above example, a *th* sound is somewhat difficult to make quickly in four consecutive words, so the phrase conveys a little of the difficulty of moving through tall grass. If the author is indeed trying to suggest this difficulty, then the alliteration is a success. Consider, however, the description of eyes as "glassy globes of glitter." This is definitely alliteration, since the initial *gl* sound is used three times. However, one might question whether this awkward sound is appropriate for a description of pretty eyes. The phrase is not especially pleasant to the ear, and therefore is probably not effective as alliteration. Related to alliteration are *assonance*, the repetition of vowel sounds, and *consonance*, the repetition of consonant sounds.

A **figure of speech**, sometimes termed a rhetorical figure or device, or elocution, is a word or phrase that departs from straightforward, literal language. Figures of speech are often used and crafted for emphasis, freshness of expression, or clarity. However, clarity may also suffer from their use.

Note that not all theories of meaning necessarily have a concept of "literal language" (see literal and figurative language). Under theories that do not, figure of speech is not an entirely coherent concept.

As an example of the figurative use of a word, consider the sentence, "I am going to crown you." It may mean:

- I am going to place a literal crown on your head.
- I am going to symbolically exalt you to the place of kingship.
- I am going to punch you in the head with my clenched fist.
- I am going to put a second checker on top of your checker to signify that it has become a king.

A **metaphor** is a type of figurative language in which the writer equates one thing with a different thing. For instance, in the sentence "The bird was an arrow arcing through the sky," the arrow is serving as a metaphor for the bird. The point of a metaphor is to encourage the reader to think about the thing being described in a different way. Using this example, we are being asked to envision the bird's flight as being similar to the arc of an arrow, so we will imagine it to be swift, bending, etc. Metaphors are a way for the author to describe without being direct and obvious. Metaphors are a more lyrical and suggestive way of providing information. Note that the thing to which a metaphor refers will not always be mentioned explicitly by the author. For instance, consider the following description of a forest in winter: "Swaying skeletons reached for the sky and groaned as the wind blew through them." The author is clearly using *skeletons* as a metaphor for leafless trees. This metaphor creates a spooky tone while inspiring the reader's imagination.

**Metonymy** is referring to one thing in terms of another, closely related thing. This is similar to metaphor, but there is less distance between the description and the thing being described. An example of metonymy is referring to the news media as the "press," when of course the press is only the device by which newspapers are printed. Metonymy is a way of referring to something without having to repeat its name constantly. **Synecdoche**, on the other hand, is referring to a whole by one of its parts. An example of synecdoche would be calling a police officer a "badge." Synecdoche, like metonymy, is a handy way of referring without having to overuse certain words. It also allows the writer to emphasize aspects of the thing being described. For instance, referring to businessmen as "suits" suggests professionalism, conformity, and drabness.

**Hyperbole** is overstatement for effect. The following sentence is an example of hyperbole: *He jumped ten feet in the air when he heard the good news.* Obviously, no person has the ability to jump ten feet in the air. The author hyperbolizes not because he believes the statement will be taken literally, but because the exaggeration conveys the extremity of emotion. Consider how much less colorful the sentence would be if the author simply said, "He jumped when he heard the good news." Hyperbole can be dangerous if the author does not exaggerate enough. For instance, if the author wrote, "He jumped two feet in the air when he heard the good news," the reader might not be sure whether this is actually true or just hyperbole. Of course, in many situations this distinction will not really matter. However, an author should avoid confusing or vague hyperbole when he needs to maintain credibility or authority with readers.

**Understatement** is the opposite of hyperbole: that is, it is describing something as less than it is, for effect. As an example, consider a person who climbs Mount Everest and then describes the journey as "a little stroll." This is an almost extreme example of understatement. Like other types of figurative language, understatement has a range of uses. It may convey self-deprecation or modesty, as in the above example. Of course, some people might interpret understatement as false modesty, a deliberate attempt to call attention to the magnitude of what is being discussed. For example, a woman is complimented on her enormous diamond engagement ring and says, "Oh, this little thing?" Her understatement might be viewed as snobby or insensitive. Understatement can have various effects, but it always calls attention to itself.

A **simile** is a figurative expression similar to a metaphor, though it requires the use of a distancing word like *like* or *as*. Some examples are "The sun was like an orange," "eager as a beaver," and "nimble as a mountain goat." Because a simile includes *like* or *as,* it creates a little space between the description and the thing being described. If an author says that a house was "like a shoebox," the tone is slightly different than if the author said that the house *was* a shoebox. In a simile, the author indicates an awareness that the description is not the same thing as the thing being described. In a metaphor, there is no such distinction, even though one may safely assume that the author is aware of it. This is a subtle difference, but authors will alternately use metaphors and similes depending on their intended tone.

Another type of figurative language is **personification.** This is the description of the nonhuman as if it were human. Literally, the word means the process of making something into a person. There is a wide range of approaches to personification, from common expressions like "whispering wind" to full novels like *Animal Farm*, by George Orwell, in which the Bolshevik Revolution is reenacted by farmyard animals. The general intent of personification is to describe things in a manner that will be comprehensible to readers. When an author states that a tree "groans" in the wind, she of course does not mean that the tree is emitting a low, pained sound from its mouth. Instead, she means that the tree is making a noise similar to a human groan. Of course, this personification establishes a tone of sadness or suffering. A different tone would be established if the author said the tree was "swaying" or "dancing."

**Irony** is a statement that suggests its opposite. In other words, it is when an author or character says one thing but means another. For example, imagine a man walks in his front door, covered in mud and in tattered clothes. His wife asks him, "How was your day?" and he says "Great!" The man's comment is an example of irony. As in this example, irony often depends on information the reader obtains elsewhere. There is a fine distinction between irony and sarcasm. Irony is any statement in which the literal meaning is opposite from the intended meaning, while sarcasm is a statement of this type that is also insulting to the person at whom it is directed. A sarcastic statement suggests that the other person is stupid enough to believe an obviously false statement is true. Irony is a bit more subtle than sarcasm.

The more words a person is exposed to, the greater their vocabulary will become. By reading on a regular basis, a person can increase the number of ways they have seen a word in context. Based on experience, a person can recall how a word was used in the past and apply that knowledge to a new context. For example, a person may have seen the word *gull* used to mean a bird that is found near the seashore. However, a *gull* can also be a person who is easily tricked. If the word is used in context in reference to a character, the reader can recognize that the character is being called a bird that is not seen as extremely intelligent. Using what the reader knows about a word can be useful when making comparisons or figuring out the meaning of a new use of a word, as in figurative language, idioms, analogies, and multiple-meaning words.

# *English Language Skills*

## Choosing topics

Very often the choice of a subject may be assigned or determined by someone besides the writer. When the choice is left to the writer, it is sometimes wise to allow the topic itself to "select" the writer. That is to say those topics that interest, engage, puzzle, or stimulate someone may be good choices. Engaging the writer is the most important factor in choosing a topic. Engagement notes a strong interest and spirit of inquiry about the subject. It is a signal that the subject and author are interacting in some creative sense, which usually encourages good writing. Even with an assigned topic, a particular aspect of the subject may interest the writer more than others. The key to any writer's choice of topic is the ability of a subject to inspire the author to question, speculate, inquire and interact. From this natural interest and attraction, some of the most creative writing develops.

A common problem is limiting the scope of a writing assignment. Narrowing the scope is not always enough, because the new subject may itself be too broad. Focusing on an aspect of a topic often effectively results in a topic both interesting and manageable. For example narrowing a topic like the "Civil War" to the "Battle of Antietam" may still leave an unwieldy topic. To sharpen the focus, an aspect such as "The use of artillery by Confederates at the battle of Antietam" could be selected.

## Understanding assignments

Many writing assignments address specific audiences (physicians, attorneys, and teachers) and have specific goals. These writers know for whom and why they are writing. This can clarify the writing significantly. Other assignments, particularly in academic settings, may appear with no specific subject, audience, or apparent purpose. Assignments may come with some variables; a specified audience, subject, or approach and leave the rest up to the writer. Because of these variables, it is useful to consider the following questions:

1. What specifically is the assignment asking the writer to do?
2. What information or knowledge in necessary to fulfill the assignment?
3. Can the topic be broadened or limited to more effectively complete the project?
4. Are there specific parameters or other requirements for the project?
5. What is the purpose of the assignment?
6. Who is the intended audience for the work?
7. What is the length of the assignment? Does it limit or require a certain number of pages? If so, what are the parameters?
8. What is the deadline for the assignment? Sometimes preliminary materials are to be submitted before the main assignment. Considering these factors will give a writer information needed to set a schedule for the project.

<u>Length and document design</u>

Writers seldom have control over length and document design. Usually a academic assignment has a specified length, while journalists work within tight word count parameters. Document design often follows the purpose of a writing project. Specific formats are required for lab reports, research papers, and abstracts. The business world operates within fairly narrow format styles, the business letter, memo, and report allowing only a small departure from the standard format.

There are some assignments that allow the writer to choose the specific format for the work. The increased flourishes provided by computers allow a great deal of creativity in designing an visually stimulating and functional document. Improving readability is always a worthwhile goal for any project, and this is becoming much easier with available software.

Deadlines

Deadlines are a critical element in any writing assignment. They help a writer budget their time to complete the assignment on schedule. For elaborate or complex writing projects, it is useful to create a working schedule that includes time for research, writing, revising, and editing. Breaking the process down into more workable parts with their own deadlines, helps keep a writer aware of the progress being made.

**Purposes of writing**

What is the main purpose of the proposed piece? This may be very clear and focused, or ambiguous. A writer should be clear about the purpose of his writing, as this will determine the direction and elements of the work. Generally purposes may be divided into three groups:

1. To entertain.
2. To persuade or convince.
3. To educate or inform.

Some or all of these purposes may be the goal in a given writing assignment. It is helpful to try and identify the major purpose of a writing piece, as well as any secondary purposes involved. Purpose in writing must be linked closely to the writer's goals in undertaking the assignment. In academic settings, it is usually more accurate to think in terms of several goals. A student may wish to convince the audience in an entertaining and informative fashion. However one goal should be paramount. Expectations of the instructor play an important role in an academic assignment.

**Recursive nature**

The process of writing is described as recursive; This means that the goals and parts of the writing process are often a seamless flow, constantly influencing each other without clear boundaries. The "steps' in the writing process occur organically, with planning, drafting and revising all taking place simultaneously, in no necessary or orderly fashion. The writer rarely pays attention to the recursive patterns. The process unfolds naturally, without attention or dependence on a predetermined sequence. The writing process is a series of recursive activities, which rarely occur in a linear fashion, rather moving back and forth between planning, drafting, revising, more planning, more drafting, polishing until the writing is complete. Forthcoming topics will cover many parts of the process individually, but they go on together as a seamless flow.

**Considering an audience**

The careful consideration of the anticipated audience is a requisite for any project. Although much of this work is intuitive, some guidelines are helpful in the analysis of an audience:

1. Specifically identify your audience. Are they eclectic or share common characteristics?
2. Determine qualities of the audience such as age, education, sex, culture, and special interests.
3. Understand what the audience values; brevity, humor, originality, honesty are examples.
4. What is the audience's attitude toward the topic; skeptical, knowledgeable, pro or con?
5. Understand the writer's relationship to the audience; peer, authority, advocate, or antagonist?

Understanding the qualities of an audience allows the writer to form an organizational plan tailored to achieve the objectives of the writing with the audience in mind. It is essential to effective writing.

## Level of formality

In choosing a level of formality in writing, the subject and audience should be carefully considered. The subject may require a more dignified tone, or perhaps an informal style would be best. The relationship between writer and reader is important in choosing a level of formality. Is the audience one with which you can assume a close relationship, or should a more formal tone prevail?

Most student or business writing requires some degree of formality. Informal writing is appropriate for private letters, personal e-mails, and business correspondence between close associates. Vocabulary and language should be relatively simple.

It is important to be consistent in the level of formality in a piece of writing. Shifts in levels of formality can confuse readers and detract from the message of the writing.

## Understanding the topic

Easily overlooked is the basic question of ascertaining how knowledgeable the writer is about the subject. A careful evaluation should be made to determine what is known about the topic, and what information must be acquired to undertake the writing assignment. Most people have a good sense of how to go about researching a subject, using the obvious available resources: libraries, the internet, journals, research papers and other sources. There are however some specific strategies that can help a writer learn more about a subject, and just as importantly, what is not known and must be learned. These strategies or techniques not only are useful in researching a subject, they can also be used when problems come up during the actual writing phase of the assignment. These strategies include brainstorming, free writing, looping, and questioning.

<u>Brainstorming</u>

Brainstorming is a technique used frequently in business, industry, science, and engineering. It is accomplished by tossing out ideas, usually with several other people, in order to find a fresh approach or a creative way to approach a subject. This can be accomplished by an individual by simply free-associating about a topic. Sitting with paper and pen, every thought about the subject is written down in a word or phrase. This is done without analytical thinking, just recording what arises in the mind about the topic. The list is then read over carefully several times. The writer looks for patterns, repetitions, clusters of ideas, or a recurring theme. Although brainstorming can be done individually, it works best when several people are involved. Three to five people is ideal. This allows an exchange of ideas, points of view, and often results in fresh ideas or approaches.

<u>Free writing</u>

Free writing is a form of brainstorming in a structured way. The method involves exploring a topic by writing about it for a certain period of time without stopping. A writer sets a time limit, and begins writing in complete sentences everything that comes to mind about the topic. Writing continues without interruption until the set period expires. When time expires, read carefully everything that has been written down. Much of it may make little or no sense, but insights and observations may emerge that the free writer did not know existed in his mind. Writing has a unique quality about it of jogging loose ideas, and seeing a word or idea appear may trigger others. Freewrtiting usually results in a fuller expression of ideas than brainstorming, because thoughts and associations are written in a more comprehensive manner. Both techniques can be used to complement one another and can yield much different results.

Looping

Looping is a variation of freewriting that focuses a topic in short five-minute stages, or loops. Looping is done as follows:

1. With a subject in mind, spend five minutes freewriting without stopping. The results are the first loop.
2. Evaluate what has been written in the first loop. Locate the strongest or most recurring thought which should be summarized in a single sentence. This is the "center of gravity", and is the starting point of the next loop.
3. Using the summary sentence as a starting point, another five minute cycle of freewriting takes place. Evaluate the writing and locate the "center of gravity" for the second loop, and summarize it in a single sentence. This will be the start of the third loop.
4. Continue this process until a clear new direction to the subject emerges. Usually this will yield a starting point for a whole new approach to a topic.

Looping can be very helpful when a writer is blocked or unable to generate new ideas on a subject.

Questioning

Asking and answering questions provides a more structured approach to investigating a subject. Several types of questions may be used to illuminate an issue.

1. Questions to describe a topic. Questions such as "What is It?", "What caused it?", "What is it like or unlike?", "What is it a part of"? What do people say about it?" help explore a topic systematically.
2. Questions to explain a topic. Examples include" Who, how, and what is it?", "Where does it end and begin?" What is at issue?", and "How is it done?".
3. Questions to persuade include "What claims can be made about it?", "What evidence supports the claims?", "Can the claims be refuted?", and "What assumptions support the claims?"

Questioning can be a very effective device as it leads the writer through a process in a systematic manner in order to gain more information about a subject.

**Thesis**

A thesis states the main idea of the essay. A working or tentative thesis should be established early on in the writing process. This working thesis is subject to change and modification as writing progresses. It will serve to keep the writer focused as ideas develop.

The working thesis has two parts: a topic and a comment. The comment makes an important point about the topic. A working thesis should be interesting to an anticipated audience; it should be specific and limit the topic to a manageable scope. Theses three criteria are useful tools to measure the effectiveness of any working thesis. The writer applies these tools to ascertain:

1. Is the topic of sufficient interest to hold an audience?
2. Is the topic specific enough to generate interest?
3. Is the topic manageable? Too broad? Too narrow? Can it be adequately researched?

Creating an effective thesis is an art. The thesis should be a generalization rather than a fact, and should be neither too broad or narrow in scope. A thesis prepares readers for facts and details, so it may not be a fact itself. It is a generalization that requires further proof or supporting points. Any thesis too broad may be an unwieldy topic and must be narrowed. The thesis should have a sharp focus, and avoid vague, ambivalent language. The process of bringing the thesis into sharp focus may help in outlining major sections of the work. This process is known as blueprinting, and helps the writer control the shape and sequence of the paper. Blueprinting outlines major points and supporting arguments that are used in elaborating on the thesis. A completed blueprint often leads to a development of an accurate first draft of a work. Once the thesis and opening are complete, it is time to address the body of the work.

**Formal outlines**

A formal outline may be useful if the subject is complex, and includes many elements. here is a guide to preparing formal outlines:

1. Always put the thesis at the top so it may be referred to as often as necessary during the outlining.
2. Make subjects similar in generality as parallel as possible in the formal outline.
3. Use complete sentences rather than phrases or sentence fragments in the outline.
4. Use the conventional system of letters and numbers to designate levels of generality.
5. There should be at least two subdivisions for each category in the formal outline.
6. Limit the number of major sections in the outline. If there are too many major sections, combine some of them and supplement with additional sub-categories.
7. Remember the formal outline is still subject to change; remain flexible throughout the process.

**Research**

Research is a means of critical inquiry, investigations based on sources of knowledge. Research is the basis of scientific knowledge, of inventions, scholarly inquiry, and many personal and general decisions. Much of work consists of research - finding something out and reporting on it. We can list five basic precepts about research:

1. Everyone does research. To buy an car, go to a film, to investigate anything is research. We all have experience in doing research.
2. Good research draws a person into a "conversation" about a topic. Results are more knowledge about a subject, understanding different sides to issues, and be able to discuss intelligently nuances of the topic.
3. Research is always driven by a purpose. Reasons may vary from solving a problem to advocating a position, but research is almost always goal oriented.
4. Research is shaped by purpose, and in turn the fruits of research refine the research further.
5. Research is usually not a linear process; it is modified and changed by the results it yields.

Many writing assignments require research. Research is basically the process of gathering information for the writer's use. There are two broad categories of research:

1. Library research should be started after a research plan is outlined. Topics that require research should be listed, and catalogues, bibliographies, periodical indexes checked for references. Librarians are usually an excellent source of ideas and information on researching a topic.
2. Field research is based on observations, interviews, and questionnaires. This can be done by an individual or a team, depending on the scope of the field research.

The specific type and amount of research will vary widely with the topic and the writing assignment. A simple essay or story may require only a few hours of research, while a major project can consume weeks or months.

Research material

- Primary sources are the raw material of research. This can include results of experiments, notes, and surveys or interviews done by the researcher. Other primary sources are books, letters, diaries, eyewitness accounts, and performances attended by the researcher.
- Secondary sources consist of oral and written accounts prepared by others. This includes reports, summaries, critical reviews, and other sources not developed by the researcher.

Most research writing uses both primary and secondary sources. Primary sources from first-hand accounts and secondary sources for background and supporting documentation. The research process calls for active reading and writing throughout. As research yields information, it often calls for more reading and research, and the cycle continues.

Organizing information

Organizing information effectively is an important part of research. The data must be organized in a useful manner so that it can be effectively used. Three basic ways to organize information are:

1. Spatial organization - this is useful as it lets the user "see" the information, to fix it in space. This has benefits for those individuals who are visually adept at processing information.
2. Chronological organization is the most common presentation of information. This method places information in the sequence with which it occurs. Chronological organization is very useful in explaining a process that occurs in a step-by-step pattern.
3. Logical organization includes presenting material in a logical pattern that makes intuitive sense. Some patterns that are frequently used are illustrated, definition, compare/contrast, cause/effect, problem/solution, and division/classification. Each of these methods is discussed next.

Logical organization

There are six major types of logical organization that are frequently used:

1. Illustrations may be used to support the thesis. Examples are the most common form of this organization.
2. Definitions say what something is or is not is another way of organization. What are the characteristics of the topic?
3. Dividing or classifying information into separate items according to their similarities is a common and effective organizing method.
4. Comparing, focusing on the similarities of things, and contrasting, highlighting the differences between things is an excellent tool to use with certain kinds of information.
5. Cause and effect is a simple tool to logically understand relationships between things. A phenomena may be traced to its causes for organizing a subject logically.
6. Problem and solution is a simple and effective manner of logically organizing material. It is very commonly used and lucidly presents information.

**Writing**

An initial plan

After information gathering has been completed and the fruits of the research organized effectively, the writer now has a rough or initial plan for the work. A rough plan may be informal, consisting of a few elements such as "Introduction, Body, and Conclusions", or a more formal outline. The rough plan may include multiple organizational strategies within the over-all piece, or it may isolate one or two that can be used exclusively. At this stage the plan is just that, a rough plan subject to change as new ideas appear, and the organization takes a new approach. In these cases, the need for more research sometimes becomes apparent, or existing information should be considered in a new way. A more formal outline leads to an easier transition to a draft, but it can also limit the new possibilities that may arise as the plan unfolds. Until the outlines of the piece become clear, it is usually best to remain open to possible shifts in approaching the subject.

<u>Supporting the thesis</u>

It is most important that the thesis of the paper be clearly expounded and adequately supported by additional points. The thesis sentence should contain a clear statement of the major theme and a comment about the thesis. The writer has an opportunity here to state what is significant or noteworthy of this particular treatment of the subject. Each sentence and paragraph in turn, should build on the thesis and support it.

Particular attention should be paid to insuring the organization properly uses the thesis and supporting points. It can be useful to outline the draft after writing, to insure that each paragraph leads smoothly to the next, and that the thesis is continually supported. The outline may highlight a weakness in flow or ideation that can be repaired. It will also spatially illustrate the flow of the argument, and provide a visual representation of the thesis and its supporting points. Often things become clearer when outlined than with a block of writing.

<u>First draft</u>

Drafting is a mysterious art, and does not easily lend itself to rules. Generally, the more detailed the formal or informal outline, the easier is the transition to a first draft. The process of drafting is a learning one, and planning, organizing, and researching may be ongoing. Drafting is an evaluative process as well, and the whole project will be under scrutiny as the draft develops. The scope may be narrowed or widened, the approach may change, and different conclusions may emerge.

The process itself is shaped by the writer's preferences for atmosphere during the writing process. Time of day or night, physical location, ambient conditions, and any useful rituals can all play into the writer's comfort and productivity. The creation of an atmosphere conducive to the writer's best work is a subtle but important aspect of writing that is often overlooked. Although excellent writing has often been done in difficult situations, it is not the best prescription for success.

<u>Evaluating the draft</u>

Once a draft is finished, an evaluation is in order. This can often mean reviewing the entire process with a critical eye. There is no formal checklist that insures a complete and effective evaluation, but there are some elements that can be considered:

1. It should be determined whether sufficient research was done to properly develop the assignment. Are there areas that call for additional information? If so, what type?
2. What are the major strengths of the draft? Are there any obvious weaknesses? How can these be fixed?
3. Who is the audience for this work and how well does the material appeal to them?
4. Does the material actually accomplish the goals of the assignment? If not, what needs to be done?

This is a stage for stepping back from the project and giving it an objective evaluation. Changes made now can improve the material significantly. Take time here to formulate a final approach to the subject.

Objective criticism

Now is the time to obtain objective criticisms of the draft. It is helpful to provide readers with a list of questions to be answered about the draft. Some examples of effective questions are:

1. Does the introduction catch the reader's attention? How can it be improved?
2. Is the thesis clearly stated and supported by additional points?
3. What type of organizational plan is used? Is it appropriate for the subject?
4. Are paragraphs well developed and is there a smooth transition between them?
5. Are the sentences well written and convey the appropriate meaning?
6. Are words used effectively and colorfully in the text?
7. What is the tone of the writing? Is it appropriate to the audience and subject?
8. Is the conclusion satisfactory? Is there a sense of completion that the work is finished?
9. What are main strengths and weaknesses of the writing? Are there specific suggestions for improvement?

Title, introduction, and conclusion

1. A good title can identify the subject, describe it in a colorful manner, and give clues to the approach and sometimes conclusion of the writing. It usually defines the work in the mind of the reader.
2. A strong introduction follows the lead of the title; it draws the readers into the work, and clearly states the topic with a clarifying comment. A common style is to state the topic, and then provide additional details, finally leading to a statement of the thesis at the end. An introduction can also begin with an arresting quote, question, or strong opinion, which grabs the reader's attention.
3. A good conclusion should leave readers satisfied and provide a sense of closure. Many conclusions restate the thesis and formulate general statements that grow out of it. Writers often find ways to conclude in a dramatic fashion, through a vivid image, quotation, or a warning. This in an effort to give the ending the "punch" to tie up any existing points.

An introduction announces the main point of the work. It will usually be a paragraph of 50 to 150 words, opening with a few sentences to engage the reader, and conclude with the essay's main point. The sentence stating the main point is called the thesis. If possible, the sentences leading to the thesis should attract the reader's attention with a provocative question, vivid image, description, paradoxical statement, quotation, anecdote, or a question. The thesis could also appear at the beginning of the introduction. There are some types of writing that do not lend themselves to stating a thesis in one sentence. Personal narratives and some types of business writing may be better served by conveying an overriding purpose of the text, which may or may not be stated directly. The important point is to impress the audience with the rationale for the writing.

The body of the essay should fulfill the promise of the introduction and thesis. If an informal outline has not been done, now is the time for a more formal one. Constructing the formal outline will create a "skeleton" of the paper. Using this skeleton, it is much easier to fill out the body of an essay. It is useful to block out paragraphs based on the outline, to insure they contain all the supporting points, and are in the appropriate sequence.

The conclusion of the essay should remind readers of the main point, without belaboring it. It may be relatively short, as the body of the text has already "made the case" for the thesis. A conclusion can summarize the main points, and offer advice or ask a question. Never introduce new ideas in a conclusion. Avoid vague and desultory endings, instead closing with a crisp, often positive, note. A dramatic or rhetorical flourish can end a piece colorfully.

Examining paragraphs
Paragraphs are a key structural unit of prose utilized to break up long stretches of words into more manageable subsets, and to indicate a shift in topics or focus. Each paragraph may be examined by identifying the main point of the section, and insuring that every sentence supports or relates to the main theme. Paragraphs may be checked to make sure the organization used in each is appropriate, and that the number of sentences are adequate to develop the topic.

Examining sentences
Sentences are the building blocks of the written word, and they can be varied by paying attention to sentence length, sentence structure, and sentence openings. These elements should be varied so that writing does not seem boring, repetitive, or choppy. A careful analysis of a piece of writing will expose these stylistic problems, and they can be corrected before the final draft is written. Varying sentence structure and length can make writing more inviting and appealing to a reader.

Examining words
A writer's choice of words is a signature of their style. A careful analysis of the use of words can improve a piece of writing. Attention to the use of specific nouns rather than general ones can enliven language. Verbs should be active whenever possible to keep the writing stronger and energetic, and there should be an appropriate balance between numbers of nouns and verbs. Too many nouns can result in heavy, boring sentences.

Examining tone
Tone may be defined as the writer's attitude toward the topic, and to the audience. This attitude is reflected in the language used in the writing. If the language is ambiguous, tone becomes very difficult to ascertain. The tone of a work should be appropriate to the topic and to the intended audience. Some writing should avoid slang and jargon, while it may be fine in a different piece. Tone can range from humorous, to serious, and all levels in between. It may be more or less formal depending on the purpose of the writing, and its intended audience. All these nuances in tone can flavor the entire writing and should be kept in mind as the work evolves.

Tone is distinguished from mood, which is the feeling the writing evokes. Tone and mood may often be similar, but can also be significantly different. Mood often depends on the manner in which words and language are employed by the writer. In a sense tone and mood are two sides of a coin which color and language enliven the total approach of a writer to his subject. Mood and tone add richness and texture to words, bringing them alive in a deliberate strategy by the writer.

Examining point-of-view
Point-of-view is the perspective from which writing occurs. There are several possibilities:

1. First Person - Is written so that the "I" of the story is a participant or observer.
2. Second Person - Is a device to draw the reader in more closely. It is really a variation or refinement of the first person narrative.
3. Third Person - The most traditional form of third-person point-of-view is the "omniscient narrator", in which the narrative voice, (presumed to be the writer), is presumed to know everything about the characters, plot, and action. Most novels use this point-of-view.
4. A Multiple Point-Of-View - The narration is delivered from the perspective of several characters.

In modern writing, the "stream-of consciousness" technique developed fully by James Joyce where the interior monologue provides the narration through the thoughts, impressions, and fantasies of the narrator.

Voice
Writers should find an appropriate voice that is appropriate for the subject, appeals to the intended audience, and conforms to the conventions of the genre in which the writing is done. If there is doubt about the conventions of the genre, lab reports, informal essays, research papers, business memos, and so on - a writer may examine models of these works written by experts in the field. These models can serve as examples for form and style for a particular type of writing.

Voice can also include the writer's attitude toward the subject and audience. Care should be taken that the language and tone of the writing is considered in terms of the purpose of the writing and it intended audience.

Gauging the appropriate voice for a piece is part art, and part science. It can be a crucial element in the ultimate effectiveness of the writing.

**Writing conventions**

Conventions in writing are traditional assumptions or practices used by authors of all types of text. Some basic conventions have survived through the centuries - for example the assumption that a first person narrator in a work is telling the truth - others such as having characters in melodramas speak in asides to the audience have become outmoded. Conventions are particularly important in specialized types of writing which demand specific formats and styles. This is true of scientific and research papers, as well as much of academic and business writing. This formality has relaxed somewhat in several areas but still holds true for many fields of technical writing. Conventions are particularly useful for writers working in various types of nonfiction writing, where guidelines help the writer conform to the rules expected for that field. Conventions are part of the unspoken contract between writer and audience, and should be respected.

**Writing preparation**

Effective writing requires preparation. The planning process includes everything done prior to drafting. Depending on the project, this could take a few minutes or several months. Elements in planning, and include considering the purpose of the writing, exploring a topic, developing a working thesis, gathering necessary materials, and developing a plan for organizing the writing. The organizational plan may vary in length and components, from a detailed outline or a stack of research cards. The organizational plan is a guide to help draft a writing project, and may change as writing progresses, but having a guide to refer to can keep a project on track. Planning is usually an ongoing process throughout the writing, but it is essential to begin with a structure.

**Editing**

Time must always be allowed for thorough and careful editing in order to insure clean and error-free work. It is helpful to create a checklist of editing to use as the manuscript is proofed. Patterns of editing problems often become apparent and understanding these patterns can eliminate them. Examples of patterns of errors include misuse of commas, difficulty in shifting tenses, and spelling problems. Once these patterns are seen, it is much easier to avoid them in the original writing. A checklist should be prepared based on every piece of writing, and should be cumulative. In this manner. progress may be checked regularly and the quantity and type of errors should be reduced over time. It is often helpful to have peer proof a manuscript, to get a fresh set of eyes on the material. Editing should be treated as an opportunity to polish and perfect a written work, rather than a chore that must be done. A good editor usually turns into a better writer over time.

Proofreading
As a proofreader, the goal is always to eliminate all errors. This includes typographical errors as well as any inconsistencies in spelling and punctuation. Begin by reading the prose aloud, calling out all punctuation marks and insuring that all sentences are complete and no words are left out. It is helpful to read the material again, backwards, so the focus is on each individual word, and the tendency to skip ahead is avoided.

A computer is a blessing to writers who have trouble proofreading their work. Spelling and grammar check programs may be utilized to reduce errors significantly. However it is still important for a writer to do the manual proofing necessary to insure errors of pattern are not repeated. Computers are a wonderful tool for writers but they must be employed by the writer, rather than as the writer. Skillful use of computers should result in a finely polished manuscript free of errors.

**Evaluating student writing**

The evaluation of student writing should be structured to include three basic goals:

1. To provide students a description of what they are doing when they respond.
2. To provide a pathway for potential improvement.
3. To help students learn to evaluate themselves.

To fulfill these goals it is necessary for the concept of evaluation be broadened beyond correcting or judging students. Any teacher response to a student's response should be considered part of the evaluation. In responding to student's responses, a teacher may use written or taped comments, dialogue with students, or conferencing between teachers and students to discuss classroom performance. Students may be asked to evaluate themselves and a teacher and student can review past progress and plan directions for potential improvement.

Teacher's response:
There are seven basic components of teacher's responses to be considered:

1. Praise - To provide positive reinforcement for the student. Praise should be specific enough to bolster student's confidence.
2. Describing - Providing feedback on teacher's responses to student responses. This is best done in a conversational, non-judgmental mode.
3. Diagnosing - Determining the student's unique set of strengths, attitudes, needs, and abilities. This evaluation should take into consideration all elements of the student.
4. Judging - Evaluating the level, depth, insightfulness, completeness, and validity of a student's responses. This evaluation will depend on the criteria implied in the instructional approach.
5. Predicting - Predicting the potential improvement of student's responses based on specific criteria.
6. Record-keeping - The process of recording a student's reading interests, attitudes, and use of literary strategies, in order to chart student progress across time. Both qualitative and quantitative assessments may be used.
7. Recognition - Giving students recognition for growth and progress.

**Assessments**

Preparing for literary tests
Literary tests are measures of a student's individual performance. Literary assessments are measures of performance of a group of students without reference to individuals. Tests take into consideration what the teachers have taught the students, while assessments do not.

For either tests or assessments, the teacher needs a clear purpose on which to base their questions or activities. Students should be told of the purpose of the tests or assessments so they will know what to expect. Tests should be used sparingly as a one tool among many that can be used to evaluate students. Tests should encourage students on formulation of responses rather than rote answers. They should evaluate students on the basis of their responses rather than 'correct answers". Improvement over time may be noted and the student given praise for specific responses.

Standardized achievement tests
These multiple choice tests measure student's ability to understand text passages or apply literary concepts to texts. Although these tests are widely used, they have many limitations. They tend to be based on a simplistic model that ignores the complex nature of a reader's engagement with a text. These tests also do not measure student's articulation of responses. The purpose of these tests is to rank students in group norms, so that half the students are below the norm.

To accurately measure a student's abilities teachers should employ open ended written or oral response activities. In developing such tests, teachers must know what specific response patterns they wish to measure. The steps involved in measuring these response patterns must be clearly outlined. Teachers may wish to design questions that encourage personal expressions of responses. This would obviate the pitfall of testing primarily facts about literature rather than how students relate and use this information to engage texts.

Assessing attitudes toward literature
An important element in teaching literature is to understand the attitudes of students about reading and studying text. This may be done by group or individual interviews encouraging students to discuss their feelings about literature. Another way to measure attitudes is with a paper and pencil rating scale using six or eight point Liker scales. This type of assessment can be refined to explore preferences in form and genre.

Another type of assessment is done by using semantic scales to indicate students interest (or lack thereof) in reading in general and favored forms and genres.

Questionnaires can be developed to learn more about student's habits regarding literature. Do they use the library regularly, read books or periodicals, and what types of reading is done. Comparisons before and after instruction can indicate the effect of the instruction on habits and attitudes about literature.

Assessing instructional methods
Assessing instructional methods within a school, district, or state can help determine instructional goals and techniques relative to overall system goals. Results can indicate needed changes in the curriculum and can help an accreditation process measure the quality of an English or literature program.

An effective assessment usually includes interviews, questionnaires, and class-room observation. Trained observers rate the general type of instruction being provided, (lectures, modeling, small groups, and so on), the focus of instruction (novels, poetry, drama, and so on), the critical approach used, the response strategies used, and the response activities employed. Observers may also analyze the statements of goals and objectives in a curriculum, as well as the scope and sequence of the curriculum.

Interviews of both students and teachers are helpful in getting first hand accounts of instruction and results.

**Classroom based research**

Teacher's can conduct their own informal descriptive research to assess the effects of their teaching on student's responses. This allows teachers an opportunity to review and reflect on their instructional methods and results. This research can take many forms including:

- An analysis of student's perception of guided response- activities to determine which were most effective.
- An analysis of student's small and large group discussions.
- A teacher self analysis of their own taped, written, or conference feedback to students writing.
- Interviews with students about their responses and background experiences and attitudes.
- Evaluating student's responses to texts commonly used in their instruction.

These are only a few possibilities for effective classroom based research. Any research that provides insight into student needs and preferences can be a valuable tool.

Conducting classroom research:

1. Create a research question related to literature instruction or responses.
2. Summarize the theory and research related to the topic.
3. Describe the participants, setting, tasks, and methods of analysis.
4. Summarize the results of the research in a graph, table, or report.
5. Interpret or give reasons for the results.
6. Draw conclusions from the results that suggest ways to improve instruction and evaluation of students.

Teachers must always keep in mind the purposes driving the research. Evaluation itself is relatively easy, the challenge is using the evaluations to help both students and teachers to grow, and become better at what they are doing.

**Reviewers**

Many professional and business writers work with editors who provide advice and support throughout the writing process. In academic situations, the use of reviewers is increasing, either by instructors or perhaps at an academic writing center. Peer review sessions are sometimes scheduled for class, and afford an opportunity to hear what other students feel about a piece of writing. This gives a writer a chance to serve as a reviewer.

**Perspective**

Textual perspective

A textual knowledge of literature implies readers are taking a perspective or stance on the text. They are examining ways in which separate parts of the text relate to its overall form or structure. Textual perspectives must be used as a part of overall learning, not as an isolated feature. Textual perspective alone excludes both the author's life and the emotional experiences and attitudes of the reader. It fails to account for the readers' prior knowledge in their engagement with the work. A textual approach may include the ways in which the text shapes students' experience and emotional engagement. Based on previous reading, social acculturation, attitudes, and a host of other factors, students bring a wealth of information into any encounter with a text. Students may compare and contrast elements of their text with other works they have read or seen to form a more rounded engagement with a work.

Social perspective
A rich resource for students' of literature is their own developing social knowledge. For adolescent students', social relationships are of primary importance. It is common for younger students' to impose their own social attitudes on a text, which is fertile ground for exploring how the understanding of texts is colored by social attitudes and experiences. Student's attitudes can help them reflect on the characters in a work, and can determine their relationship with the text itself.

Social perspectives can shed light on a number of important ways which can effect a reader's engagement with the text. A skillful teacher may probe these attitudes and experiences and make students' more aware of the impact of social attitudes to reading and studying a work of literature. This knowledge can become cumulative and promote more careful understanding of a literature over a period of time.

Cultural and historical context
The cultural knowledge and background of readers effects their response to texts. They can relate the works in a context of subcultures such as peer group, mass media, school, religion, and politics, social and historical communities. Engaging with the texts, readers can better understand how characters and authors are shaped by cultural influences. Cultural elements influence reader's reactions to events, including their responses to literature.

Cultural and historical context is important in understanding the roles of women and minorities in literature. Placing works of literature in their proper cultural setting can make a work more understandable and provoke reader interest in the milieu of the day. These factors can stimulate a reader's interest in how their own cultural background impacts the engagement with the text. Thus, the cultural aspects of literature become an opportunity for the reader to gain insight into their own attitudes.

Topical perspective
In using a topical perspective, students apply their background in a variety of different fields, for instance sports, science, politics or cooking, to the literary work they are studying. Students may then engage the text in a holistic manner, bringing all their knowledge to bear on a work. It is useful to encourage students to determine how their own information pool relates to the work. There are an infinite number of fields or topics that relate to literature.

Students are most likely to integrate topics they are currently studying into their engagement with a text. These topics would include history, science, art, and music among others. Thinking about literature from these other topical point-of-view can help students ' understand that what they are learning in other courses enhances their experience of both literature and life.

**Effects of prior knowledge**

History
When students employ topical knowledge of history in their study of literature, they may do much more than remember date, events, and historical figures in relation to a text. They may well apply what they know about a historical period to better understand the attitudes and relationships in a work of literature. Students learn to think historically, considering different explanations for events, or cause and effect relationships in tracing a sequence of events. For example in reading Steinbeck's novels, students may draw on what they know about the historical period of the depression. Hemingway's "Farewell To Arms" may evoke a historical picture of Europe embroiled in World War I.

Literature offers an opportunity to apply historical knowledge in the context of a work. Students understand that both literary and historical accounts of an event or character may differ significantly, and that one may illuminate the other.

Scientific knowledge

Students can apply their knowledge of science when reading literature. Their description of carefully observed phenomena can be used to describe a piece of writing. after reading essays by science writers, students' may be encouraged to transpose this knowledge into reading other texts. Understanding the scientific method gives readers' an opportunity to impose this process on events narrated in literature. The validity of events may be tested in the students' mind to assess the "reality" of the text.

There are many texts that take as their subject the role of the scientist in society. In reading "Frankenstein" or "Dr. Faustus", many issues can be raised about the responsibilities of scientists in conducting experiments.

The blending of science and literature is particularly compelling to some students' when they read science fiction or futuristic texts. An example would be "1984" which posits a authoritarian government controlling the lives of people.

**Research papers**

Hypothesis

The result of a focusing process is a research question, a question or problem that can be solved by through research data. A hypothesis is a tentative answer to the research question that must be supported by the research. A research question must be manageable, specific, and interesting. Additionally, it must be argumentative, capable of being proved or disproved by research.

It is helpful to explore a topic with background reading and notes before formulating a research question and a hypothesis. Create a data base where all the knowledge of a topic is written down to be utilized in approaching the task of identifying the research question. This background work will allow a narrowing to a specific question, and formulate a tentative answer, the hypothesis. The process of exploring a topic can include brainstorming, freewriting, and scanning your memory and experience for information.

Observing data

Collecting data in the field begins with direct observation, noting phenomena in a totally objective manner, and recording it. This requires a systematic approach to observation and recording information. Prior to beginning the observation process, certain steps must be accomplished:

1. Determine the purpose of the observation and review the research question and hypothesis to see that they relate to each other.
2. Set a limited time period for the observations.
3. Develop a system for recording information in a useful manner.
4. Obtain proper materials for taking notes.
5. Consider the use of cameras, video recorders, or audio tape recorders.
6. Use the journalistic technique of asking "who, what, where, when, and why" to garner information.

Research interviews

After determining the exact purpose of the interview, check it against the research question and hypothesis. Set up the interview in advance, specifying the amount of time needed. Prepare a written list of questions for the interview, and try out questions on peers before the interview. Prepare a copy of your questions leaving room for notes. Insure that all the necessary equipment is on hand, and record the date, time, and subject of the interview.

The interview should be businesslike, and take only the allotted time. A flexible attitude will allow for questions or comments that have not been planned for, but may prove helpful to the process. Follow-up questions should be asked whenever appropriate. A follow-up thank you note is always appreciated and may pave the way for further interviews. Be mindful at all times of the research question and hypothesis under consideration.

Surveys

Surveys are usually in the form of questionnaires which have the advantage of speed and rapid compilation of data. Preparation of the questionnaire is of critical importance. Tie the questionnaire to the research question as closely as possible, and include questions which will bear on the hypothesis. Questions that can be answered "yes" or "no" can be easily tabulated. The following checklist may be helpful:

1. Determine the audience for the questionnaire and how best to reach them.
2. Draft questions that will provide short, specific answers.
3. Test the questions on friends or peers.
4. Remember to include a deadline for return of the questionnaire.
5. Format the questionnaire so that it is clear and easily completed.
6. Carefully proofread the questionnaire and insure that it is neatly reproduced.

Library research

After reviewing personal resources for information, the library is the next stop. Use index cards or notepads for documentation. Create a system for reviewing data. It is helpful to create "key words" to trigger responses from sources. Some valuable guidelines for conducting library research include:

1. Consult the reference librarian for sources and ideas.
2. Select appropriate general and specific reference books for examination. Encyclopedias are a good place to start. There are numerous specialized encyclopedias to assist in research.
3. Survey biographical dictionaries and indexes for information.
4. Review almanacs, yearbooks, and statistical data.
5. Scan periodical indexes for articles on the research topic.
6. Determine if there are specialized indexes and abstracts that may be helpful.
7. Review the computer or card catalog for relevant references.

Drafting the research essay

Before beginning the research essay, revisit the purpose, audience, and scope of the essay. An explicit thesis statement should summarize major arguments and approaches to the subject. After determining the special format of the essay, a survey of the literature on the subject is helpful. If original or first-hand research is involved, a summary of the methods and conclusions should be prepared.

A clustering strategy assembles all pertinent information on a topic in one physical place. The preparation of an outline may be based on the clusters, or a first draft may be developed without an outline. Formal outlines use a format of "Thesis statement", "Main topic", and "Supporting ideas" to shape the information. Drafting the essay can vary considerably among researchers, but it is useful to use an outline or information clusters to get started. Drafts are usually done on a point-to-point basis.

Introduction

The introduction to a research essay is particularly important as it sets the context for the essay. It needs to draw the reader into the subject, and also provide necessary background to understand the subject. It is sometimes helpful to open with the research question, and explain how the question will be answered. The major points of the essay may be forecast or previewed to prepare readers for the coming arguments.

In a research essay it is a good idea to establish the writer's credibility by reviewing credentials and experience with the subject. Another useful opening involves quoting several sources that support the points of the essay, again to establish credibility. The tone should be appropriate to the audience and subject, maintaining a sense of careful authority while building the arguments. Jargon should be kept to a minimum, and language carefully chosen to reflect the appropriate tone.

Conclusion
The conclusion to a research essay helps readers' summarize what they have learned. Conclusions are not meant to convince, as this has been done in the body of the essay. It can be useful to leave the reader with a memorable phrase or example that supports the argument. Conclusions should be both memorable but logical restatements of the arguments in the body of the essay.

A specific-to-general pattern can be helpful, opening with the thesis statement and expanding to more general observations. A good idea is to restate the main points in the body of the essay, leading to the conclusion. An ending that evokes a vivid image or asks a provocative question makes the essay memorable. The same effect can be achieved by a call for action, or a warning. Conclusions may be tailored to the audience's background, both in terms of language, tone, and style.

Reviewing the draft
A quick checklist for reviewing a draft of a research essay includes:

1. Introduction - Is the reader's attention gained and held by the introduction?
2. Thesis - Does the essay fulfill the promise of the thesis? Is it strong enough?
3. Main Points - List the main points and rank them in order of importance.
4. Organization - What is the organizing principle of the essay? Does it work?
5. Supporting Information - Is the thesis adequately supported? Is the thesis convincing?
6. Source Material - Are there adequate sources and are they smoothly integrated into the essay?
7. Conclusion - Does the conclusion have sufficient power? Does it summarize the essay well?
8. Paragraphs, Sentences, and Words - Review all these for effectiveness in promoting the thesis.
9. Overall Review - Evaluate the essay's strengths and weaknesses. What revisions are needed?

**Modern Language Association style**

The Modern Language Association style is widely used in literature and languages as well as other fields. The MLA style calls for noting brief references to sources in parentheses in the text of an essay, and adding an alphabetical list of sources, called "Works Cited", at the end. Specific recommendations of the MLA include:

1. Works Cited - Includes only works actually cited. List on a separate page with the author's name, title, and publication information, which must list the location of the publisher, the publishers' name, and the date of publication.
2. Parenthetical Citations - MLA style uses parenthetical citations following each quotation, reference, paraphrase, or summary to a source. Each citation is made up of the author's last name and page reference, keyed to a reference in "Works Cited".
3. Explanatory Notes - Explanatory notes are numbered consecutively, and identified by superscript numbers in the text. The full notes may appear as endnotes or as footnotes at the bottom of the page.

**American Psychological Association style**

The American Psychological Association style is widely followed in the social sciences. The APA parenthetical citations within the text directs readers to a list of sources. In APA style this list is called "References". References are listed on a separate page, and each line includes the author's name, publication date, title, and publication information. Publication information includes the city where the publisher is located, and the publisher's name. Underline the titles of books and periodicals , but not articles.

APA parenthetical expressions citations include the author's last name, the date of publication, and the page number. APA style allows for content footnotes for information needed to be expanded or supplemented, marked in the text by superscript numbers in consecutive order. Footnotes are listed under a separate page, headed "Footnotes" after the last page of text. All entries should be double-spaced.

**Revisions**

Revising sentences

Revising sentences is done to make writing more effective. Editing sentences is done to correct any errors. Revising sentences is usually best done on a computer, where it is possible to try several versions easily. Some writers prefer to print out a hard copy and work with this for revisions. Each works equally well and depends on the individual preference.

Spelling and grammar checks on software are a great aid to a writer but not a panacea. Many grammatical problems, such as faulty parallelism, mixed constructions, and misplaced modifiers can slip past the programs. Even if errors are caught, the writing still must be evaluated for effectiveness. A combination of software programs and writer awareness is necessary to insure an error free manuscript.

Global revisions

Global revisions address the larger elements of writing. They usually affect paragraphs or sections, and may involve condensing or merging sections of text to improve meaning and flow. Sometimes material may be rearranged to better present the arguments of the essay. It is usually better for the writer to get some distance from the work before starting a global revision. Reviewers and editors can be usefully employed to make suggestions for revision. If reviewers are utilized, it is helpful to emphasize the focus on the larger themes of the work, rather than the finer points. When undertaking a global review, the writer might wish to position himself as the audience, rather than the writer. This provides some additional objectivity, and can result in a more honest appraisal of the writing and revisions that should be made. Global revisions are the last major changes a writer will make in the text. seal to persuade, inform, or entertain them. Answering these questions as objectively as possible will allow for a useful global revision.

1. Purpose - Does the draft accomplish its purpose? Is the material and tone appropriate for the intended audience? Does it account for the audience's knowledge of the subject? Does it seek to persuade, inform, or entertain them?
2. Focus - Does the introduction and the conclusion focus on the main point? Are all supporting arguments focused on the thesis?
3. Organization and Paragraphing - Are there enough organizational cues to guide the reader? Are any paragraphs too long or too short?
4. Content - Is the supporting material persuasive? Are all ideas adequately developed? Is there any material that could be deleted?
5. Point -of-view - Is the draft free of distracting sifts in point-of-view? Is the point-of-view appropriate for the subject and intended audience?

**Paragraphs**

A paragraph should be unified around a main point. A good topic sentence summarizing the paragraphs main point. A topic sentence is more general than subsequent supporting sentences. Sometime the topic sentence will be used to close the paragraph if earlier sentences give a clear indication of the direction of the paragraph. Sticking to the main point means deleting or omitting unnecessary sentences that do not advance the main point.

The main point of a paragraph deserves adequate development, which usually means a substantial paragraph. A paragraph of two or three sentences often does not develop a point well enough, particularly if the point is a strong supporting argument of the thesis. An occasional short paragraph is fine, particularly it is used as a transitional device. A choppy appearance should be avoided.

Methods of development:

1. Examples are a common method of development and may be effectively used when a reader may ask "For Example?" Examples are selected instances, not an inclusive catalog. They may be used to suggest the validity of topic sentences.
2. Illustrations are extended examples, sometimes presented in story form for interest. They usually require several sentences each, so they are used sparingly. Well selected illustrations can be a colorful and vivid way of developing a point.
3. Stories that command reader interest, developed in a story form, can be powerful methods of emphasizing key points in a essay. Stories and illustrations should be very specific and relate directly to a point or points being made in the text. They allow more colorful language and instill a sense of human interest in a subject. Used judiciously, illustrations and stories are an excellent device.
4. Analogies draw comparisons between items that appear to have nothing in common. Analogies are employed by writers to attempt to provoke fresh thoughts and changed feelings about a subject. They may be used to make the unfamiliar more familiar, to clarify an abstract point, or to argue a point. Although analogies are effective literary devices, they should be used thoughtfully in arguments. Two things may be alike in some respects but completely different in others.
5. Cause and effect is a excellent device and are best used when the cause and effect are generally accepted as true. As a matter of argument, cause and effect is usually too complex and subject to other interpretations to be used effectively. A valid way of using cause and effect is to state the effect in the topic sentence of a paragraph, and add the causes in the body of the paragraph. This adds logic and form to a paragraph, and usually makes it more effective.

Types of paragraphs:

1. A paragraph of narration tells a story or part of a story. They are usually arranged in chronological order, but sometimes include flashbacks, taking the story back to an earlier time.
2. A descriptive paragraph paints a verbal portrait of a person, place, or thing, using specific details that appeal to one or more of our senses - sight, sound, smell, taste, and touch. It conveys a real sense of being present and observing phenomena.
3. A process paragraphs is related in time order, generally chronological. It usually describes a process or teaches readers how to perform the process.
4. Comparing two subjects draws attention to their similarities but can also indicate a consideration of differences. To contrast is to focus only on differences. Both comparisons and contrasts may be examined point-by-point, or in succeeding paragraphs.

Organizing information:

1. A grouping of items into categories based on some consistent criteria is called classification. The principle of classification a writer chooses will depend on the purpose of the classification. Most items can be classified by a number of criteria, and the selection of the specific classification will depend on the writer's aims in using this device.
2. Division, on the other hand, takes one item and divides it into parts. Just as with classification, the division must be based on a valid and consistent principle. For example a body may be divided into various body systems easily, but not as easily divided into body functions, because the categories overlap
3. Definition classifies a concept or word in a general group, then distinguishes it from other members of the class. Usually simple definitions can be provided in a sentence or two, while more complex ones may need a paragraph or two to adequately define them.

**Coherence**

A smooth flow of sentences and paragraphs without gaps, shifts, or bumps leads to paragraph coherence. Ties between old information and new, can be smoothed by several strategies.

1. Linking ideas clearly, from the topic sentence to the body of the paragraph is essential for a smooth transition. The topic sentence states the main point, and this should be followed by specific details, examples, and illustrations that support the topic sentence. The support may be direct or indirect. In indirect support the illustrations and examples may support a sentence that in turn supports the topic directly.
2. The repetition of key words adds coherence to a paragraph. To avoid dull language, variations of the key words may be used.
3. Parallel structures are often used within sentences to emphasize the similarity of ideas and connect sentences giving similar information.
4. Minimize shifting sentences from one verb tense to another. These shifts affect the smooth flows of words and can disrupt the coherence of the paragraph.

**Transitions**

Transitions are bridges between what has been read and what is about to be read. Transitions smooth the reader's path between sentences, and inform readers of major connections to new ideas forthcoming in the text. Transitional phrases should be used with care, selecting the appropriate phrase for a transition. Tone is another important consideration in using transitional phrases, varying the tone for different audiences. For example in a scholarly essay, "in summary" would be preferable to the more informal "in short".

When working with transitional words and phrases, writers usually find a natural flow that indicates when a transition is needed. In reading a draft of the text, it should become apparent where the flow is uneven or rough. At this point, the writer can add transitional elements during the revision process. Revising can also afford an opportunity to delete transitional devices that seem heavy-handed or unnecessary.

<u>Lengths of paragraphs</u>

The comfort level for readers is paragraphs of between 100 and 200 words. Shorter paragraphs cause too much starting and stopping, and give a "choppy" effect. Paragraphs that are too long often test the attention span of the reader. Two notable exceptions to this rule exist. In scientific or scholarly papers, longer paragraphs suggest seriousness and depth. In journalistic writing, constraints are placed on paragraph size by the narrow columns in a newspaper format.

The first and last paragraphs of a text will usually be the introduction and conclusion. These special purpose paragraphs are likely to be shorter than paragraphs in the body of the work. Paragraphs in the body of the essay follow the subject's outline; one paragraph per point in short essays, and a group of paragraphs per point in longer works. Some ideas require more development than others, so it is good for a writer to remain flexible. A too long paragraph may be divided, while shorter ones may be combined.

Paragraph breaks are used for many reasons, usually as devices to improve the flow or content of the text. Some examples for beginning new paragraphs include:

1. To mark off the introduction and concluding paragraphs.
2. To signal a shift to a new idea or topic.
3. To indicate an important shift in time or place.
4. To emphasize a point by repositioning a major sentence.
5. To highlight a comparison, contrast, or cause and effect relationship.
6. To signal a change in speakers, voice, or tense.

**Argumentative writing**

Constructing a reasonable argument, the goal is not to "win" or have the last word, but rather to reveal current understanding of the question, and propose a solution to the perceived problem. The purpose of argument in a free society or a research field is to reach the best conclusion possible at the time.

Conventions of arguments vary from culture to culture. In America arguments tend to be direct rather than subtle, carefully organized rather than discursive, spoken plainly rather than poetically. Evidence presented is usually specific and factual, while appeals to intuition or communal wisdom are rare.

Argumentative writing takes a stand on a debatable issue , and seeks to explore all sides of the issue and reach the best possible solution. Argumentative writing should not be combative, at it's strongest it is assertive.

A prelude to argumentative writing is an examination of the issue's social and intellectual contexts.

<u>Introducion</u>
The introduction of an essay arguing an issue should end with a thesis sentence that states a position on the issue. A good strategy is to establish credibility with readers by showing both expert knowledge and fair-mindedness. Building common ground with undecided or neutral readers is helpful.

The thesis should be supported by strong arguments that support the stated position. The main lines of argument should have a cumulative effect of convincing readers that the thesis has merit. The sum of the main lines of argument will outline the overall argumentative essay. The outline will clearly illustrate the central thesis, and subordinate claims that support it.

Evidence must be provided that support both the thesis and supporting arguments. Evidence based on reading should be documented, to show the sources. Readers must know how to check sources for accuracy and validity.

<u>Supporting evidence</u>
Most arguments must be supported by facts and statistics. Facts are something that is known with certainty, and have been objectively verified. Statistics may be used in selective ways to for partisan purposes. It is good to check statistics by reading authors writing on both sides of an issue. This will give a more accurate idea of how valid are the statistics cited.

Examples and illustrations add an emotional component to arguments, reaching readers in ways that facts and figures cannot. They are most effective when used in combination with objective information that can be verified.

Expert opinion can contribute to a position on a question. The source should be an authority whose credentials are beyond dispute. Sometimes it is necessary to provide the credentials of the expert. Expert testimony can be quoted directly, or may be summarized by the writer. Sources must be well documented to insure their validity.

Counter arguments

In addition to arguing a position, it is a good practice to review opposing arguments and attempt to counter them. This process can take place anywhere in the essay, but is perhaps best placed after the thesis is stated. Objections can be countered on a point-by-point analysis, or in a summary paragraph. Pointing out flaws in counter arguments is important, as is showing the counter arguments to have less weight than the supported thesis.

Building common ground with neutral or opposed readers can make a strong case. Sharing values with undecided readers can allow people to switch positions without giving up what they feel is important. People who may oppose a position need to feel they can change their minds without compromising their intelligence or their integrity. This appeal to open-mindedness can be a powerful tool in arguing a position without antagonizing opposing views.

Fallacious arguments

A number of unreasonable argumentative tactics are known as logical fallacies. Most fallacies are misguided uses of legitimate argumentative arguments.

Generalizing is drawing a conclusion from an array of facts using inductive reasoning. These conclusions are a probability, not a certainty. The fallacy known as a "hasty generalization" is a conclusion based on insufficient or unrepresentative evidence. Stereotyping is a hasty generalization about a group. This is common because of the human tendency to perceive selectively. Observations are made through a filter of preconceptions, prejudices, and attitudes.

Analogies point out similarities between disparate things. When an analogy is unreasonable, it is called a "false analogy". This usually consists of assuming if two things are alike in one respect, they must be alike in others. This, of course, may or may not be true. Each comparison must be independently verified to make the argument valid.

Post Hoc Fallacy

Tracing cause and effect can be a complicated matter. Because of the complexity involved, writers often over-simplify it. A common error is to assume that because one event follows another, the first is the cause of the second. This common fallacy is known as "post hoc", from the Latin meaning "after this,therefore because of this".

A post hoc fallacy could run like this: "Since Abner Jones returned to the Giants lineup, the team has much better morale". The fact that Jones returned to the lineup may or may not have had an effect on team morale. The writer must show there is a cause and effect relationship between Jones' return and team morale. It is not enough to note that one event followed another. It must be proved beyond a reasonable doubt that morale was improved by the return of Jones to the lineup. The two may be true but do not necessarily follow a cause and effect pattern.

Assumptions
When considering problems and solutions, the full range of possible options should be mentioned before recommending one solution above others. It is unfair to state there are only two alternatives, when in fact there are more options. Writers who set up a choice between their preferred option and a clearly inferior one are committing the "either...or" fallacy. All reasonable alternatives should be included in the possible solutions.

Assumptions are claims that are taken to be true without proof. If a claim is controversial, proof should be provided to verify the assumption. When a claim is made that few would agree with, the writer is guilty of a "non sequitur" (Latin for "does not follow") fallacy. Thus any assumption that is subject to debate cannot be accepted without supporting evidence is suspect.

Syllogism
Deductive reasoning is constructed in a three-step method called a syllogism. The three steps are the major premise, the minor premise, and the conclusion. The major premise is a generalization, and the minor premise is a specific case. The conclusion is deduced from applying the generalization to the specific case. Deductive arguments fail if either the major or minor premise is not true, or if the conclusion does not logically follow from the premises. This means a deductive argument must stand on valid, verifiable premises, and the conclusion is a logical result of the premises.

"Straw man" fallacy
The "straw man" fallacy consists of an oversimplification or distortion of opposing views. This fallacy is one of the most obvious and easily uncovered since it relies on gross distortions. The name comes from a side setting up a position so weak (the straw man) that is easily refuted.

**Composition**

Composition refers to a range of activities which include the achievement of literacy, transmission of culture, preparation for writing skills in the workplace, and writing as a mode of personal expression and identity. Composition has evolved into an interdisciplinary study and an eclectic practice. Writing is always a process, performing a critical role in education.

Composition studies, like its companion, rhetoric, is a practical and theoretical study Originally it was limited to teaching and correction of student's grammar. Composition has come of age as a writing process, a complex network of interweaving social, political, and individual components.

The field now includes collaborative writing, two or more students writing together, each assuming specific responsibilities with a heavy emphasis on joint revisions. Continued innovations and experimentation are an ongoing part of composition studies.

**Literary devices**

Allusions
An allusion is a reference within a text to some person, place, or event outside the text. Allusions that refer to events more or less contemporary with the text are called topical allusions. Those referring to specific persons are called personal allusions. An example of personal allusion is William Butler Yeat's reference to "golden thighed Pythagoras" in his poem " Among School Children".

Allusions may be used to summarize an important idea or point out a contrast between contemporary life and a heroic past. An example of this would be James Joyce's classical parallels in "Ulysses" in which heroic deeds in the "Odyssey" are implicitly compared to the banal aspects of everyday life in Dublin.

Allusions may also be used to summarize an important idea such as the concluding line from "King Kong", "It was beauty killed the beast".

Jargon

Jargon is a specialized language used among members of a trade, profession, or group. Jargon should be avoided and used only when the audience will be familiar with the language. Jargon includes exaggerated language usually designed to impress rather than inform. Sentences filled with jargon are both wordy and difficult to understand. Jargon is commonly used in such institutions as the military, politics, sports, and art.

Clichés

Clichés are sentences and phrases that have been overused to the point of triviality. They have no creativity or originality and add very little to modern writing. Writers should avoid clichés whenever possible. When editing writing, the best solution for clichés is to delete them. If this does not seem easily accomplished, a cliché can be modified so that it is not dully predictable and trite. This often means adding phrases or sentences to change the cliché.

Slang

Slang is an informal and sometimes private language that connotes the solidarity and exclusivity of a group such as teenagers, sports fans, ethnic groups, or rock musicians. Slang has a certain vitality, but it is not always widely understood and should be avoided in most writing. An exception could be when the audience is a specialized group who understand the jargon and slang commonly used by the members.

Sexist language

Sexist language is language that stereotypes or demeans women or men, usually women. Such language is derived from stereotypical thinking, traditional pronoun use, and from words used to refer indefinitely to both sexes. Writers should avoid referring to a profession as being basically male or female, and using different conventions when referring to men and women. Pronouns "he,him,and his"should be avoided by using a pair of pronouns or revising the sentence to obviate the sexist language.

Pretentious language

In an attempt to sound elegant, profound, poetic, or impressive, some writers embroider their thoughts with flowery phrases, inflated language, and generally pretentious wordage. Pretentious language is often so ornate and wordy that it obscures the true meaning of the writing.

Euphemisms

Euphemisms are pleasant sounding words that replace language that seems overly harsh or ugly. Euphemisms are wordy and indirect, clouding meaning through "pretty" words. However euphemisms are sometimes uses as conventions, when speaking about subjects such as death, bodily functions and sex.

Doublespeak

The term "doublespeak" was coined by George Orwell in his futuristic novel "1984". It applies to any evasive or deceptive language, particularly favored by politicians. Doublespeak is evident in advertising, journalism, and in political polemics. it should be avoided by serious writers.

Figures of speech

A figure of speech is an expression that uses words imaginatively rather than literally to make abstract ideas concrete. Figures of speech compare unlike things to reveal surprising similarities. The pitfalls of using figures of speech is the failure of writers to think through the images they evoke. The result can be a mixed metaphor, a combination of two or more images that do not make sense together.

In a simile the writer makes an explicit comparison, usually by introducing it with "like" or "as". An example would be " white as a sheet" or "my love is like a red, red, rose". Effective use of similes can add color and vivid imagery to language. Used carefully and sparingly, they provide a writer with an effective device to enhance meaning and style.

Figures of speech are particularly effective when used with discretion and selectively. Examples of figures of speech can be found in all genres of writing.

<u>Allegories</u>
Allegories are a type of narrative in which the story reflects at least one other meaning. Traditional allegory often employs personification, the use of human characters to represent abstract ideas. Early examples of the use of allegory were the medieval mystery plays in which abstractions such as Good, Evil, Penance, and Death appeared as characters.

Another type of allegory uses a surface story to refer to historical or political events. Jonathan Swift was a master at using allegory in this manner, particularly in his "Tale of a Tub" (1704), a satirical allegory of the reformation.

Allegory has been largely replaced by symbolism by modern writers. Although they are sometimes confused, symbolism bears a natural relationship to the events in a story, while in allegory the surface story is only an excuse for the secondary and more important meaning. Allegory has had a revival in postmodern writing, and is seen in much contemporary literature.

<u>Ambiguity</u>
In writing historically, ambiguity is generally viewed as an error or flaw. The word now means a literary technique in which a word or phrase conveys two or more different meanings. William Empson defines ambiguity as " any verbal nuance, however slight, which gives room for alternative reactions to the same piece of language." Empons chief purpose in defining ambiguity was to note how this device affects the interpretation of poetry. Empson identified seven types of ambiguity including the traditional meaning. These seven types of ambiguity each provided a different view of possible interpretation of text in writing. Empsons's "Seven Types of Ambiguity" was the first detailed analysis of the phenomena of multiple meanings, sometimes called plurisignation. Ambiguity can be a useful device for some types of writing but does lend itself to informative or persuasive text.

**Phonetics**

Phonetics seeks to provide a descriptive terminology for the sounds of spoken language. This includes the physiology for the production of speech sounds, the classification of speech sounds including vowels and consonants, the dynamic features of speech production, and the study of instrumental phonetics, the investigation of human speech by laboratory techniques. The dynamic aspects of phonetics include voice quality, stress, rhythm, and speech melody.

Instrumental phonetics underlines both the complexity of speech production, and the subtlety of the human brain in interpreting a constantly changing flow of acoustic data as recognizable speech-sounds. The correlation between acoustic quality, auditory perception, and articulatory position is a complex and not yet fully understood process. It represents a fertile area of research for phoneticians, psychologists, and perhaps philosophers.

General phonetics classifies the speech sounds of all languages. Any one language uses only possibilities of the selections available. Sounds and how they are used in a language is the phonology of a language. Dynamic features of phonology include speech melody, stress, rhythmic organization, length and syllabicity. The central unit of phonology is the phoneme, the smallest distinct sound in a given language. Two words are composed of different phonemes only if they differ phonetically in ways that are found to make a difference in meaning. Phonemic transcription of a word or phrase is its representation as a sequence or other combinations of phonemes.

Phonology

Phonology is a controversial and enigmatic part of linguistics. It is widely studied and defined but there is no agreement on the definition of a phoneme or phonology theory. There may be as many theories as there are phonologies in linguistics.

**Linguistics**

Linguistics is the branch of knowledge that deals with language. Grammar, an integral part of linguistics, in its widest sense, includes the study of the structure of words and syntactic constructions, and that of sound systems. Linguistics is concerned with the lexical and grammatical categories of individual languages, and the differences between languages and the historical relations between families of languages. Each lexical entry informs us about the linguistic properties of the word. It will indicate a word's phonological, grammatical, and somatic properties.

1. Grammar may be said to generate a set of phrases and sentences, so linguistics is also the study of generative grammar. Grammar must also contain a phonological component, since this determines the phonetic form of words in speech.
2. Phonology, the study of sound systems and processes affecting the way words are pronounced, is another aspect of linguistics.

Psycholinguistics

Psycholinguistics is concerned with how linguistic competence is employed in the production and comprehension of speech.

1. The first step in language comprehension is to use the phonological processor to identify sounds.
2. Then the lexical processor identifies the component words.
3. Finally the syntactic processor provides a syntactic representation of the sentence.
4. The last step is for the semantic processor to compute a meaning representation for the sentence, on the basis of syntactical and lexical information supplied by previous steps in the process.

The relevant meaning of the words serves as the end-product of the process, and once this has been computed the sentence is understood. All stages of the psycholinguistic process take place in real time, so that measurements of each specific part of the process may be compared to the level of complexity of the grammar itself. Such is the experimental study of psycholinguistics applied.

Developmental linguistics

Neurolinguistics is concerned with the physical representations of linguistic processes in the brain. The most effective way to study this is to observe the effects on language capacity in brain-injured individuals. The frontal lobe of the brain appears to be the area responsible for controlling the production of speech. As research has become more refined over the years, it is evident that language functions are located in different parts of the brain. As improved diagnostic and sophisticated imaging techniques are developed, it is anticipated that the mysteries of language capacity and competence corresponding to specific parts of the brain will become clearer. For now, our knowledge in this field is imperfect, and the process of mapping the brain for linguistic capacity and performance is limited. Neurolinguistics is closely tied to neurology and neuro-physiology.

Sociolinguistics

Sociolinguistics is the study of the relationship between language and the structure of society. It takes into account the social backgrounds of both the speaker and the addressee, the relationship between the speaker and the addressee, and the context and manner of the interaction. Because the emphasis in sociolinguistics is on language use, the analysis of language in this field is typically based on taped recordings of everyday interactions. The sociolinguists seek to discover universal properties of languages, attempting to analyze questions such as "do all languages change in the same ways"? Answers are sought to the larger questions about universals in society in which language plays a major role. The multifaceted nature of language and its broad impact on many areas of society make this field an exciting and cutting edge part of linguistics.

Meaning

Meaning is traditionally something said to be expressed by a sentence. Modern theories in linguistics often elaborate on this. The four major theories are:

1. The meaning of a sentence is different depending on the context of the utterance.
2. Sentence meanings are part of the language system and form a level of semantic representation independent of other levels.
3. Representations are derivable from the level of syntax, given a lexicon which specifies the meaning of words and a set of semantic rules.
4. The meaning of utterances follows from separate principles that are in the domain of context or pragmatics.

Other theories assert that neither words or sentences can be assigned meanings independently of situations in which they are uttered. These theories all seek to establish a standard understanding of meaning so that linguists can refine and extend their research.

Etmology

Etymology is the study of the historical relation between a word and earlier form or forms from which it has developed. Etymology can be loosely defined as the study of the origins of words. This study may occur on different levels of linguistic approach. Word meanings and their historical antecedents are often a complicated and controversial source of study. Tracing the meaning of words often includes understanding the social, political, and cultural time that the definition existed. The evolution of words from earlier forms suggests a cross-fertilization of social contexts and common usage that is a fascinating field of study.

An etymological fallacy is that the notion that a true meaning of a word can be derived from it etymology. Modern linguistic theory provides a substantial body of knowledge that compares and evaluates etymology and provides numerous avenues for new research.

Lexicology

Lexicon is the aspect of a language that is centered on individual words or similar units. Its scope varies widely from one theory to another. In some systems, lexicon is a simple component of generative grammar. In others it is the basis for all grammatical patterns. some view a lexicon as an unstructured list, while others see it as an elaborate network of entries governed by lexical rules and shared features. Lexicon in linguistics is to be distinguished as a theory from a dictionary or part of a practical description.

Lexicology is the branch of linguistics concerned with the semantic structure of the lexicon. Lexical diffusion is the gradual spread of a phonetic or other change across the vocabulary of a language or across a speech community? The term may also refer to the diffusion of individual lexical units within a lexicon. Lexical decomposition is the analysis of word meanings into smaller units.

**Grammar**

Grammar may be practically defined as the study of how words are put together or the study of sentences. There are multiple approaches to grammar in modern linguistics. Any systematic account of the structure of a language and the patterns it describes is grammar. Modern definitions of grammar state grammar is the knowledge of a language developed in the minds of the speakers.

A grammar in the broadest sense is a set of rules internalized by members of a speech community, and an account, by a linguist, of such a grammar. This internalized grammar is what is commonly called a language. Grammar is often restricted to units that have meaning. The expanded scope of grammar includes morphology and syntax, and a lexicon. Grammatical meaning is described as part of the syntax and morphology of a language as distinct from its lexicon.

The ability to learn language is determined by a biologically determined innate language facility. This widely accepted theory is known as the innateness hypothesis. The knowledge of adult grammar appears to go far beyond anything supplied by the child's linguistic experience, implying an innate ability to learn language. A language facility must incorporate a set of Universal Grammar principles which enable a child to form and interpret sentences in any natural language. Children have the ability to acquire any natural language so it follows that the contents of the innate language facility must not be specific to any one human language. Developmental linguistics is concerned with examining children's grammar and the conditions under which they emerge. The language faculty is species-specific and the ability to develop a grammar of a language is unique to human beings. The study of non-human communication forms a different field of study.

Structuralized grammar

Structuralize grammar tends to be formal in nature as it is concerned with grammatical and phonological considerations, rather than semantics. The chief goal is to uncover the structure of a language. There are valid criticisms of the structural approach to grammar. problems exist in the available descriptive frameworks to manage, difficulties with definitions, and inconsistency and contradiction between theory and practice. These concerns have not invalidated the study of structural grammar, but have been utilized by linguists to perfect the analysis.

**Transformational grammar**

Transformational grammar is any grammar in which different syntactic structures are related by transformations. The main role of transformations was to relate the sentences of a language as a whole to a small set of kernel sentences. A base component of a grammar generated a deep structure for each sentence. these structures were an input to a transformational component, which was an ordered structure of transformational rules. Its output was a set of surface structures, which combined with the deep structures, formed its syntactic description. Further rules supplied its semantic representation and phonetic representation.

Transformational grammar was invented and promulgated by Noam Chomsky, a revolutionary figure in linguistics. Much of Chomsky's work has been directed to the development of a universal grammar, conceived as an account of what is inherited by the individual. Chomsky remains the dominant figure of the 20th century in linguistics.

**Sentences**

The largest structural unit normally recognized by grammar is the sentence. Any attempt to accurately define the sentence is in error. Any such definition will not bear up under Linguistic Analysis. In every language, there are a limited number of favorite sentence-types to which most others can be related. They vary from language to language. Certain utterances, while not immediately conforming to favorite sentence types, can be expanded in their context to become one sentence of a particular type. These can be called referable sentences. Other utterances that do not conform to favorite sentence types may reveal obsolete sentence types; these are proverbial sayings and are called gnomic or fossilized sentences. A very small number of utterances not conforming to the favorite sentence-types are found in prescribed social situations, such as "Hello" or "Bye".

Sentence patterns

Sentence patterns fall into five common modes with some exceptions. They are:

1. Subject / linking verb / subject complement
2. Subject / transitive verb / direct object
3. Subject / transitive verb / indirect object / direct object
4. Subject / transitive verb / direct object / object complement
5. Subject / intransitive verb

Common exceptions to these patterns are questions and commands, sentences with delayed subjects, and passive transformations. Writers sometimes use the passive voice when the active voice would be more appropriate.

Sentences classification

Sentences are classified in two ways:

1. according to their structure
2. according to their purpose

Writers use declarative sentences to make statements, imperative sentences to issue requests or commands, interrogative sentences to ask questions, and exclamatory sentences to make exclamations. Depending on the number and types of clauses they contain, sentences may be classified as simple, compound, complex, or compound-complex.

Clauses come in two varieties: independent and subordinate.

1. An independent clause is a full sentence pattern that does not function within another sentence pattern; it contains a subject and modifiers plus a verb and any objects, complements, and modifiers of that verb. It either stands alone or could stand alone.
2. A subordinate clause is a full sentence pattern that functions within a sentence as an adjective, an adverb, or a noun but that cannot stand alone as a complete sentence.

Sentence structures

The four major types of sentence structure are:

1. Simple sentences - Simple sentences have one independent clause with no subordinate clauses. a simple sentence may contain compound elements,- a compound subject, verb, or object for example, but does not contain more than one full sentence pattern.
2. Compound sentences - Compound sentences are composed of two or more independent clauses with no subordinate clauses. The independent clauses are usually joined with a comma and a coordinating conjunction, or with a semicolon.
3. Complex sentences - A complex sentence is composed of one independent clause with one or more dependent clauses.
4. Compound-complex sentences - A compound-complex sentence contains at least two independent clauses and at least one subordinate clause. sometimes they contain two full sentence patters that can stand alone. When each independent clause contains a subordinate clause, this makes the sentence both compound and complex.

Chomsky's sentence structure

Deep structure is a representation of the syntax of a sentence distinguished by various criteria from its surface structure. Initially defined by Noam Chomsky as the part of the syntactic description of a of a sentence that determines its semantic interpretation by the base component of a generative grammar.

Surface sentence structure is a representation of the syntax of a sentence seen as deriving by one ore more transformations, from a an underlying deep structure. Such a sentence is in the order in which the corresponding phonetic forms are spoken. Surface structure was later broadened by Chomsky to include semantic structure. Chomsky's later minimalist program no longer takes this for granted. Minimalist theory assumes no more than a minimum of types of statements and levels of representation.

The technical analysis outlined by Chomsky over three decades forms an integral part of transformational grammar.

**Language investigation**

The investigation of a language by classification is the goal of the modern linguist. When the observer has determined the phonemic structure of a language, and has classified all its constructions, both morphological and syntactic, the resulting description will be an accurate and usable grammar of the language, accounting in the simplest way for all the utterances of the speech community.

**Language families**

A language family is a group of languages that have been developed from a single ancestor. An example would be Indo-European, of which English is one of many members. Language families are identified whenever a common origin can be accepted as certain. When a family origin in speculative or uncertain, it may be called a projected family, a proposed family, or a probable family.

Some linguists have tried to apply a biological method of classification of language families, following the genus, order, species model. They have classed languages as beginning with "superficies", “macro families", "stocks", "super stocks", or "phyla" at the top. Below those will be "subfamilies", "branches", and "groups". This attempt has proved faulty as the classifications imply more than is known about family origins. It has been difficult and largely unaccepted to class language families in these descending modes of importance.

**Language descriptions**

The levels of language descriptions represent a distinct phase in the description of a language at which specific types of elements and the relations between them are studied or investigated.

1. At the level of phonology, one studies the sound structure of a language, words or larger units that are specific to that level.
2. At the level of syntax, sentences are represented as the configuration of words or morphemes standing in specific construction in relationship to one another.

Levels of language are an important part of structural linguistics, whether they focus on formal analyses or representation. Some give an order of procedures which govern the formal structural analysis of language. Others propose a hierarchy of greater or lesser degrees of abstraction, ranging from phonetics as the highest and semantics as the lowest. In many of these levels are defined by the different components of an integrated structural grammar.

## Morphology

Morphology is the grammatical structure of words and their categories. The morphological process includes any of the formal processes or operations by which the forms of words are derived from stems or roots. Types of morphological processes include affix, any element in the structure of a word other than a root; reduplication, where all or part of a form is duplicated; subtraction, where part of a form is deleted; supple ton, where one part of the morphological process replaces another; compound, where two parts of the morphological process are joined; and modification, where one part of a form is modified. Forms of morphological classification distinguished isolating, in which each grammatical classification is represented by a single word, agglutinating, where words are easily divided into separate sections, and inflectional, concerned with inflections in languages.

## Functions of language

1. Language is a means of social control making human society possible. The communication of thoughts is but a small part of this.
2. Language acts as an index to various things about the speaker - age, sex, physical and mental wellbeing, and personality characteristics.
3. Language acts to limit classes within a society, either by accent, dialect, choice of words and grammatical features.
4. Language brings human beings into relationship with the external world. It mediates between man and his environment.
5. Language is the material of artistic creation, including not only literary works but poetic and oral traditions.

Any list of languages functions is arbitrary. There are dozens of other possible classifications of language functions in the literature of linguistics. The classification given above includes the basic elements of language and their societal effect.

## Semantics

Semantics studies the meaning of utterances and why particular utterances have the meanings they do. Semantics originally covered grammar, the account of meaningful forms, and the lexicon or body of words contained in a language. When the study of forms was separated from that of meanings, the field of generative grammar became associated with semantics. Currently, the scope of semantics will cover word meanings or lexical semantics, and the meaning of utterances studied in pragmatics, the meaning of language in everyday life. Some narrow definitions of semantics understand the term to mean the study of problems encounted in formal semantics, excluding lexical meaning completely. This last definition is an extreme one, and is included to illustrate the broad vistas that are opened when we discuss semantics. What can be asserted is that semantics in its broadest and most common usage is the field of study in linguistics that deals with meaning in all its forms.

## Spoken and written language

The relationship of spoken language and written form has been the subject of differences of attitudes among linguists. The spoken form is historically prior, both for the language community and the individual. It is also more complicated. For these reasons, emphasis is placed on the sound systems of languages which has led some linguists to describe the spoken form as language, and the written form as written language. Both are equal examples of language. The relationship is not a straightforward case of deriving the written from the spoken form. When a written form evolves, it tends to take on a life of its own and acquires usages different from the spoken. Linguists are concerned with the analysis and development of language as a whole, both written and spoken.

**Parts of speech**

Nouns

Nouns are the name of a person, place, or thing, and are usually signaled by an article (a, an, the). Nouns sometimes function as adjectives modifying other nouns. Nouns used in this manner are called noun/adjectives. Nouns are classified for a number of purposes: capitalization, word choice, count/no count nouns, and collective nouns are examples.

Pronouns

Pronouns is a word used in place of a noun. Usually the pronoun substitutes for the specific noun, called the antecedent. Although most pronouns function as substitutes for nouns, some can function as adjectives modifying nouns. pronouns may be classed as personal, possessive, intensive, relative, interrogative, demonstrative, indefinite, and reciprocal. pronouns can cause a number of problems for writers including pronoun-antecedent agreement, distinguishing between who and whom, and differentiating pronouns such as I and me.

Problems with pronouns

Pronouns are words that substitute for nouns: he, it, them, her, me, and so on. Four frequently encountered problems with pronouns include:

1. Pronoun - antecedent agreement - The antecedent of a pronoun is the word the pronoun refers to. A pronoun and its antecedent agree when they are both singular or plural.
2. Pronoun reference - A pronoun should refer clearly to its antecedent. A pronoun's reference will be unclear if it id ambiguous, implied, vague, or indefinite.
3. Personal pronouns - Some pronouns change their case form according to their grammatical structure in a sentence. Pronouns functioning as subjects appear in the subjective case, those functioning as objects appear in the objective case, and those functioning as possessives appear in the possessive case.
4. Who or whom - Who, a subjective-case pronoun, can only be used subjects and subject complements. Whom, an objective case pronoun, can only be used for objects. The words who and whom appear primarily in subordinate clauses or in questions.

Verbs

The verb of a sentence usually expresses action or being. It is composed of a main verb and sometimes supporting verbs. These helping verbs are forms of have, do, and be, and nine modals. The modals are "can, could, may, might, shall, should, will, would, and ought". Some verbs are followed by words that look like prepositions, but are so closely associated with the verb to be part of its meaning. These words are known as particles, and examples include "call off", "look up", and "drop off". The main verb of a sentence is always one that would change form from base form to past tense, past participle, present participle and, -s forms. When both the past-tense and past-participle forms of a verb end in "ed", the verb is regular. In all other cases the verb is irregular. The verb "be" is highly irregular, having eight forms instead of the usual five.

1. Linking verbs link the subject to a subject complement, a word or word group that completes the meaning of the subject by renaming or describing it.
2. A transitive verb takes a direct object, a word or word group that names a receiver of the action. The direct object of a transitive verb is sometimes preceded by an indirect object. Transitive verbs usually appear in the active voice, with a subject doing the action and a direct object receiving the action. The direct object of a transitive verb is sometimes followed by an object complement, a word or word group that completes the direct object's meaning by renaming or describing it.
3. Intransitive verbs take no objects or complements. Their pattern is subject verb.

A dictionary will disclose whether a verb is transitive or intransitive. Some verbs have both transitive and intransitive functions.

Verb phrases
A verbal phrase is a verb form that does not function as the verb of a clause. There are three major types of verbal phrases:

1. Participial phrases - These always function as adjectives. Their verbals are always present participles, always ending in "ing", or past participles frequently ending in "-d,-ed,-n.-en,or -t". Participial phrases frequently appear immediately following the noun or pronoun they modify.
2. Gerund phrases - Gerund phrases are built around present participles and they always function as nouns. : usually as subjects subject complements, direct objects, or objects of a preposition.
3. Infinitive phrases are usually structured around "to" plus the base form of the verb. they can function as nouns, as adjectives, or as adverbs. When functioning as a noun, an infinitive phrase may appear in almost any noun slot in a sentence, usually as a subject, subject complement, or direct object. Infinitive phrases functioning as adjectives usually appear immediately following the noun or pronoun they modify. adverbial phrases usually qualify the meaning of the verb.

Problems with verbs
The verb is the heart of the sentence. Verbs have several potential problems including:

1. Irregular verbs - Verbs that do not follow usual grammatical rules.
2. Tense - Tenses indicate the time of an action in relation to the time of speaking or writing about the action.
3. Mood - There are three moods in English: the indicative, used for facts, opinions, and questions; the imperative, used for orders or advice, and the subjunctive, used for wishes. The subjective mood is the most likely to cause problems. The subjective mood is used for wishes, and in "if"clauses expressing conditions contrary to facts. The subjective in such cases is the past tense form of the verb; in the case of "be", it is always "were", even if the subject is singular. The subjective mood is also used in "that' clauses following verbs such as "ask, insist, recommend, and request. The subjunctive in such cases is the base or dictionary form of the verb.

Adjectives
An adjective is a word use to modify or describe a noun or pronoun. An adjective usually answers one of these question: "Which one?, What kind of?, and How many?" Adjectives usually precede the words they modify, although they sometimes follow linking verbs, in which case they describe the subject. Most adjectives have three forms: the positive, the comparative, and the superlative. The comparative should be used to compare two things, the superlative to compare three or more things.

Articles
Articles, sometimes classed as adjectives, are used to mark nouns. There are only three: the definite article “the” and the indefinite articles “a” and “an.”

Adverbs
An adverb is a word used to modify or qualify a verb, adjective, or another adverb. It usually answers one of these questions: "When?, where?, how?, and why?" Adverbs modifying adjectives or other adverbs usually intensify or limit the intensity of words they modify. The negators "not" and "never" are classified as adverbs. Writers sometimes misuse adverbs, and multilingual speakers have trouble placing them correctly. Most adverbs also have three forms: the positive, the comparative, and the superlative. The comparative should be used to compare two things, the superlative to compare three or more things.

Prepositions

A preposition is a word placed before a noun or pronoun to form a phrase modifying another word in the sentence. The prepositional phrase usually functions as an adjective or adverb. There are a limited number of prepositions in English, perhaps around 80. Some prepositions are more than one word long. "Along with", "listen to", and "next to" are some examples.

Conjunctions

Conjunctions join words, phrases, or clauses, and they indicate the relationship between the elements that are joined. There are coordinating conjunctions that connect grammatically equal element, correlative conjunctions that connect pairs, subordinating conjunctions that introduces a subordinate clause, and conjunctive adverbs which may be used with a semicolon to connect independent clauses. The most common conjunctive adverbs include "then, thus, and however". Using adverbs correctly helps avoid sentence fragments and run-on sentences.

Subjects

The subject of a sentence names who or what the sentence is about. The complete subject is composed of the simple subject and all of its modifiers. To find the complete subject, ask "Who" or "What", and insert the verb to complete the question. The answer is the complete subject. To find the simple subject, strip away all the modifiers in the complete subject.

In imperative sentences, the verb's subject is understood but not actually present in the sentence. Although the subject ordinarily comes before the verb, sentences that begin with "There are" or "There was", the subject follows the verb.

The ability to recognize the subject of a sentence helps in editing a variety of problems such as sentence fragments and subject-verb agreement, as well as the choice of pronouns.

Subordinate word groups

Subordinate word groups cannot stand alone. They function only within sentences, as adjectives, adverbs, or nouns.

1. Prepositional phrases begins with a preposition and ends with a noun or noun equivalent called its object. Prepositional phrases function as adjectives or adverbs.
2. Subordinate clauses are patterned like sentences, having subject, verbs, and objects or complements. They function within sentences as adverbs, adjectives, or nouns.
3. Adjective clauses modify nouns or pronouns and begin with a relative pronoun or relative adverb.
4. Adverb clauses modify verbs, adjectives, and other adverbs.
5. Noun clauses function as subjects, objects, or complements. In both adjective and noun clauses words may appear out of their normal order. The parts of a noun clause may also appear in their normal order.

Appositive and absolute phrases

Strictly speaking, appositive phrases are not subordinate word groups. Appositive phrases function somewhat as adjectives do, to describe nouns or pronouns. Instead of modifying nouns or pronouns however, appositive phrases rename them. In form they are nouns or nouns equivalents. Appositives are said to be in " in apposition" to the nouns or pronouns they rename. For example, in the sentence "Terriers, hunters at heart, have been dandled up to look like lap dogs", "hunters at heart" is apposition to the noun "terriers".

An absolute phrase modifies a whole clause or sentence, not just one word, and it may appear nearly anywhere in the sentence. It consists of a noun or noun equivalent usually followed by a participial phrase. Both appositive and absolute phrases can cause confusion in their usage in grammatical structures. They are particularly difficult for a person whose first language is not English.

**Common problems with sentences**

Subject-verb agreement
In the present tense, verbs agree with their subjects in number, (singular or plural), and in person, (first ,second, or third). The present tense ending -s is used on a verb if its subject is third person singular; otherwise the verb takes no ending. The verb "be" varies from this pattern, and alone among verbs it has special forms in both the present and past tense.

Problems with subject-verb agreement tend to arise in certain contexts:

1. Words between subject and verbs.
2. Subjects joined by "and".
3. Subjects joined by "or" or "nor".
4. Indefinite pronouns such as "someone".
5. Collective nouns.
6. Subject after verb.
7. Who, which, and that.
8. Plural form, singular meaning.
9. Titles, company names, and words mentioned as words.

Sentence fragments
As a rule a part of a sentence should not be treated as a complete sentence. A sentence must be composed of at least one full independent clause. An independent clause has a subject, a verb, and can stand alone as a sentence. Some fragments are clauses that contain a subject and a verb, but begin with a subordinating word. Other fragments lack a subject, verb, or both.

A sentence fragment can be repaired by combining the fragment with a nearby sentence, punctuating the new sentence correctly, or turn the fragment into a sentence by adding the missing elements. Some sentence fragments are used by writers for emphasis. Although sentence fragments are sometimes acceptable, readers and writers do not always agree on when they are appropriate. A conservative approach is to write in complete sentences only unless a special circumstance dictates otherwise.

Run-on sentences
Run-on sentences are independent clauses that have not been joined correctly. An independent clause is a word group that does or could stand alone in a sentence. When two or more independent clauses appear in one sentence, they must be joined in one of these ways:

1. Revision with a comma and a coordinating conjunction.
2. Revision with a semicolon, a colon, or a dash. Used when independent clauses are closely related and their relationship is clear without a coordinating conjunction.
3. Revision by separating sentences. This approach may be used when both independent clauses are long,
4. or if one is a question and one is not. Separate sentences may be the best option in this case.
5. Revision by restructuring the sentence. For sentence variety, consider restructuring the sentence, perhaps by turning one of the independent clauses into a subordinate phrase or clause.

Usually one of these choices will be an obvious solution to the run-on sentence. The fourth technique above is often the most effective solution, but requires the most revision.

Double negatives
Standard English allows two negatives only if a positive meaning is intended. "The team was not displeased with their performance" is an example. Double negatives used to emphasize negation are nonstandard.

Negative modifiers such as "never, no, and not" should not be paired with other negative modifiers or negative words such as " none, nobody, nothing, or neither". The modifiers "hardly, barely, and scarcely" are also considered negatives in standard English, so they should not be used with other negatives such as "not, no one, or never".

Double superlatives
Do not use double superlatives or comparatives. When "er" or "est" has been added to an adjective or adverb, avoid using "more" or "most". Avoid expressions such as "more perfect", and "very round". Either something is or is not. It is not logical to suggest that absolute concepts come in degrees. Use the comparative to compare two things, and the superlative to compare three or more things.

**Punctuation**

Commas
The comma was invented to help readers. Without it, sentence parts can run together, making meanings unclear. Various rules for comma use include:

1. Use a comma between a coordinating conjunction joining independent clauses.
2. Use a comma after an introductory clause or phrase.
3. Use a comma between items in a series.
4. Use a comma between coordinate adjectives not joined with "and". Do not use a comma between cumulative adjectives.
5. Use commas to set off nonrestrictive elements. Do not use commas to set off restrictive elements.
6. Use commas to set off transitional and parenthetical expressions, absolute phrases, and elements expressing contrast.
7. Use commas to set off nouns of direct address, the words yes and no, interrogative tags, and interjections.
8. Use commas with dates, addresses, titles, and numbers.

Some situations where commas are unnecessary include:

1. Do not use a comma between compound elements that are not independent clauses.
2. Do not use a comma after a phrase that begins with an inverted sentence.
3. Do not use a comma between the first or after the last item in a series or before the word "although".
4. Do not use a comma between cumulative adjectives, between an adjective and a noun, or between an adverb and an adjective.
5. Do not use commas to set off restrictive or mildly parenthetical elements or to set off an indirect quotation.
6. Do not use a comma to set off a concluding adverb clause that is essential to the meaning of the sentence or after the word "although".
7. Do not use a comma to separate a verb from its subject or object. Do not use a comma after a coordinating conjunction or before a parenthesis.
8. Do not use a comma with a question mark or an exclamation point.
9. Use commas to prevent confusion.
10. Use commas to set off direct quotations.

Semicolons
The semicolon is used to connect major sentence elements of equal grammatical rank. Some rules regarding semicolons include:

1. Use a semicolon between closely related independent clauses not joined with a coordinating conjunction.
2. Use a semicolon between independent clauses linked with a transitional expression.
3. Use a semicolon between items in a series containing internal punctuation.
4. Avoid using a semicolon between a subordinate clause and the rest of the sentence.
5. Avoid using a semicolon between an appositive word and the word it refers to.
6. Avoid using a semicolon to introduce a list.
7. Avoid using a semicolon between independent clauses joined by "and, but, or, nor, for, so, or yet".

Colons
The colon is used primarily to call attention to the words that follow it. In addition the colon has some other conventional uses:

1. Use a colon after an independent clause to direct attention to a list, an appositive, or a quotation.
2. Use a colon between independent clauses if the second summarizes or explains the first.
3. Use a colon after the salutation in a formal letter, to indicate hours and minutes, to show proportions between a title and subtitle, and between city and publisher in bibliographic entries.

A colon must be preceded by a full independent clause. Avoid using colons in the following situations:

1. Avoid using a colon between a verb and its object or complement.
2. Avoid using a colon between a preposition and its object.
3. Avoid using a colon after "such as, including, or for example"

Apostrophes
An apostrophe is used to indicate that a noun is possessive. Possessive nouns usually indicate ownership, as in Bill's coat or the dog's biscuit. Sometimes ownership is only loosely implied, as in the dog's coat or the forest's trees. If it is unclear whether a noun is possessive, turning into phrase may clarify it.

If the noun is plural and ends in-s, add only an apostrophe. To show joint possession, use -'s with the last noun only. To show individual possession, make all nouns possessive.

An apostrophe is often optional in plural numbers, letters, abbreviations, and words mentioned as words.

Common errors in using apostrophes include:

1. Do not use an apostrophe with nouns that are not possessive.
2. Do not use an apostrophe in the possessive pronouns "its, whose, his, hers, ours, yours, and theirs".

Quotation marks
Use quotation marks to enclose direct quotations of a person's words, spoken or written. Do not use quotation marks around indirect quotations. An indirect quotation reports someone's ideas without using that person's exact words. Set off long quotations of prose or poetry by indenting. Use single quotation marks to enclose a quotation within a quotation. Quotation marks should be used around the titles of short works: newspaper and magazine articles, poems, short stories, songs, episodes of television and radio programs, and subdivisions of books or web sites.

Quotation marks may be used to set off words used as words. Punctuation is used with quotation marks according to convention. Periods and commas are placed inside quotation marks, while colons and semicolons are placed outside quotation marks. Question marks and exclamation points are placed inside quotation marks. Do not use quotation marks around the title of your own essay.

Dashes

When typing, use two hyphens to form a dash. Do not put spaces before or after the dash. Dashes are used for the following purposes:

1. To set off parenthetical material that deserves emphasis.
2. To set off appositives that contain commas.
3. To prepare for a list, a restatement, an amplification, or a dramatic shift in tone or thought.

Unless there is a specific reason for using the dash, omit it. It can give text a choppy effect.

Parentheses

Parentheses are used to enclose supplemental material, minor digressions, and afterthoughts. They are also used to enclose letters or numbers labeling them items in a series. Parentheses should be used sparingly, as they break up text in a distracting manner when overused.

Brackets

Brackets are used to enclose any words or phrases that have been inserted into an otherwise word-for-word quotation.

Ellipsis marks

The ellipsis mark consists of three spaced periods (...), and is used to indicate when certain words have been deleted from an otherwise word-for-word quotation. If a full sentence or more is deleted in the middle of quoted passage, a person should be inserted before the ellipsis dots. The ellipsis mark should not be used at the beginning of a quotation. It should also not be used at the end of a quotation unless some words have been deleted from the end of the final sentence.

Slashes

The slash, (/), may be used to separate two or three lines of poetry that have been run into a text. If there are more than three lines of poetry they should be handled as an indented quotation. The slash may occasionally be used to separate paired terms such as passed/failed or either/or. In this case, apace is not placed before or after the slash. The slash should be used sparingly, only when it is clearly appropriate.

End punctuations

1. Use a period to end all sentences except direct questions or genuine exclamations. Periods should be used in abbreviations according to convention. Problems can arise when there is a choice between a period and a question mark or exclamation point. If a sentence reports a question rather than asking it directly, it should end with a period, not a question mark.
2. Question marks should be used following a direct question. If a polite request is written in the form of a question, it may be followed by a period. Questions in a series may be followed by question marks even when they are not in complete sentences.
3. Exclamation marks are used after a word group or sentence that expresses exceptional feeling or deserves special emphasis. Exclamation marks should not be overused, being reserved for appropriate exclamatory interjections.

**Essays**

Essays are generally defined to describe a prose composition, relatively brief (rarely exceeding 25 pages), dealing with a specific topic. Originally, essays tended to be informal in tone and exploratory and tentative in approach and conclusions. In more modern writing, essays have divided into the formal and informal. The formal essays have dominated the professional and scientific fields, while the informal style is written primarily to entertain or give opinions. Writers should be mindful of the style of essay their subject lends itself to, and conform to the conventions of that style.

Some types of essays, particularly scientific and academic writing, have style manuals to guide the format and conventions of the writing. The Modern Language Association and the American Psychological Association have two of the most widely followed style manuals. They are widely available for writers' reference.

# *Mathematics*

**Numbers and their classifications**

Numbers are the basic building blocks of mathematics. Specific features of numbers are identified by the following terms:

Integers – The set of whole positive and negative numbers, including zero. Integers do not include fractions ($\frac{1}{3}$), decimals (0.56), or mixed numbers ($7\frac{3}{4}$).

Prime number – A whole number greater than 1 that has only two factors, itself and 1; that is, a number that can be divided evenly only by 1 and itself.

Composite number – A whole number greater than 1 that has more than two different factors; in other words, any whole number that is not a prime number. For example: The composite number 8 has the factors of 1, 2, 4, and 8.

Even number – Any integer that can be divided by 2 without leaving a remainder. For example: 2, 4, 6, 8, and so on.

Odd number – Any integer that cannot be divided evenly by 2. For example: 3, 5, 7, 9, and so on.

Decimal number – a number that uses a decimal point to show the part of the number that is less than one. Example: 1.234.

Decimal point – a symbol used to separate the ones place from the tenths place in decimals or dollars from cents in currency.

Decimal place – the position of a number to the right of the decimal point. In the decimal 0.123, the 1 is in the first place to the right of the decimal point, indicating tenths; the 2 is in the second place, indicating hundredths; and the 3 is in the third place, indicating thousandths.

The decimal, or base 10, system is a number system that uses ten different digits $(0, 1, 2, 3, 4, 5, 6, 7, 8, 9)$. An example of a number system that uses something other than ten digits is the binary, or base 2, number system, used by computers, which uses only the numbers 0 and 1. It is thought that the decimal system originated because people had only their 10 fingers for counting.

Rational, irrational, and real numbers can be described as follows:

Rational numbers include all integers, decimals, and fractions. Any terminating or repeating decimal number is a rational number.

Irrational numbers cannot be written as fractions or decimals because the number of decimal places is infinite and there is no recurring pattern of digits within the number. For example, pi ($\pi$) begins with 3.141592 and continues without terminating or repeating, so pi is an irrational number.

Real numbers are the set of all rational and irrational numbers.

**Operations**

There are four basic mathematical operations:

Addition increases the value of one quantity by the value of another quantity. Example: $2 + 4 = 6; 8 + 9 = 17$. The result is called the sum. With addition, the order does not matter. $4 + 2 = 2 + 4$.

Subtraction is the opposite operation to addition; it decreases the value of one quantity by the value of another quantity. Example: $6 - 4 = 2; 17 - 8 = 9$. The result is called the difference. Note that with subtraction, the order does matter. $6 - 4 \neq 4 - 6$.

Multiplication can be thought of as repeated addition. One number tells how many times to add the other number to itself. Example: $3 \times 2$ (three times two) $= 2 + 2 + 2 = 6$. With multiplication, the order does not matter. $2 \times 3 = 3 \times 2$ or $3 + 3 = 2 + 2 + 2$.

Division is the opposite operation to multiplication; one number tells us how many parts to divide the other number into. Example: $20 \div 4 = 5$; if 20 is split into 4 equal parts, each part is 5. With division, the order of the numbers does matter. $20 \div 4 \neq 4 \div 20$.

An exponent is a superscript number placed next to another number at the top right. It indicates how many times the base number is to be multiplied by itself. Exponents provide a shorthand way to write what would be a longer mathematical expression. Example: $a^2 = a \times a$; $2^4 = 2 \times 2 \times 2 \times 2$. A number with an exponent of 2 is said to be "squared," while a number with an exponent of 3 is said to be "cubed." The value of a number raised to an exponent is called its power. So, $8^4$ is read as "8 to the 4th power," or "8 raised to the power of 4." A negative exponent is the same as the reciprocal of a positive exponent. Example: $a^{-2} = \frac{1}{a^2}$.

Parentheses are used to designate which operations should be done first when there are multiple operations. Example: 4 – (2 + 1) = 1; the parentheses tell us that we must add 2 and 1, and then subtract the sum from 4, rather than subtracting 2 from 4 and then adding 1 (this would give us an answer of 3).

Order of Operations is a set of rules that dictates the order in which we must perform each operation in an expression so that we will evaluate at accurately. If we have an expression that includes multiple different operations, Order of Operations tells us which operations to do first. The most common mnemonic for Order of Operations is PEMDAS, or "Please Excuse My Dear Aunt Sally." PEMDAS stands for Parentheses, Exponents, Multiplication, Division, Addition, Subtraction. It is important to understand that multiplication and division have equal precedence, as do addition and subtraction, so those pairs of operations are simply worked from left to right in order.

Example: Evaluate the expression $5 + 20 \div 4 \times (2 + 3)^2 - 6$ using the correct order of operations.

P: Perform the operations inside the parentheses, $(2 + 3) = 5$.
E: Simplify the exponents, $(5)^2 = 25$.
The equation now looks like this: $5 + 20 \div 4 \times 25 - 6$.

MD: Perform multiplication and division from left to right, $20 \div 4 = 5$; then $5 \times 25 = 125$.
The equation now looks like this: $5 + 125 - 6$.

AS: Perform addition and subtraction from left to right, $5 + 125 = 130$; then $130 - 6 = 124$.

The laws of exponents are as follows:

1. Any number to the power of 1 is equal to itself: $a^1 = a$.
2. The number 1 raised to any power is equal to 1: $1^n = 1$.
3. Any number raised to the power of 0 is equal to 1: $a^0 = 1$.
4. Add exponents to multiply powers of the same base number:$a^n \times a^m = a^{n+m}$.
5. Subtract exponents to divide powers of the same number; that is $a^n \div a^m = a^{n-m}$.
6. Multiply exponents to raise a power to a power: $(a^n)^m = a^{n\times m}$.
7. If multiplied or divided numbers inside parentheses are collectively raised to a power, this is the same as each individual term being raised to that power: $(a \times b)^n = a^n \times b^n$; $(a \div b)^n = a^n \div b^n$.

Note: Exponents do not have to be integers. Fractional or decimal exponents follow all the rules above as well. Example: $5^{\frac{1}{4}} \times 5^{\frac{3}{4}} = 5^{\frac{1}{4}+\frac{3}{4}} = 5^1 = 5$.

A root, such as a square root, is another way of writing a fractional exponent. Instead of using a superscript, roots use the radical symbol ($\sqrt{\ }$) to indicate the operation. A radical will have a number underneath the bar, and may sometimes have a number in the upper left: $\sqrt[n]{a}$, read as "the $n^{\text{th}}$ root of *a*." The relationship between radical notation and exponent notation can be described by this equation: $\sqrt[n]{a} = a^{\frac{1}{n}}$. The two special cases of $n = 2$ and $n = 3$ are called square roots and cube roots. If there is no number to the upper left, it is understood to be a square root ($n = 2$). Nearly all of the roots you encounter will be square roots. A square root is the same as a number raised to the one-half power. When we say that *a* is the square root of *b* ($a = \sqrt{b}$), we mean that *a* multiplied by itself equals *b*: ($a \times a = b$).

A perfect square is a number that has an integer for its square root. There are 10 perfect squares from 1 to 100: 1, 4, 9, 16, 25, 36, 49, 64, 81, 100 (the squares of integers 1 through 10).

Scientific notation is a way of writing large numbers in a shorter form. The form $a \times 10^n$ is used in scientific notation, where *a* is greater than or equal to 1, but less than 10, and *n* is the number of places the decimal must move to get from the original number to *a*. Example: The number 230,400,000 is cumbersome to write. To write the value in scientific notation, place a decimal point between the first and second numbers, and include all digits through the last non-zero digit ($a = 2.304$). To find the appropriate power of 10, count the number of places the decimal point had to move ($n = 8$). The number is positive if the decimal moved to the left, and negative if it moved to the right. We can then write 230,400,000 as $2.304 \times 10^8$. If we look instead at the number 0.00002304, we have the same value for *a*, but this time the decimal moved 5 places to the right ($n = -5$). Thus, 0.00002304 can be written as $2.304 \times 10^{-5}$. Using this notation makes it simple to compare very large or very small numbers. By comparing exponents, it is easy to see that $3.28 \times 10^4$ is smaller than $1.51 \times 10^5$, because 4 is less than 5.

**Factors and multiples**

Factors are numbers that are multiplied together to obtain a product. For example, in the equation $2 \times 3 = 6$, the numbers 2 and 3 are factors. A prime number has only two factors (1 and itself), but other numbers can have many factors.

A common factor is a number that divides exactly into two or more other numbers. For example, the factors of 12 are 1, 2, 3, 4, 6, and 12, while the factors of 15 are 1, 3, 5, and 15. The common factors of 12 and 15 are 1 and 3.

A prime factor is also a prime number. Therefore, the prime factors of 12 are 2 and 3. For 15, the prime factors are 3 and 5.

The greatest common factor (GCF) is the largest number that is a factor of two or more numbers. For example, the factors of 15 are 1, 3, 5, and 15; the factors of 35 are 1, 5, 7, and 35. Therefore, the greatest common factor of 15 and 35 is 5.

The least common multiple (LCM) is the smallest number that is a multiple of two or more numbers. For example, the multiples of 3 include 3, 6, 9, 12, 15, etc.; the multiples of 5 include 5, 10, 15, 20, etc. Therefore, the least common multiple of 3 and 5 is 15.

**Fractions, percentages, and related concepts**

A fraction is a number that is expressed as one integer written above another integer, with a dividing line between them ($\frac{x}{y}$). It represents the quotient of the two numbers "*x* divided by *y*." It can also be thought of as *x* out of *y* equal parts.

The top number of a fraction is called the numerator, and it represents the number of parts under consideration. The 1 in $\frac{1}{4}$ means that 1 part out of the whole is being considered in the calculation. The bottom number of a fraction is called the denominator, and it represents the total number of equal parts. The 4 in $\frac{1}{4}$ means that the whole consists of 4 equal parts. A fraction cannot have a denominator of zero; this is referred to as "undefined."

Fractions can be manipulated, without changing the value of the fraction, by multiplying or dividing (but not adding or subtracting) both the numerator and denominator by the same number. If you divide both numbers by a common factor, you are reducing or simplifying the fraction. Two fractions that have the same value, but are expressed differently are known as equivalent fractions. For example, $\frac{2}{10}, \frac{3}{15}, \frac{4}{20}, \text{and} \frac{5}{25}$ are all equivalent fractions. They can also all be reduced or simplified to $\frac{1}{5}$.

When two fractions are manipulated so that they have the same denominator, this is known as finding a common denominator. The number chosen to be that common denominator should be the least common multiple of the two original denominators. Example: $\frac{3}{4} \text{ and } \frac{5}{6}$; the least common multiple of 4 and 6 is 12. Manipulating to achieve the common denominator: $\frac{3}{4} = \frac{9}{12}; \frac{5}{6} = \frac{10}{12}$.

If two fractions have a common denominator, they can be added or subtracted simply by adding or subtracting the two numerators and retaining the same denominator. Example: $\frac{1}{2} + \frac{1}{4} = \frac{2}{4} + \frac{1}{4} = \frac{3}{4}$. If the two fractions do not already have the same denominator, one or both of them must be manipulated to achieve a common denominator before they can be added or subtracted.

Two fractions can be multiplied by multiplying the two numerators to find the new numerator and the two denominators to find the new denominator. Example: $\frac{1}{3} \times \frac{2}{3} = \frac{1 \times 2}{3 \times 3} = \frac{2}{9}$.

Two fractions can be divided flipping the numerator and denominator of the second fraction and then proceeding as though it were a multiplication. Example: $\frac{2}{3} \div \frac{3}{4} = \frac{2}{3} \times \frac{4}{3} = \frac{8}{9}$.

A fraction whose denominator is greater than its numerator is known as a proper fraction, while a fraction whose numerator is greater than its denominator is known as an improper fraction. Proper fractions have values less than one and improper fractions have values greater than one.

A mixed number is a number that contains both an integer and a fraction. Any improper fraction can be rewritten as a mixed number. Example: $\frac{8}{3} = \frac{6}{3} + \frac{2}{3} = 2 + \frac{2}{3} = 2\frac{2}{3}$. Similarly, any mixed number can be rewritten as an improper fraction. Example: $1\frac{3}{5} = 1 + \frac{3}{5} = \frac{5}{5} + \frac{3}{5} = \frac{8}{5}$.

Percentages can be thought of as fractions that are based on a whole of 100; that is, one whole is equal to 100%. The word percent means "per hundred." Fractions can be expressed as percents by finding equivalent fractions with a denomination of 100. Example: $\frac{7}{10} = \frac{70}{100} = 70\%$; $\frac{1}{4} = \frac{25}{100} = 25\%$.

To express a percentage as a fraction, divide the percentage number by 100 and reduce the fraction to its simplest possible terms. Example: $60\% = \frac{60}{100} = \frac{3}{5}$; $96\% = \frac{96}{100} = \frac{24}{25}$.

Converting decimals to percentages and percentages to decimals is as simple as moving the decimal point. To convert from a decimal to a percent, move the decimal point two places to the right. To convert from a percent to a decimal, move it two places to the left. Example: 0.23 = 23%; 5.34 = 534%; 0.007 = 0.7%; 700% = 7.00; 86% = 0.86; 0.15% = 0.0015.

It may be helpful to remember that the percentage number will always be larger than the equivalent decimal number.

A percentage problem can be presented three main ways: (1) Find what percentage of some number another number is. Example: What percentage of 40 is 8? (2) Find what number is some percentage of a given number. Example: What number is 20% of 40? (3) Find what number another number is a given percentage of. Example: What number is 8 20% of? The three components in all of these cases are the same: a whole (*W*), a part (*P*), and a percentage (%). These are related by the equation: $P = W \times \%$. This is the form of the equation you would use to solve problems of type (2). To solve types (1) and (3), you would use these two forms: $\% = \frac{P}{W}$ and $W = \frac{P}{\%}$.

The thing that frequently makes percentage problems difficult is that they are most often also word problems, so a large part of solving them is figuring out which quantities are what. Example: In a school cafeteria, 7 students choose pizza, 9 choose hamburgers, and 4 choose tacos. Find the percentage that chooses tacos. To find the whole, you must first add all of the parts: 7 + 9 + 4 = 20. The percentage can then be found by dividing the part by the whole ($\% = \frac{P}{W}$): $\frac{4}{20} = \frac{20}{100} = 20\%$.

A ratio is a comparison of two quantities in a particular order. Example: If there are 14 computers in a lab, and the class has 20 students, there is a student to computer ratio of 20 to 14, commonly written as 20:14. Ratios are normally reduced to their smallest whole number representation, so 20:14 would be reduced to 10:7 by dividing both sides by 2.

A proportion is a relationship between two quantities that dictates how one changes when the other changes. A direct proportion describes a relationship in which a quantity increases by a set amount for every increase in the other quantity, or decreases by that same amount for every decrease in the other quantity. Example: Assuming a constant driving speed, the time required for a car trip increases as the distance of the trip increases. The distance to be traveled and the time required to travel are directly proportional.

Inverse proportion is a relationship in which an increase in one quantity is accompanied by a decrease in the other, or vice versa. Example: the time required for a car trip decreases as the speed increases, and increases as the speed decreases, so the time required is inversely proportional to the speed of the car.

**Data analysis**

Statistics is the branch of mathematics that deals with collecting, recording, interpreting, illustrating, and analyzing large amounts of data. The following terms are often used in the discussion of data and statistics:

- Continuous data – information (such as time and temperature) that can be expressed by any value within a given range
- Data – the collective name for pieces of information (singular is datum).
- Discrete data – information that can be expressed only by a specific value, such as whole or half numbers; For example, since people can be counted only in whole numbers, a population count would be discrete data.
- Nominal data – information that cannot be placed in numerical order, such as names or places
- Ordinal data – information that can be placed in numerical order, such as age or weight
- Primary data – information that has been collected directly from a survey, investigation, or experiment, such as a questionnaire or the recording of daily temperatures; Primary data that has not yet been organized or analyzed is called raw data.
- Quantitative data – measurements (such as length, mass, and speed) that provide information about quantities in numbers
- Qualitative data – information (such as colors, scents, tastes, and shapes) that cannot be measured using numbers
- Secondary data – information that has been collected, sorted, and processed by the researcher

**Measures of central tendency**

The quantities of mean, median, and mode are all referred to as measures of central tendency. They can each give a picture of what the whole set of data looks like with just a single number. Knowing what each of these values represents is vital to making use of the information they provide.

The mean, also known as the arithmetic mean or average, of a data set is calculated by summing all of the values in the set and dividing that sum by the number of values. For example, if a data set has 6 numbers and the sum of those 6 numbers is 30, the mean is calculated as 30/6 = 5.

The median is the middle value of a data set. The median can be found by putting the data set in numerical order, and locating the middle value. In the data set (1, 2, 3, 4, 5), the median is 3. If there is an even number of values in the set, the median is calculated by taking the average of the two middle values. In the data set, (1, 2, 3, 4, 5, 6), the median would be (3 + 4)/2 = 3.5.

The mode is the value that appears most frequently in the data set. In the data set (1, 2, 3, 4, 5, 5, 5), the mode would be 5 since the value 5 appears three times. If multiple values appear the same number of times, there are multiple values for the mode. If the data set were (1, 2, 2, 3, 4, 4, 5, 5), the modes would be 2, 4, and 5. If no value appears more than any other value in the data set, then there is no mode.

**Measures of dispersion**

The standard deviation expresses how spread out the values of a distribution are from the mean. Standard deviation is given in the same units as the original data and is represented by a lower case sigma ($\sigma$).

A high standard deviation means that the values are very spread out. A low standard deviation means that the values are close together.

If every value in a distribution is increased or decreased by the same amount, the mean, median, and mode are increased or decreased by that amount, but the standard deviation stays the same.

If every value in a distribution is multiplied or divided by the same number, the mean, median, mode, and standard deviation will all be multiplied or divided by that number.

The range of a distribution is the difference between the highest and lowest values in the distribution. For example, in the data set (1, 3, 5, 7, 9, 11), the highest and lowest values are 11 and 1, respectively. The range then would be calculated as $11 - 1 = 10$.

The three quartiles are the three values that divide a data set into four equal parts. Quartiles are generally only calculated for data sets with a large number of values. As a simple example, for the data set consisting of the numbers 1 through 99, the first quartile (Q1) would be 25, the second quartile (Q2), always equal to the median, would be 50, and the third quartile (Q3) would be 75. The difference between Q1 and Q3 is known as the interquartile range.

**Probability**

Probability is a branch of statistics that deals with the likelihood of something taking place. One classic example is a coin toss. There are only two possible results: heads or tails. The likelihood, or probability, that the coin will land as heads is 1 out of 2 (1/2, 0.5, 50%). Tails has the same probability. Another common example is a 6-sided die roll. There are six possible results from rolling a single die, each with an equal chance of happening, so the probability of any given number coming up is 1 out of 6.

Terms frequently used in probability:

- Certain outcome – probability of outcome is 100% or 1
- Compound event – event that involves two or more items (rolling a pair of dice; taking the sum)
- Dependent events – two or more events whose outcomes affect one another (two cards drawn consecutively from the same deck)
- Desired outcome (or success) – an outcome that meets a particular set of criteria (a roll of 1 or 2 if we are looking for numbers less than 3)
- Event – a situation that produces results of some sort (a coin toss)
- Impossible outcome – probability of outcome is 0% or 0
- Mutually exclusive outcomes – two or more outcomes whose criteria cannot all be satisfied in a single event (a coin coming up heads and tails on the same toss)
- Outcome – a possible result in an experiment or event (heads, tails)
- Independent events – two or more events whose outcomes do not affect one another (two coins tossed at the same time)

**Probability** is the likelihood of a certain outcome occurring for a given event. The **theoretical probability** can usually be determined without actually performing the event. The likelihood of a outcome occurring, or the probability of an outcome occurring, is given by the formula

$$P(A) = \frac{\text{Number of acceptable outcomes}}{\text{Total number of possible outcomes}}$$

where $P(A)$ is the probability of an outcome $A$ occurring, and each outcome is just as likely to occur as any other outcome. If each outcome has the same probability of occurring as every other possible outcome, the outcomes are said to be equally likely to occur. The total number of acceptable outcomes must be less than or equal to the total number of possible outcomes. If the two are equal, then the outcome is certain to occur and the probability is 1. If the number of acceptable outcomes is zero, then the outcome is impossible and the probability is 0.

Example: There are 20 marbles in a bag and 5 are red. The theoretical probability of randomly selecting a red marble is 5 out of 20, (5/20 = 1/4, 0.25, or 25%).

When trying to calculate the probability of an event using the (desired outcomes)/(total outcomes formula), you may frequently find that there are too many outcomes to individually count them. Permutation and combination formulas offer a shortcut to counting outcomes. The primary distinction between permutations and combinations is that permutations take into account order, while combinations do not. To calculate the number of possible groupings, there are two necessary parameters: the number of items available for selection and the number to be selected. The number of **permutations** of *r* items given a set of *n* items can be calculated as $_nP_r = \frac{n!}{(n-r)!}$. The number of **combinations** of *r* items given a set of *n* items can be calculated as $_nC_r = \frac{n!}{r!(n-r)!}$ or $_nC_r = \frac{_nP_r}{r!}$.

Example: Suppose you want to calculate how many different 5-card hands can be drawn from a deck of 52 cards. This is a combination since the order of the cards in a hand does not matter. There are 52 cards available, and 5 to be selected. Thus, the number of different hands is $_{52}C_5 = \frac{52!}{5!\times 47!} = 2{,}598{,}960$.

Sometimes it may be easier to calculate the possibility of something not happening, or the **complement of an event**. Represented by the symbol $\bar{A}$, the complement of *A* is the probability that event *A* does not happen. When you know the probability of event *A* occurring, you can use the formula $P(\bar{A}) = 1 - P(A)$, where $P(\bar{A})$ is the probability of event *A* not occurring, and $P(A)$ is the probability of event *A* occurring.

The **addition rule** for probability is used for finding the probability of a compound event. Use the formula $P(A \text{ or } B) = P(A) + P(B) - P(A \text{ and } B)$, where *P*(*A*) is the probability of the event *A* occurring, *P*(*B*) is the probability of event *B* occurring, and *P*(*A* and *B*) is the probability of both events occurring to find the probability of a compound event. The probability of both events occurring at the same time must be subtracted to eliminate any overlap in the first two probabilities.

**Conditional probability** is the probability of a dependent event occurring once the original event has already occurred. Given event *A* and dependent event *B*, the probability of event *B* occurring when event *A* has already occurred is represented by the notation $P(A|B)$. To find the probability of event *B* occurring, take into account the fact that event *A* has already occurred and adjust the total number of possible outcomes. For example, suppose you have ten balls numbered 1–10 and you want ball number 7 to be pulled in two pulls. On the first pull, the probability of getting the 7 is $\frac{1}{10}$ because there is one ball with a 7 on it and 10 balls to choose from. Assuming the first pull did not yield a 7, the probability of pulling a 7 on the second pull is now $\frac{1}{9}$ because there are only 9 balls remaining for the second pull.

The **multiplication rule** can be used to find the probability of two independent events occurring using the formula *P*(*A* and *B*) = *P*(*A*) *P*(*B*), where *P*(*A* and *B*) is the probability of two independent events occurring, *P*(*A*) is the probability of the first event occurring, and *P*(*B*) is the probability of the second event occurring.

The multiplication rule can also be used to find the probability of two dependent events occurring using the formula $P(A \text{ and } B) = P(A) \cdot P(B|A)$, where *P*(*A* and *B*) is the probability of two dependent events occurring, *P*(*A*) is the probability of the first event occurring, and $P(B|A)$ is the probability of the second event occurring after the first event has already occurred.

Before using the multiplication rule, you MUST first determine whether the two events are dependent or independent.

Use a combination of the multiplication rule and the rule of complements to find the probability that at least one outcome of the element will occur. This given by the general formula $P(\text{at least one event occurring}) = 1 - P(\text{no outcomes occurring})$. For example, to find the probability that at least one even number will show when a pair of dice is rolled, find the probability that two odd numbers will be rolled (no even numbers) and subtract from one. You can always use a tree diagram or make a chart to list the possible outcomes when the sample space is small, such as in the dice-rolling example, but in most cases it will be much faster to use the multiplication and complement formulas.

**Expected value** is a method of determining expected outcome in a random situation. It is really a sum of the weighted probabilities of the possible outcomes. Multiply the probability of an event occurring by the weight assigned to that probability (such as the amount of money won or lost). A practical application of the expected value is to determine whether a game of chance is really fair. If the sum of the weighted probabilities is equal to zero, the game is generally considered fair because the player has a fair chance to at least to break even. If the expected value is less than zero, then players lose more than they win. For example, a lottery drawing might allow the player to choose any three-digit number, 000–999. The probability of choosing the winning number is 1:1000. If it costs $1 to play, and a winning number receives $500, the expected value is
$\left(-\$1 \cdot \frac{999}{1,000}\right) + \left(\$500 \cdot \frac{1}{1,000}\right) = -0.499 \text{ or } -\$0.50$

You can expect to lose on average 50 cents for every dollar you spend.

Most of the time, when we talk about probability, we mean theoretical probability. **Experimental probability**, or empirical probability or relative frequency, is the number of times an outcome occurs in a particular experiment or a certain number of observed events. While theoretical probability is based on what *should* happen, experimental probability is based on what *has* happened. Experimental probability is calculated in the same way as theoretical, except that actual outcomes are used instead of possible outcomes.

Theoretical and experimental probability do not always line up with one another. Theoretical probability says that out of 20 coin tosses, 10 should be heads. However, if we were actually to toss 20 coins, we might record just 5 heads. This doesn't mean that our theoretical probability is incorrect; it just means that this particular experiment had results that were different from what was predicted. A practical application of empirical probability is the insurance industry. There are no set functions that define life span, health, or safety. Insurance companies look at factors from hundreds of thousands of individuals to find patterns that they then use to set the formulas for insurance premiums.

**Objective probability** is based on mathematical formulas and documented evidence. Examples of objective probability include raffles or lottery drawings where there is a pre-determined number of possible outcomes and a predetermined number of outcomes that correspond to an event. Other cases of objective probability include probabilities of rolling dice, flipping coins, or drawing cards. Most gambling games are based on objective probability.

**Subjective probability** is based on personal or professional feelings and judgments. Often, there is a lot of guesswork following extensive research. Areas where subjective probability is applicable include sales trends and business expenses. Attractions set admission prices based on subjective probabilities of attendance based on varying admission rates in an effort to maximize their profit.

**Common charts and graphs**

A bar graph is a graph that uses bars to compare data, as if each bar were a ruler being used to measure the data. The graph includes a scale that identifies the units being measured.

A line graph is a graph that connects points to show how data increases or decreases over time. The time line is the horizontal axis. The connecting lines between data points on the graph are a way to more clearly show how the data changes.

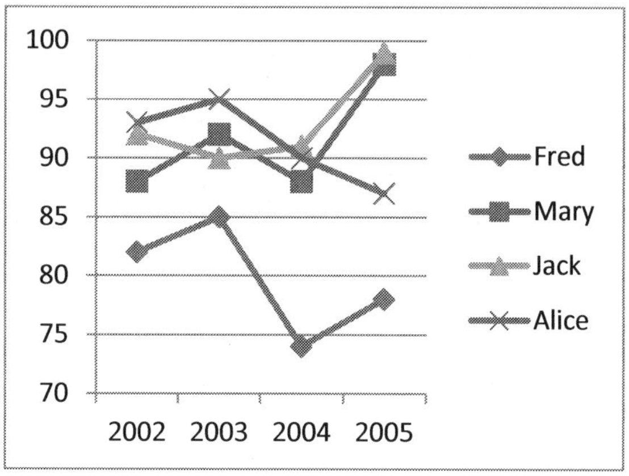


A pictograph is a graph that uses pictures or symbols to show data. The pictograph will have a key to identify what each symbol represents. Generally, each symbol stands for one or more objects.

A pie chart or circle graph is a diagram used to compare parts of a whole. The full pie represents the whole, and it is divided into sectors that each represent something that is a part of the whole. Each sector or slice of the pie is either labeled to indicate what it represents, or explained on a key associated with the chart. The size of each slice is determined by the percentage of the whole that the associated quantity represents. Numerically, the angle measurement of each sector can be computed by solving the proportion: x/360 = part/whole.

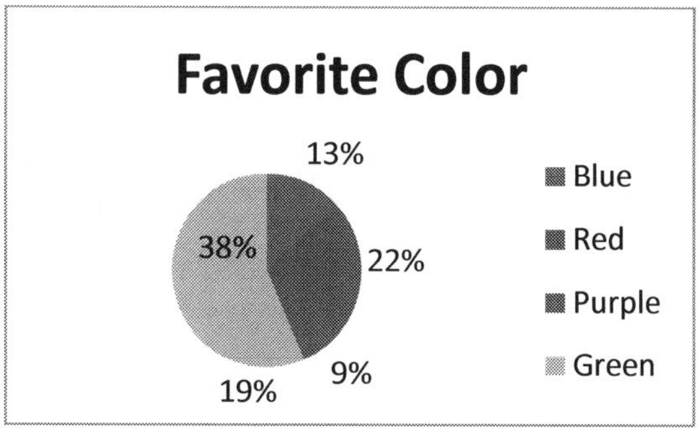

A histogram is a special type of bar graph where the data are grouped in intervals (for example 20-29, 30-39, 40-49, etc.). The frequency, or number of times a value occurs in each interval, is indicated by the height of the bar. The intervals do not have to be the same amount but usually are (all data in ranges of 10 or all in ranges of 5, for example). The smaller the intervals, the more detailed the information.

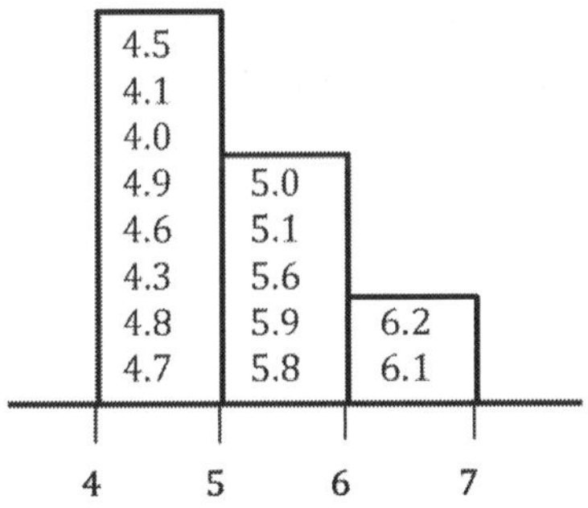


A stem-and-leaf plot is a way to organize data visually so that the information is easy to understand. A stem-and-leaf plot is simple to construct because a simple line separates the stem (the part of the plot listing the tens digit, if displaying two-digit data) from the leaf (the part that shows the ones digit). Thus, the number 45 would appear as 4 | 5. The stem-and-leaf plot for test scores of a group of 11 students might look like the following:

| | |
|---|---|
| 9 | 5 |
| 8 | 1, 3, 8 |
| 7 | 0, 2, 4, 6, 7 |
| 6 | 2, 8 |

A stem-and-leaf plot is similar to a histogram or other frequency plot, but with a stem-and-leaf plot, all the original data is preserved. In this example, it can be seen at a glance that nearly half the students scored in the 70's, yet all the data has been maintained. These plots can be used for larger numbers as well, but they tend to work better for small sets of data as they can become unwieldy with larger sets.

## Equations and graphing

When algebraic functions and equations are shown graphically, they are usually shown on a *Cartesian Coordinate Plane*. The Cartesian coordinate plane consists of two number lines placed perpendicular to each other, and intersecting at the zero point, also known as the origin. The horizontal number line is known as the *x*-axis, with positive values to the right of the origin, and negative values to the left of the origin. The vertical number line is known as the *y*-axis, with positive values above the origin, and negative values below the origin. Any point on the plane can be identified by an ordered pair in the form (*x*,*y*), called coordinates. The *x*-value of the coordinate is called the abscissa, and the *y*-value of the coordinate is called the ordinate. The two number lines divide the plane into four quadrants: I, II, III, and IV.

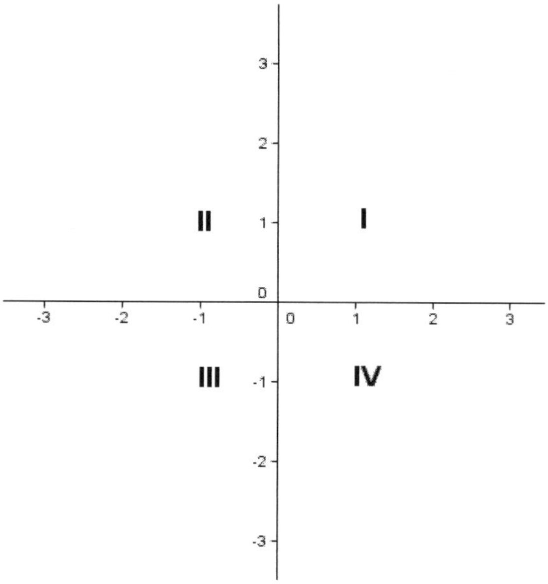


Before learning the different forms equations can be written in, it is important to understand some terminology. A ratio of the change in the vertical distance to the change in horizontal distance is called the *Slope*. On a graph with two points, $(x_1, y_1)$ and $(x_2, y_2)$, the slope is represented by the formula $= \frac{y_2 - y_1}{x_2 - x_1}$ ; $x_1 \neq x_2$. If the value of the slope is positive, the line slopes upward from left to right. If the value of the slope is negative, the line slopes downward from left to right. If the *y*-coordinates are the same for both points, the slope is 0 and the line is a *Horizontal Line*. If the *x*-coordinates are the same for both points, there is no slope and the line is a *Vertical Line*. Two or more lines that have equal slopes are *Parallel Lines*. *Perpendicular Lines* have slopes that are negative reciprocals of each other, such as $\frac{a}{b}$ and $\frac{-b}{a}$.

Equations are made up of monomials and polynomials. A *Monomial* is a single variable or product of constants and variables, such as *x*, 2*x*, or $\frac{2}{x}$ . There will never be addition or subtraction symbols in a monomial. Like monomials have like variables, but they may have different coefficients. *Polynomials* are algebraic expressions which use addition and subtraction to combine two or more monomials. Two terms make a binomial; three terms make a trinomial; etc.. The *Degree of a Monomial* is the sum of the exponents of the variables. The *Degree of a Polynomial* is the highest degree of any individual term.

As mentioned previously, equations can be written many ways. Below is a list of the many forms equations can take.

- *Standard Form*: $Ax + By = C$; the slope is $\frac{-A}{B}$ and the *y*-intercept is $\frac{C}{B}$
- *Slope Intercept Form*: $y = mx + b$, where *m* is the slope and *b* is the *y*-intercept
- *Point-Slope Form*: $y - y_1 = m(x - x_1)$, where *m* is the slope and $(x_1, y_1)$ is a point on the line
- *Two-Point Form*: $\frac{y-y_1}{x-x_1} = \frac{y_2-y_1}{x_2-x_1}$, where $(x_1, y_1)$ and $(x_2, y_2)$ are two points on the given line
- *Intercept Form*: $\frac{x}{x_1} + \frac{y}{y_1} = 1$, where $(x_1, 0)$ is the point at which a line intersects the *x*-axis, and $(0, y_1)$ is the point at which the same line intersects the *y*-axis

Equations can also be written as $ax + b = 0$, where $a \neq 0$. These are referred to as *One Variable Linear Equations*. A solution to such an equation is called a *Root*. In the case where we have the equation $5x + 10 = 0$, if we solve for $x$ we get a solution of $x = -2$. In other words, the root of the equation is -2. This is found by first subtracting 10 from both sides, which gives $5x = -10$. Next, simply divide both sides by the coefficient of the variable, in this case 5, to get $x = -2$. This can be checked by plugging -2 back into the original equation $(5)(-2) + 10 = -10 + 10 = 0$.

The *Solution Set* is the set of all solutions of an equation. In our example, the solution set would simply be -2. If there were more solutions (there usually are in multivariable equations) then they would also be included in the solution set. When an equation has no true solutions, this is referred to as an *Empty Set*. Equations with identical solution sets are *Equivalent Equations*. An *Identity* is a term whose value or determinant is equal to 1.

**Calculations using points**

Sometimes you need to perform calculations using only points on a graph as input data. Using points, you can determine what the midpoint and distance are. If you know the equation for a line you can calculate the distance between the line and the point.

To find the *Midpoint* of two points $(x_1, y_1)$ and $(x_2, y_2)$, average the *x*-coordinates to get the *x*-coordinate of the midpoint, and average the *y*-coordinates to get the *y*-coordinate of the midpoint. The formula is midpoint $= \left(\frac{x_1+x_2}{2}, \frac{y_1+y_2}{2}\right)$.

The *Distance* between two points is the same as the length of the hypotenuse of a right triangle with the two given points as endpoints, and the two sides of the right triangle parallel to the *x*-axis and *y*-axis, respectively. The length of the segment parallel to the *x*-axis is the difference between the *x*-coordinates of the two points. The length of the segment parallel to the *y*-axis is the difference between the *y*-coordinates of the two points. Use the Pythagorean Theorem $a^2 + b^2 = c^2$ or $c = \sqrt{a^2 + b^2}$ to find the distance. The formula is: distance $= \sqrt{(x_2 - x_1)^2 + (y_2 - y_1)^2}$.

When a line is in the format $Ax + By + C = 0$, where *A*, *B*, and *C* are coefficients, you can use a point ($x_1$, $y_1$) not on the line and apply the formula $d = \frac{|Ax_1+By_1+C|}{\sqrt{A^2+B^2}}$ to find the distance between the line and the point ($x_1$, $y_1$).

**Systems of equations**

*Systems of Equations* are a set of simultaneous equations that all use the same variables. A solution to a system of equations must be true for each equation in the system. *Consistent Systems* are those with at least one solution. *Inconsistent Systems* are systems of equations that have no solution.

To solve a system of linear equations by *substitution*, start with the easier equation and solve for one of the variables. Express this variable in terms of the other variable. Substitute this expression in the other equation, and solve for the other variable. The solution should be expressed in the form (*x, y*). Substitute the values into both of the original equations to check your answer. Consider the following problem.

Solve the system using substitution:

$$x + 6y = 15$$
$$3x - 12y = 18$$

Solving the first equation for *x*:
$x = 15 - 6y$

Substitute this value in place of *x* in the second equation, and solve for *y*:

$$3(15 - 6y) - 12y = 18$$
$$45 - 18y - 12y = 18$$
$$30y = 27$$
$$y = \frac{27}{30} = \frac{9}{10} = 0.9$$

Plug this value for *y* back into the first equation to solve for *x*:
$x = 15 - 6(0.9) = 15 - 5.4 = 9.6$

Check both equations if you have time:

$$9.6 + 6(0.9) = 9.6 + 5.4 = 15$$
$$3(9.6) - 12(0.9) = 28.8 - 10.8 = 18$$

Therefore, the solution is (9.6, 0.9).

To solve a system of equations using *elimination*, begin by rewriting both equations in standard form $Ax + By = C$. Check to see if the coefficients of one pair of like variables add to zero. If not, multiply one or both of the equations by a non-zero number to make one set of like variables add to zero. Add the two equations to solve for one of the variables. Substitute this value into one of the original equations to solve for the other variable. Check your work by substituting into the other equation. Next we will solve the same problem as above, but using the addition method.

Solve the system using elimination:

$$x + 6y = 15$$
$$3x - 12y = 18$$

If we multiply the first equation by 2, we can eliminate the *y* terms:

$$2x + 12y = 30$$
$$3x - 12y = 18$$

Add the equations together and solve for *x*:

$5x = 48$

$x = \frac{48}{5} = 9.6$

Plug the value for *x* back in to either of the original equations and solve for *y*:

$9.6 + 6y = 15$

$y = \frac{15 - 9.6}{6} = 0.9$

Check both equations if you have time:

$$9.6 + 6(0.9) = 9.6 + 5.4 = 15$$
$$3(9.6) - 12(0.9) = 28.8 - 10.8 = 18$$

Therefore, the solution is (9.6, 0.9).

**Polynomial algebra**

To multiply two binomials, follow the *FOIL* method. FOIL stands for:

- First: Multiply the first term of each binomial
- Outer: Multiply the outer terms of each binomial
- Inner: Multiply the inner terms of each binomial
- Last: Multiply the last term of each binomial

Using FOIL, $(Ax + By)(Cx + Dy) = ACx^2 + ADxy + BCxy + BDy^2$

To divide polynomials, begin by arranging the terms of each polynomial in order of one variable. You may arrange in ascending or descending order, but be consistent with both polynomials. To get the first term of the quotient, divide the first term of the dividend by the first term of the divisor. Multiply the first term of the quotient by the entire divisor and subtract that product from the dividend. Repeat for the second and successive terms until you either get a remainder of zero or a remainder whose degree is less than the degree of the divisor. If the quotient has a remainder, write the answer as a mixed expression in the form: quotient $+ \frac{\text{remainder}}{\text{divisor}}$.

*Rational Expressions* are fractions with polynomials in both the numerator and the denominator; the value of the polynomial in the denominator cannot be equal to zero. To add or subtract rational expressions, first find the common denominator, then rewrite each fraction as an equivalent fraction with the common denominator. Finally, add or subtract the numerators to get the numerator of the answer, and keep the common denominator as the denominator of the answer. When multiplying rational expressions factor each polynomial and cancel like factors (a factor which appears in both the numerator and the denominator). Then, multiply all remaining factors in the numerator to get the numerator of the product, and multiply the remaining factors in the denominator to get the denominator of the product. Remember – cancel entire factors, not individual terms. To divide rational expressions, take the reciprocal of the divisor (the rational expression you are dividing by) and multiply by the dividend.

Below are patterns of some special products to remember: *perfect trinomial squares*, the *difference between two squares*, the *sum and difference of two cubes*, and *perfect cubes.*

- Perfect Trinomial Squares: $x^2 + 2xy + y^2 = (x + y)^2$ or $x^2 - 2xy + y^2 = (x - y)^2$
- Difference Between Two Squares: $x^2 - y^2 = (x + y)(x - y)$
- Sum of Two Cubes: $x^3 + y^3 = (x + y)(x^2 - xy + y^2)$
  Note: the second factor is NOT the same as a perfect trinomial square, so do not try to factor it further.
- Difference Between Two Cubes: $x^3 - y^3 = (x - y)(x^2 + xy + y^2)$
  Again, the second factor is NOT the same as a perfect trinomial square.
- Perfect Cubes: $x^3 + 3x^2y + 3xy^2 + y^3 = (x + y)^3$ and $x^3 - 3x^2y + 3xy^2 - y^3 = (x - y)^3$

In order to *factor* a polynomial, first check for a common monomial factor. When the greatest common monomial factor has been factored out, look for patterns of special products: differences of two squares, the sum or difference of two cubes for binomial factors, or perfect trinomial squares for trinomial factors. If the factor is a trinomial but not a perfect trinomial square, look for a factorable form, such as $x^2 + (a + b)x + ab = (x + a)(x + b)$ or$(ac)x^2 + (ad + bc)x + bd = (ax + b)(cx + d)$. For factors with four terms, look for groups to factor. Once you have found the factors, write the original polynomial as the product of all the factors. Make sure all of the polynomial factors are prime. Monomial factors may be prime or composite. Check your work by multiplying the factors to make sure you get the original polynomial.

**Solving quadratic equations**

The *Quadratic Formula* is used to solve quadratic equations when other methods are more difficult. To use the quadratic formula to solve a quadratic equation, begin by rewriting the equation in standard form $ax^2 + bx + c = 0$, where *a*, *b*, and *c* are coefficients. Once you have identified the values of the coefficients, substitute those values into the quadratic formula $= \frac{-b \pm \sqrt{b^2 - 4ac}}{2a}$. Evaluate the equation and simplify the expression. Again, check each root by substituting into the original equation. In the quadratic formula, the portion of the formula under the radical $(b^2 - 4ac)$ is called the *Discriminant.* If the discriminant is zero, there is only one root: zero. If the discriminant is positive, there are two different real roots. If the discriminant is negative, there are no real roots.

To solve a quadratic equation by *Factoring*, begin by rewriting the equation in standard form, if necessary. Factor the side with the variable then set each of the factors equal to zero and solve the resulting linear equations. Check your answers by substituting the roots you found into the original equation. If, when writing the equation in standard form, you have an equation in the form $x^2 + c = 0$ or $x^2 - c = 0$, set $x^2 = -c$ or $x^2 = c$ and take the square root of *c*. If *c* = 0, the only real root is zero. If *c* is positive, there are two real roots—the positive and negative square root values. If *c* is negative, there are no real roots because you cannot take the square root of a negative number.

To solve a quadratic equation by *Completing the Square*, rewrite the equation so that all terms containing the variable are on the left side of the equal sign, and all the constants are on the right side of the equal sign. Make sure the coefficient of the squared term is 1. If there is a coefficient with the squared term, divide each term on both sides of the equal side by that number. Next, work with the coefficient of the single-variable term. Square half of this coefficient, and add that value to both sides. Now you can factor the left side (the side containing the variable) as the square of a binomial. $x^2 + 2ax + a^2 = C \Rightarrow (x + a)^2 = C$, where *x* is the variable, and *a* and *C* are constants. Take the square root of both sides and solve for the variable. Substitute the value of the variable in the original problem to check your work.

**Other important concepts**

Commonly in algebra and other upper-level fields of math you find yourself working with mathematical expressions that do not equal each other. The statement comparing such expressions with symbols such as < (less than) or > (greater than) is called an *Inequality.* An example of an inequality is $7x > 5$. To solve for $x$, simply divide both sides by $7$ and the solution is shown to be $x > \frac{5}{7}$. Graphs of the solution set of inequalities are represented on a number line. Open circles are used to show that an expression approaches a number but is never quite equal to that number.

*Conditional Inequalities* are those with certain values for the variable that will make the condition true and other values for the variable where the condition will be false. *Absolute Inequalities* can have any real number as the value for the variable to make the condition true, while there is no real number value for the variable that will make the condition false. Solving inequalities is done by following the same rules as for solving equations with the exception that when multiplying or dividing by a negative number the direction of the inequality sign must be flipped or reversed. *Double Inequalities* are situations where two inequality statements apply to the same variable expression. An example of this is $-c < ax + b < c$.

A *Weighted Mean*, or weighted average, is a mean that uses "weighted" values. The formula is weighted mean $= \frac{w_1x_1 + w_2x_2 + w_3x_3 \ldots + w_nx_n}{w_1 + w_2 + w_3 + \cdots + w_n}$. Weighted values, such as $w_1, w_2, w_3, \ldots w_n$ are assigned to each member of the set $x_1, x_2, x_3, \ldots x_n$. If calculating weighted mean, make sure a weight value for each member of the set is used.

A fraction that contains a fraction in the numerator, denominator, or both is called a *Complex Fraction.* These can be solved in a number of ways; with the simplest being by following the order of operations as stated earlier. For example, $\left(\frac{4}{7}\right) \Big/ \left(\frac{5}{8}\right) = 0.571 / 0.625 = 0.914$. Another way to solve this problem is to multiply the fraction in the numerator by the recipricol of the fraction in the denominator. For example, $\left(\frac{4}{7}\right) \Big/ \left(\frac{5}{8}\right) = \frac{4}{7} \times \frac{8}{5} = \frac{32}{35} = 0.914$.

In order to solve a *Radical Equation*, begin by isolating the radical term on one side of the equation, and move all other terms to the other side of the equation. Look at the index of the radicand. Remember, if no number is given, the index is 2, meaning square root. Raise both sides of the equation to the power equal to the index of the radical. Solve the resulting equation as you would a normal polynomial equation. When you have found the roots, you must check them in the original problem to eliminate extraneous roots.

**Lines and planes**

A point is a fixed location in space; has no size or dimensions; commonly represented by a dot.

A line is a set of points that extends infinitely in two opposite directions. It has length, but no width or depth. A line can be defined by any two distinct points that it contains. A line segment is a portion of a line that has definite endpoints. A ray is a portion of a line that extends from a single point on that line in one direction along the line. It has a definite beginning, but no ending.

A plane is a two-dimensional flat surface defined by three non-collinear points. A plane extends an infinite distance in all directions in those two dimensions. It contains an infinite number of points, parallel lines and segments, intersecting lines and segments, as well as parallel or intersecting rays. A plane will never contain a three-dimensional figure or skew lines. Two given planes will either be parallel or they will intersect to form a line. A plane may intersect a circular conic surface, such as a cone, to form conic sections, such as the parabola, hyperbola, circle or ellipse.

Perpendicular lines are lines that intersect at right angles. They are represented by the symbol $\perp$. The shortest distance from a line to a point not on the line is a perpendicular segment from the point to the line.

Parallel lines are lines in the same plane that have no points in common and never meet. It is possible for lines to be in different planes, have no points in common, and never meet, but they are not parallel because they are in different planes.

A bisector is a line or line segment that divides another line segment into two equal lengths. A perpendicular bisector of a line segment is composed of points that are equidistant from the endpoints of the segment it is dividing.

Intersecting lines are lines that have exactly one point in common. Concurrent lines are multiple lines that intersect at a single point.

A transversal is a line that intersects at least two other lines, which may or may not be parallel to one another. A transversal that intersects parallel lines is a common occurrence in geometry.

**Angles**

An angle is formed when two lines or line segments meet at a common point. It may be a common starting point for a pair of segments or rays, or it may be the intersection of lines. Angles are represented by the symbol $\angle$.

The vertex is the point at which two segments or rays meet to form an angle. If the angle is formed by intersecting rays, lines, and/or line segments, the vertex is the point at which four angles are formed. The pairs of angles opposite one another are called vertical angles, and their measures are equal.

An acute angle is an angle with a degree measure less than 90°.

A right angle is an angle with a degree measure of exactly 90°.

An obtuse angle is an angle with a degree measure greater than 90° but less than 180°.

A straight angle is an angle with a degree measure of exactly 180°. This is also a semicircle.

A reflex angle is an angle with a degree measure greater than 180° but less than 360°.

A full angle is an angle with a degree measure of exactly 360°.

Two angles whose sum is exactly 90° are said to be complementary. The two angles may or may not be adjacent. In a right triangle, the two acute angles are complementary.

Two angles whose sum is exactly 180° are said to be supplementary. The two angles may or may not be adjacent. Two intersecting lines always form two pairs of supplementary angles. Adjacent supplementary angles will always form a straight line.

Two angles that have the same vertex and share a side are said to be adjacent. Vertical angles are not adjacent because they share a vertex but no common side.

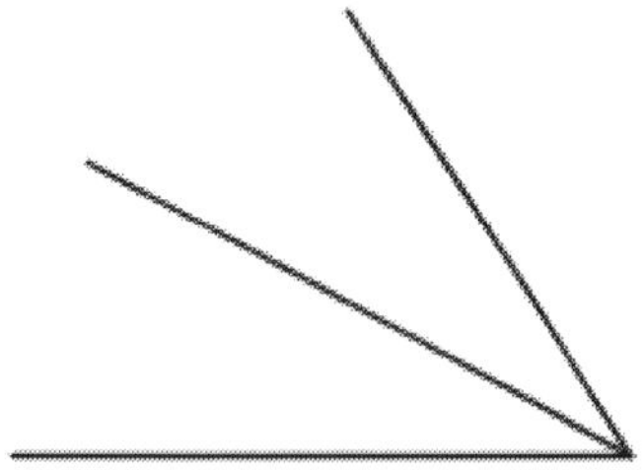

**Adjacent**

**Share vertex and side**

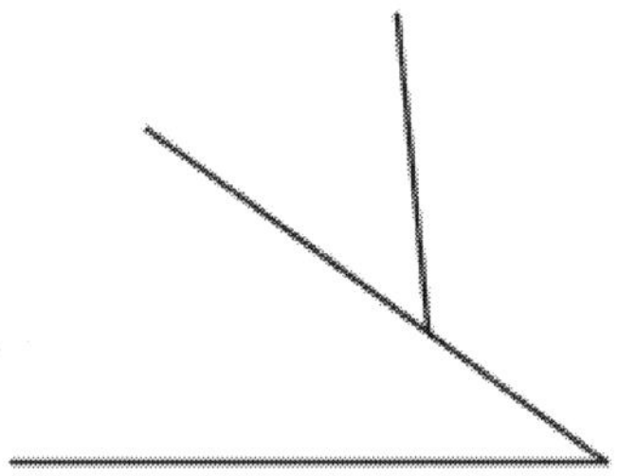

**Not adjacent**

**Share part of side, but not vertex**

When two parallel lines are cut by a transversal, the angles that are between the two parallel lines are interior angles. In the diagram below, angles 3, 4, 5, and 6 are interior angles.

When two parallel lines are cut by a transversal, the angles that are outside the parallel lines are exterior angles. In the diagram below, angles 1, 2, 7, and 8 are exterior angles.

When two parallel lines are cut by a transversal, the angles that are in the same position relative to the transversal and a parallel line are corresponding angles. The diagram below has four pairs of corresponding angles: angles 1 and 5; angles 2 and 6; angles 3 and 7; and angles 4 and 8. Corresponding angles formed by parallel lines are congruent.

When two parallel lines are cut by a transversal, the two interior angles that are on opposite sides of the transversal are called alternate interior angles. In the diagram below, there are two pairs of alternate interior angles: angles 3 and 6, and angles 4 and 5. Alternate interior angles formed by parallel lines are congruent.

When two parallel lines are cut by a transversal, the two exterior angles that are on opposite sides of the transversal are called alternate exterior angles. In the diagram below, there are two pairs of alternate exterior angles: angles 1 and 8, and angles 2 and 7. Alternate exterior angles formed by parallel lines are congruent.

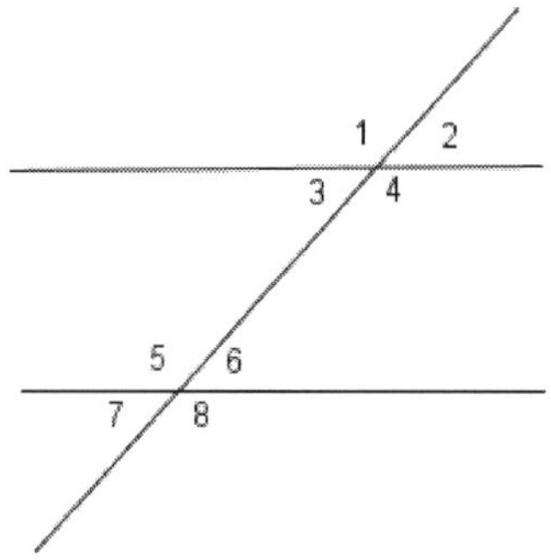


When two lines intersect, four angles are formed. The non-adjacent angles at this vertex are called vertical angles. Vertical angles are congruent. In the diagram, $\angle ABD \cong \angle CBE$ and $\angle ABC \cong \angle DBE$.

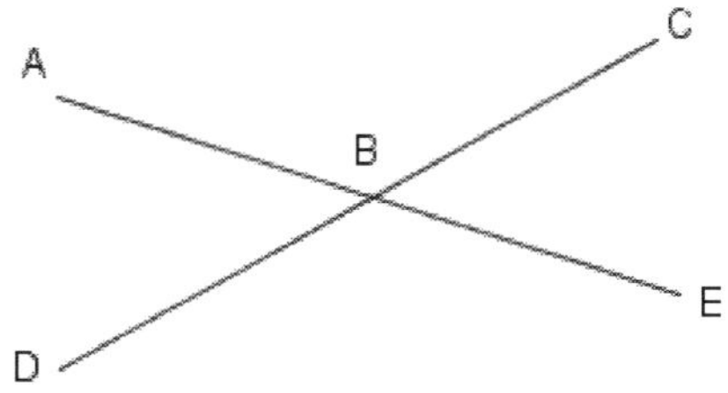


**Triangles**

An equilateral triangle is a triangle with three congruent sides. An equilateral triangle will also have three congruent angles, each 60°. All equilateral triangles are also acute triangles.

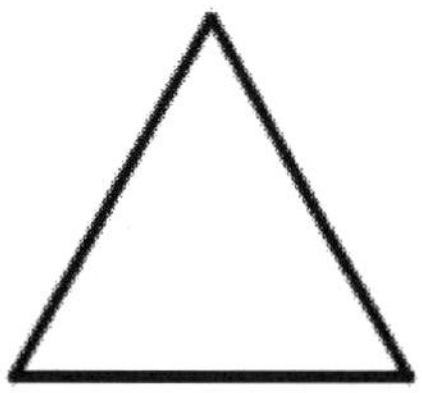

An isosceles triangle is a triangle with two congruent sides. An isosceles triangle will also have two congruent angles opposite the two congruent sides.

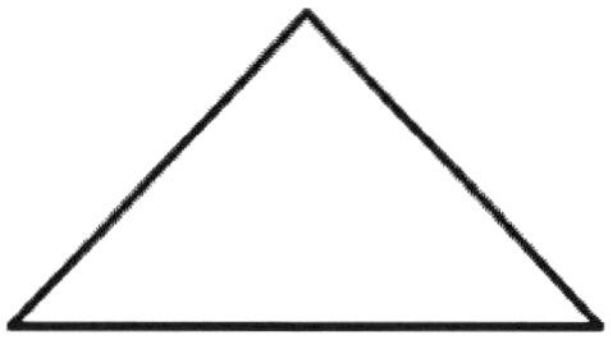

A scalene triangle is a triangle with no congruent sides. A scalene triangle will also have three angles of different measures. The angle with the largest measure is opposite the longest side, and the angle with the smallest measure is opposite the shortest side.

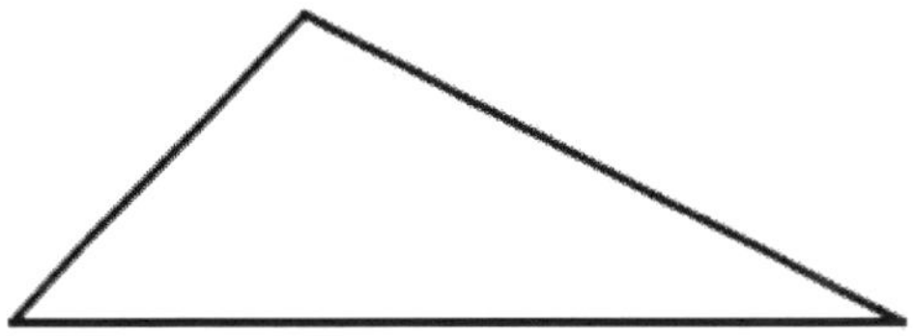

An acute triangle is a triangle whose three angles are all less than 90°. If two of the angles are equal, the acute triangle is also an isosceles triangle. If the three angles are all equal, the acute triangle is also an equilateral triangle.

A right triangle is a triangle with exactly one angle equal to 90°. All right triangles follow the Pythagorean Theorem. A right triangle can never be acute or obtuse.

An obtuse triangle is a triangle with exactly one angle greater than 90°. The other two angles may or may not be equal. If the two remaining angles are equal, the obtuse triangle is also an isosceles triangle.

**Terminology**

Altitude of a Triangle: A line segment drawn from one vertex perpendicular to the opposite side. In the diagram below, $\overline{BE}$, $\overline{AD}$, and $\overline{CF}$ are altitudes. The three altitudes in a triangle are always concurrent.

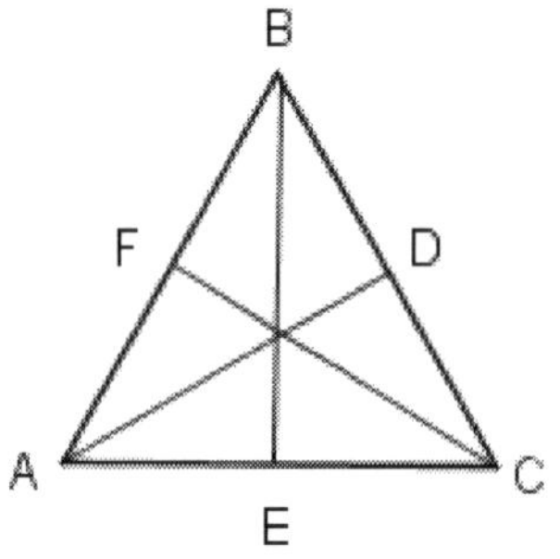


Height of a Triangle: The length of the altitude, although the two terms are often used interchangeably.

Orthocenter of a Triangle: The point of concurrency of the altitudes of a triangle. Note that in an obtuse triangle, the orthocenter will be outside the circle, and in a right triangle, the orthocenter is the vertex of the right angle.

Median of a Triangle: A line segment drawn from one vertex to the midpoint of the opposite side. This is not the same as the altitude, except the altitude to the base of an isosceles triangle and all three altitudes of an equilateral triangle.

Centroid of a Triangle: The point of concurrency of the medians of a triangle. This is the same point as the orthocenter only in an equilateral triangle. Unlike the orthocenter, the centroid is always inside the triangle. The centroid can also be considered the exact center of the triangle. Any shape triangle can be perfectly balanced on a tip placed at the centroid. The centroid is also the point that is two-thirds the distance from the vertex to the opposite side.

**Pythagorean theorem**

The side of a triangle opposite the right angle is called the hypotenuse. The other two sides are called the legs. The Pythagorean Theorem states a relationship among the legs and hypotenuse of a right triangle: $a^2 + b^2 = c^2$, where *a* and *b* are the lengths of the legs of a right triangle, and *c* is the length of the hypotenuse. Note that this formula will only work with right triangles.

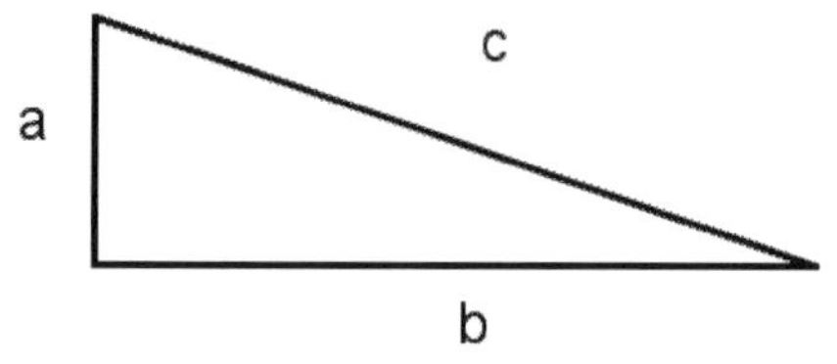


**General rules**

The Triangle Inequality Theorem states that the sum of the measures of any two sides of a triangle is always greater than the measure of the third side. If the sum of the measures of two sides were equal to the third side, a triangle would be impossible because the two sides would lie flat across the third side and there would be no vertex. If the sum of the measures of two of the sides was less than the third side, a closed figure would be impossible because the two shortest sides would never meet.

The sum of the measures of the interior angles of a triangle is always 180°. Therefore, a triangle can never have more than one angle greater than or equal to 90°.

In any triangle, the angles opposite congruent sides are congruent, and the sides opposite congruent angles are congruent. The largest angle is always opposite the longest side, and the smallest angle is always opposite the shortest side.

The line segment that joins the midpoints of any two sides of a triangle is always parallel to the third side and exactly half the length of the third side.

**Similarity and congruence rules**

Similar triangles are triangles whose corresponding angles are equal and whose corresponding sides are proportional. Represented by AA. Similar triangles whose corresponding sides are congruent are also congruent triangles.

Three sides of one triangle are congruent to the three corresponding sides of the second triangle. Represented as SSS.

Two sides and the included angle (the angle formed by those two sides) of one triangle are congruent to the corresponding two sides and included angle of the second triangle. Represented by SAS.

Two angles and the included side (the side that joins the two angles) of one triangle are congruent to the corresponding two angles and included side of the second triangle. Represented by ASA.

Two angles and a non-included side of one triangle are congruent to the corresponding two angles and non-included side of the second triangle. Represented by AAS.

Note that AAA is not a form for congruent triangles. This would say that the three angles are congruent, but says nothing about the sides. This meets the requirements for similar triangles, but not congruent triangles.

**Area and perimeter formulas**

The perimeter of any triangle is found by summing the three side lengths; $P = a + b + c$. For an equilateral triangle, this is the same as $P = 3s$, where *s* is any side length, since all three sides are the same length.

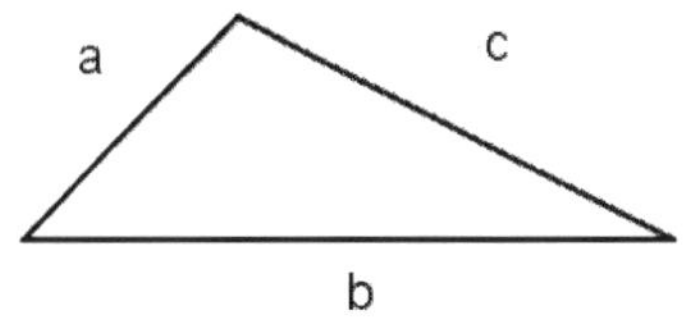


The area of any triangle can be found by taking half the product of one side length (base or *b*) and the perpendicular distance from that side to the opposite vertex (height or *h*). In equation form, $A = \frac{1}{2}bh$. For many triangles, it may be difficult to calculate *h*, so using one of the other formulas given here may be easier.

Another formula that works for any triangle is $A = \sqrt{s(s-a)(s-b)(s-c)}$, where *A* is the area, *s* is the semiperimeter $s = \frac{a+b+c}{2}$, and *a*, *b*, and *c* are the lengths of the three sides.

The area of an equilateral triangle can found by the formula $A = \frac{\sqrt{3}}{4}s^2$, where *A* is the area and *s* is the length of a side. You could use the $30° - 60° - 90°$ ratios to find the height of the triangle and then use the standard triangle area formula, but this is faster.

The area of an isosceles triangle can found by the formula, $A = \frac{1}{2}b\sqrt{a^2 - \frac{b^2}{4}}$, where *A* is the area, *b* is the base (the unique side), and *a* is the length of one of the two congruent sides. If you do not remember this formula, you can use the Pythagorean Theorem to find the height so you can use the standard formula for the area of a triangle.

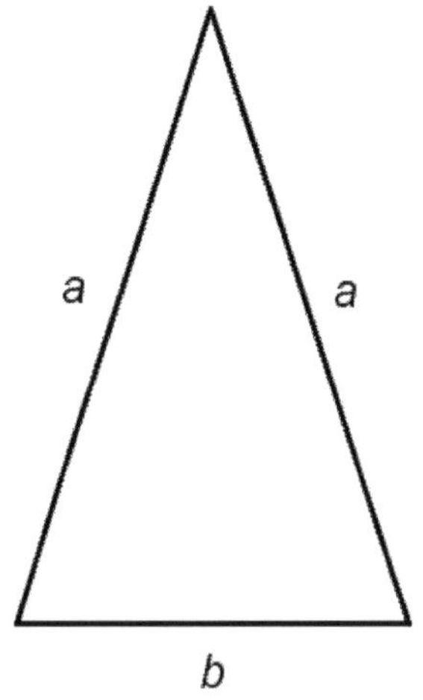

**Trigonometric formulas**

In the diagram below, angle *C* is the right angle, and side *c* is the hypotenuse. Side *a* is the side adjacent to angle *B* and side *b* is the side adjacent to angle *A*. These formulas will work for any acute angle in a right triangle. They will NOT work for any triangle that is not a right triangle. Also, they will not work for the right angle in a right triangle, since there are not distinct adjacent and opposite sides to differentiate from the hypotenuse.

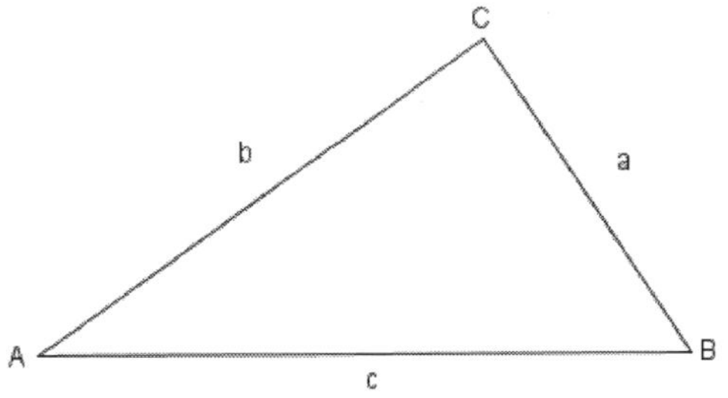


$$\sin A = \frac{\text{opposite side}}{\text{hypotenuse}} = \frac{a}{c}$$
$$\cos A = \frac{\text{adjacent side}}{\text{hypotenuse}} = \frac{b}{c}$$
$$\tan A = \frac{\text{opposite side}}{\text{adjacent side}} = \frac{a}{b}$$
$$\csc A = \frac{1}{\sin A} = \frac{\text{hypotenuse}}{\text{opposite side}} = \frac{c}{a}$$
$$\sec A = \frac{1}{\cos A} = \frac{\text{hypotenuse}}{\text{adjacent side}} = \frac{c}{b}$$
$$\cot A = \frac{1}{\tan A} = \frac{\text{adjacent side}}{\text{opposite side}} = \frac{b}{a}$$

**Laws of sines and cosines**

The Law of Sines states that $\frac{\sin A}{a} = \frac{\sin B}{b} = \frac{\sin C}{c}$, where *A*, *B*, and *C* are the angles of a triangle, and *a*, *b*, and *c* are the sides opposite their respective angles. This formula will work with all triangles, not just right triangles.

The Law of Cosines is given by the formula $c^2 = a^2 + b^2 - 2ab(\cos C)$, where *a*, *b*, and *c* are the sides of a triangle, and *C* is the angle opposite side *c*. This formula is similar to the Pythagorean Theorem, but unlike the Pythagorean Theorem, it can be used on any triangle.

**Polygons**

Each straight line segment of a polygon is called a side.

The point at which two sides of a polygon intersect is called the vertex. In a polygon, the number of sides is always equal to the number of vertices.

A polygon with all sides congruent and all angles equal is called a regular polygon.

A line segment from the center of a polygon perpendicular to a side of the polygon is called the apothem. In a regular polygon, the apothem can be used to find the area of the polygon using the formula $A = \frac{1}{2}ap$, where *a* is the apothem and *p* is the perimeter.

A line segment from the center of a polygon to a vertex of the polygon is called a radius. The radius of a regular polygon is also the radius of a circle that can be circumscribed about the polygon.

Triangle – 3 sides
Quadrilateral – 4 sides
Pentagon – 5 sides
Hexagon – 6 sides
Heptagon – 7 sides
Octagon – 8 sides
Nonagon – 9 sides
Decagon – 10 sides
Dodecagon – 12 sides

More generally, an *n*-gon is a polygon that has *n* angles and *n* sides.

The sum of the interior angles of an *n*-sided polygon is (n – 2)180°. For example, in a triangle n = 3, so the sum of the interior angles is (3 – 2)180° = 180°. In a quadrilateral, n = 4, and the sum of the angles is (4 – 2)180° = 360°. The sum of the interior angles of a polygon is equal to the sum of the interior angles of any other polygon with the same number of sides.

A diagonal is a line segment that joins two non-adjacent vertices of a polygon.

A convex polygon is a polygon whose diagonals all lie within the interior of the polygon.

A concave polygon is a polygon with a least one diagonal that lies outside the polygon. In the diagram below, quadrilateral *ABCD* is concave because diagonal $\overline{AC}$ lies outside the polygon.

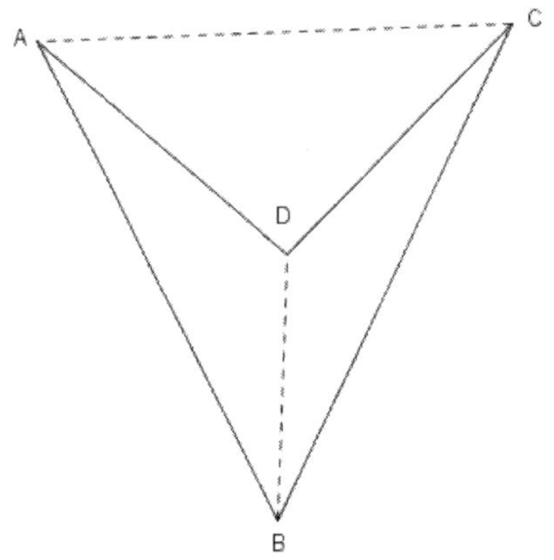

The number of diagonals a polygon has can be found by using the formula: number of diagonals $= \frac{n(n-3)}{2}$, where $n$ is the number of sides in the polygon. This formula works for all polygons, not just regular polygons.

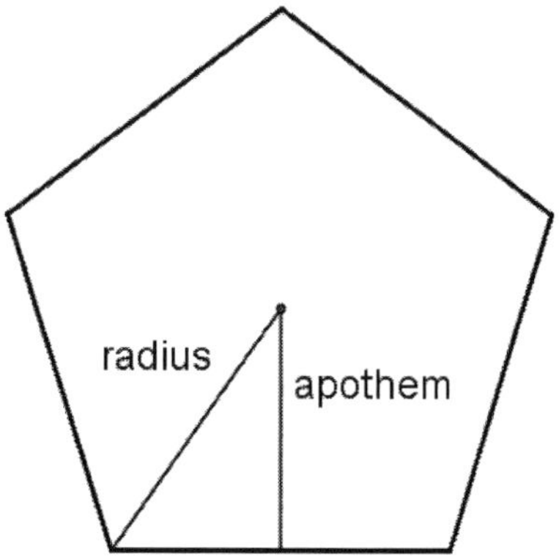


Congruent figures are geometric figures that have the same size and shape. All corresponding angles are equal, and all corresponding sides are equal. It is indicated by the symbol $\cong$.

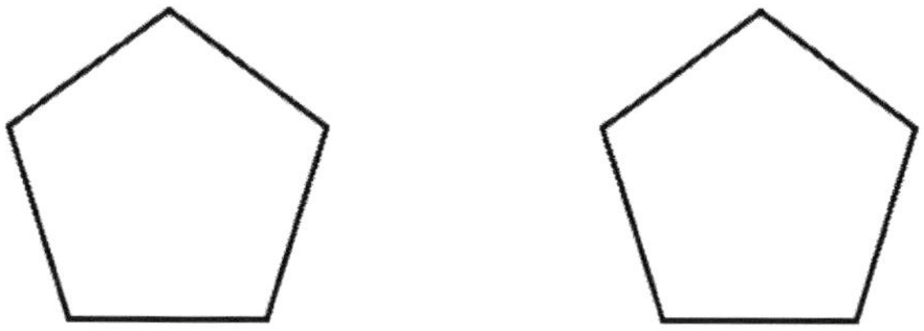

Congruent polygons

Similar figures are geometric figures that have the same shape, but do not necessarily have the same size. All corresponding angles are equal, and all corresponding sides are proportional, but they do not have to be equal. It is indicated by the symbol $\sim$.

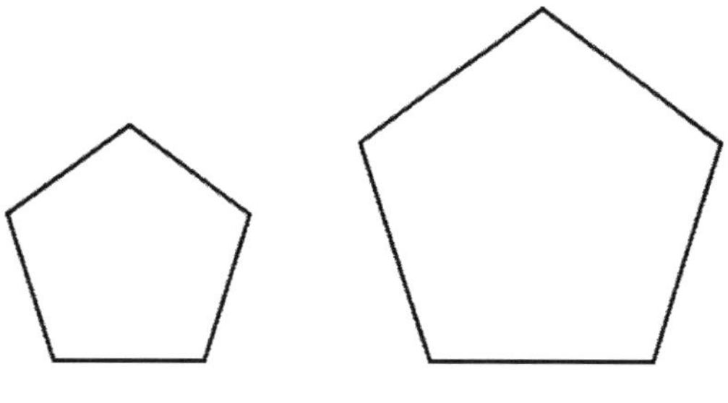

Similar polygons

Note that all congruent figures are also similar, but not all similar figures are congruent.

Line of Symmetry: The line that divides a figure or object into two symmetric parts. Each symmetric half is congruent to the other. An object may have no lines of symmetry, one line of symmetry, or more than one line of symmetry.

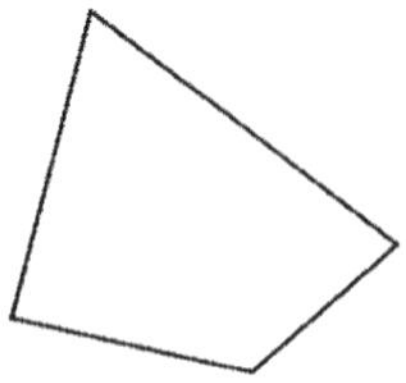

No lines of symmetry

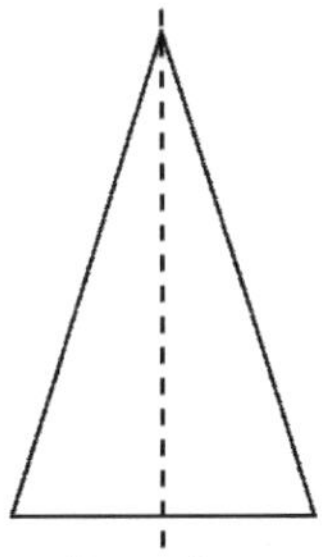

One line of symmetry

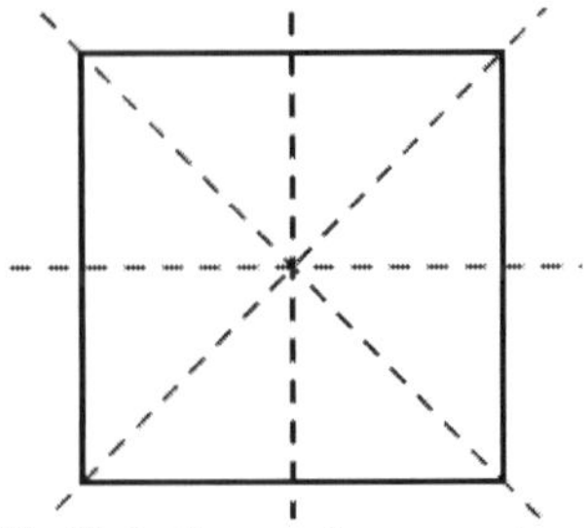

Multiple lines of symmetry

Quadrilateral: A closed two-dimensional geometric figure composed of exactly four straight sides. The sum of the interior angles of any quadrilateral is $360°$.

Parallelogram: A quadrilateral that has exactly two pairs of opposite parallel sides. The sides that are parallel are also congruent. The opposite interior angles are always congruent, and the consecutive interior angles are supplementary. The diagonals of a parallelogram bisect each other. Each diagonal divides the parallelogram into two congruent triangles.

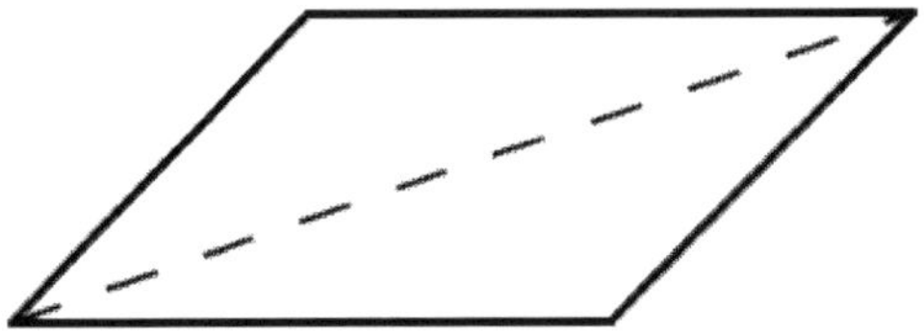

Trapezoid: Traditionally, a quadrilateral that has exactly one pair of parallel sides. Some math texts define trapezoid as a quadrilateral that has at least one pair of parallel sides. Because there are no rules governing the second pair of sides, there are no rules that apply to the properties of the diagonals of a trapezoid.

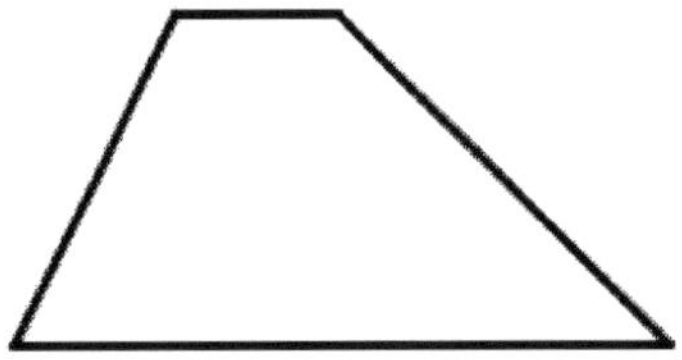

Rectangles, rhombuses, and squares are all special forms of parallelograms.

Rectangle: A parallelogram with four right angles. All rectangles are parallelograms, but not all parallelograms are rectangles. The diagonals of a rectangle are congruent.

Rhombus: A parallelogram with four congruent sides. All rhombuses are parallelograms, but not all parallelograms are rhombuses. The diagonals of a rhombus are perpendicular to each other.

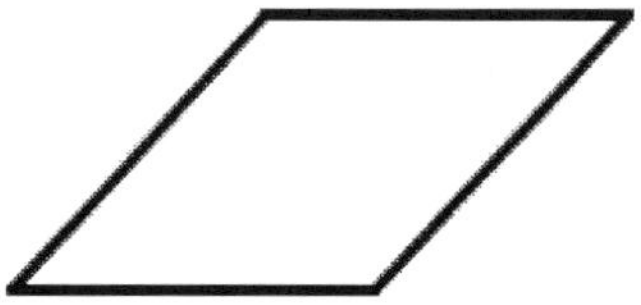

Square: A parallelogram with four right angles and four congruent sides. All squares are also parallelograms, rhombuses, and rectangles. The diagonals of a square are congruent and perpendicular to each other.

A quadrilateral whose diagonals bisect each other is a parallelogram. A quadrilateral whose opposite sides are parallel (2 pairs of parallel sides) is a parallelogram.

A quadrilateral whose diagonals are perpendicular bisectors of each other is a rhombus. A quadrilateral whose opposite sides (both pairs) are parallel and congruent is a rhombus.

A parallelogram that has a right angle is a rectangle. (Consecutive angles of a parallelogram are supplementary. Therefore if there is one right angle in a parallelogram, there are four right angles in that parallelogram.)

A rhombus with one right angle is a square. Because the rhombus is a special form of a parallelogram, the rules about the angles of a parallelogram also apply to the rhombus.

**Area and perimeter formulas**

The area of a square is found by using the formula $A = s^2$, where and *s* is the length of one side.

The perimeter of a square is found by using the formula $P = 4s$, where *s* is the length of one side. Because all four sides are equal in a square, it is faster to multiply the length of one side by 4 than to add the same number four times. You could use the formulas for rectangles and get the same answer.

The area of a rectangle is found by the formula $A = lw$, where *A* is the area of the rectangle, *l* is the length (usually considered to be the longer side) and *w* is the width (usually considered to be the shorter side). The numbers for *l* and *w* are interchangeable.

The perimeter of a rectangle is found by the formula $P = 2l + 2w$ or $P = 2(l + w)$, where *l* is the length, and *w* is the width. It may be easier to add the length and width first and then double the result, as in the second formula.

The area of a parallelogram is found by the formula $A = bh$, where *b* is the length of the base, and *h* is the height. Note that the base and height correspond to the length and width in a rectangle, so this formula would apply to rectangles as well. Do not confuse the height of a parallelogram with the length of the second side. The two are only the same measure in the case of a rectangle.

The perimeter of a parallelogram is found by the formula $P = 2a + 2b$ or $P = 2(a + b)$, where *a* and *b* are the lengths of the two sides.

The area of a trapezoid is found by the formula $A = \frac{1}{2}h(b_1 + b_2)$, where *h* is the height (segment joining and perpendicular to the parallel bases), and $b_1$ and $b_2$ are the two parallel sides (bases). Do not use one of the other two sides as the height unless that side is also perpendicular to the parallel bases.

The perimeter of a trapezoid is found by the formula $P = a + b_1 + c + b_2$, where *a*, $b_1$, *c*, and $b_2$ are the four sides of the trapezoid.

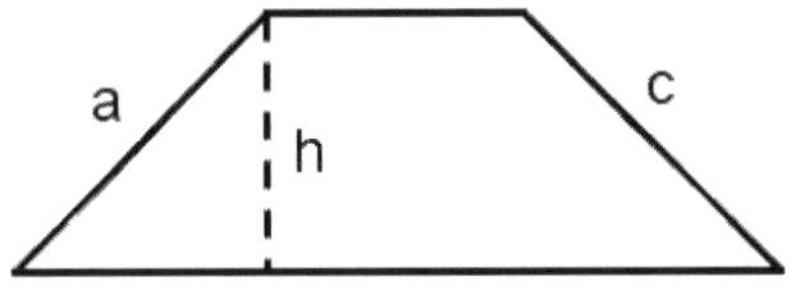


**Circles**

The center is the single point inside the circle that is equidistant from every point on the circle. (Point *O* in the diagram below.)

The radius is a line segment that joins the center of the circle and any one point on the circle. All radii of a circle are equal. (Segments *OX*, *OY*, and *OZ* in the diagram below.)

The diameter is a line segment that passes through the center of the circle and has both endpoints on the circle. The length of the diameter is exactly twice the length of the radius. (Segment *XZ* in the diagram below.)

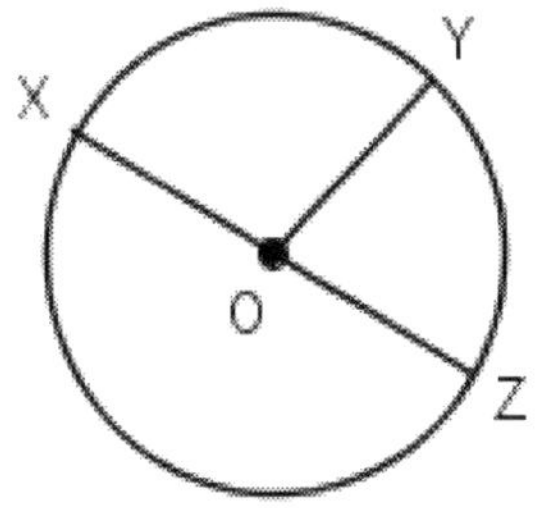


The area of a circle is found by the formula $A = \pi r^2$, where *r* is the length of the radius. If the diameter of the circle is given, remember to divide it in half to get the length of the radius before proceeding.

The circumference of a circle is found by the formula $C = 2\pi r$, where *r* is the radius. Again, remember to convert the diameter if you are given that measure rather than the radius.

Concentric circles are circles that have the same center, but not the same length of radii. A bulls-eye target is an example of concentric circles.

An arc is a portion of a circle. Specifically, an arc is the set of points between and including two points on a circle. An arc does not contain any points inside the circle. When a segment is drawn from the endpoints of an arc to the center of the circle, a sector is formed.

A central angle is an angle whose vertex is the center of a circle and whose legs intercept an arc of the circle. Angle *XOY* in the diagram above is a central angle. A minor arc is an arc that has a measure less than 180°. The measure of a central angle is equal to the measure of the minor arc it intercepts. A major arc is an arc having a measure of at least 180°. The measure of the major arc can be found by subtracting the measure of the central angle from 360°.

A semicircle is an arc whose endpoints are the endpoints of the diameter of a circle. A semicircle is exactly half of a circle.

An inscribed angle is an angle whose vertex lies on a circle and whose legs contain chords of that circle. The portion of the circle intercepted by the legs of the angle is called the intercepted arc. The measure of the intercepted arc is exactly twice the measure of the inscribed angle. In the diagram below, angle *ABC* is an inscribed angle. $\widehat{AC} = 2(\text{m}\angle ABC)$

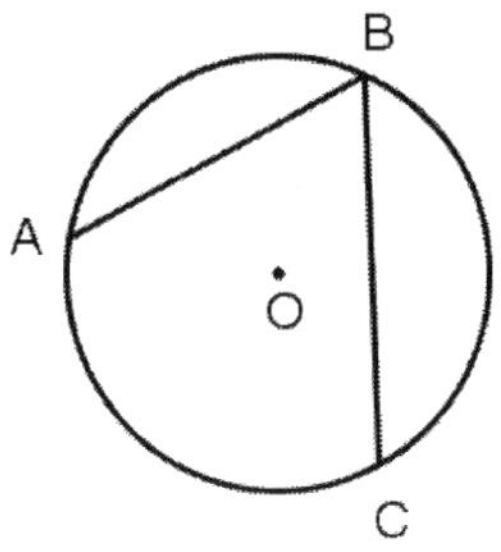


Any angle inscribed in a semicircle is a right angle. The intercepted arc is 180°, making the inscribed angle half that, or 90°. In the diagram below, angle *ABC* is inscribed in semicircle *ABC*, making angle *ABC* equal to 90°.

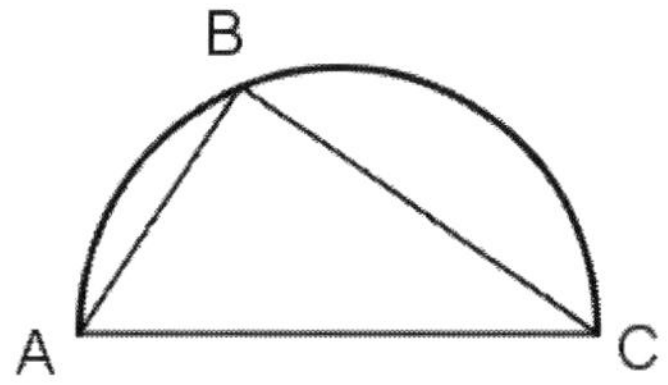


A chord is a line segment that has both endpoints on a circle. In the diagram below, $\overline{EB}$ is a chord.

Secant: A line that passes through a circle and contains a chord of that circle. In the diagram below, $\overleftrightarrow{EB}$ is a secant and contains chord $\overline{EB}$.

A tangent is a line in the same plane as a circle that touches the circle in exactly one point. While a line segment can be tangent to a circle as part of a line that is tangent, it is improper to say a tangent can be simply a line segment that touches the circle in exactly one point. In the diagram below, $\overleftrightarrow{CD}$ is tangent to circle *A*. Notice that $\overline{FB}$ is not tangent to the circle. $\overline{FB}$ is a line segment that touches the circle in exactly one point, but if the segment were extended, it would touch the circle in a second point. The point at which a tangent touches a circle is called the point of tangency. In the diagram below, point *B* is the point of tangency.

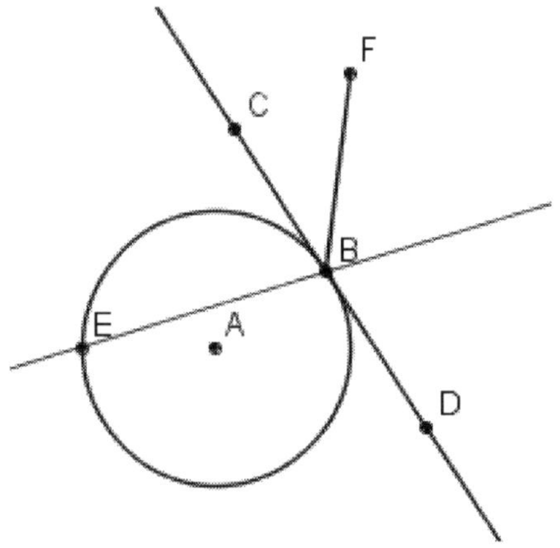


A secant is a line that intersects a circle in two points. Two secants may intersect inside the circle, on the circle, or outside the circle. When the two secants intersect on the circle, an inscribed angle is formed.

When two secants intersect inside a circle, the measure of each of two vertical angles is equal to half the sum of the two intercepted arcs. In the diagram below, $m\angle AEB = \frac{1}{2}(\widehat{AB} + \widehat{CD})$ and $m\angle BEC = \frac{1}{2}(\widehat{BC} + \widehat{AD})$.

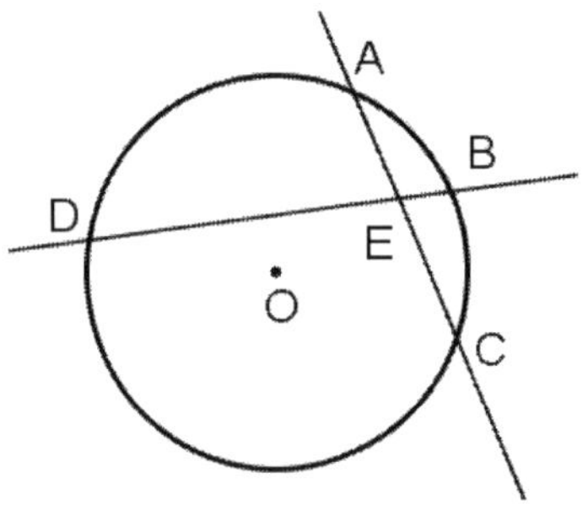

When two secants intersect outside a circle, the measure of the angle formed is equal to half the difference of the two arcs that lie between the two secants. In the diagram below, $m\angle E = \frac{1}{2}(\widehat{AB} - \widehat{CD})$.

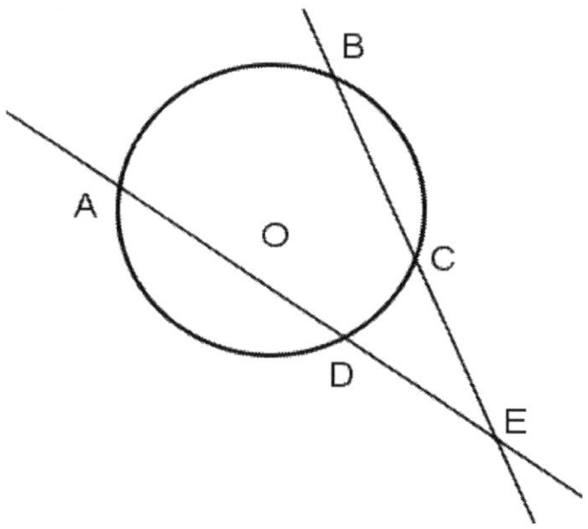


The arc length is the length of that portion of the circumference between two points on the circle. The formula for arc length is $s = \frac{\pi r\theta}{180°}$ where *s* is the arc length, *r* is the length of the radius, and $\theta$ is the angular measure of the arc in degrees, or $s = r\theta$, where $\theta$ is the angular measure of the arc in radians ($2\pi$ radians $= 360$ degrees).

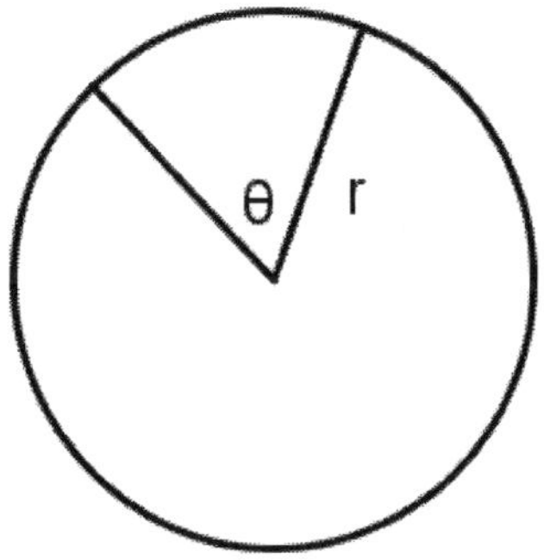


A sector is the portion of a circle formed by two radii and their intercepted arc. While the arc length is exclusively the points that are also on the circumference of the circle, the sector is the entire area bounded by the arc and the two radii.

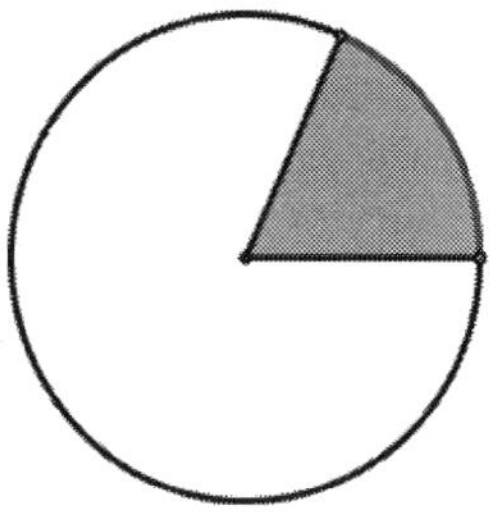

The area of a sector of a circle is found by the formula, $A = \frac{\theta r^2}{2}$, where *A* is the area, $\theta$ is the measure of the central angle in radians, and *r* is the radius. To find the area when the central angle is in degrees, use the formula, $A = \frac{\theta\pi r^2}{360}$, where $\theta$ is the measure of the central angle in degrees and *r* is the radius.

A circle is inscribed in a polygon if each of the sides of the polygon is tangent to the circle. A polygon is inscribed in a circle if each of the vertices of the polygon lies on the circle.

A circle is circumscribed about a polygon if each of the vertices of the polygon lies on the circle. A polygon is circumscribed about the circle if each of the sides of the polygon is tangent to the circle.

If one figure is inscribed in another, then the other figure is circumscribed about the first figure.

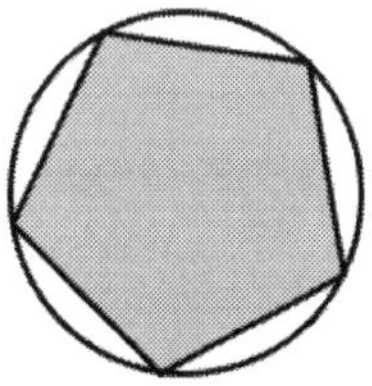

Circle circumscribed about a pentagon
Pentagon inscribed in a circle

**Other conic sections**

An ellipse is the set of all points in a plane, whose total distance from two fixed points called the foci (singular: focus) is constant, and whose center is the midpoint between the foci.

The standard equation of an ellipse that is taller than it is wide is $\frac{(y-k)^2}{a^2} + \frac{(x-h)^2}{b^2} = 1$, where *a* and *b* are coefficients. The center is the point (*h*, *k*) and the foci are the points $(h, k + c)$ and $(h, k - c)$, where $c^2 = a^2 - b^2$ and $a^2 > b^2$.

The major axis has length 2*a*, and the minor axis has length 2*b*.

Eccentricity (*e*) is a measure of how elongated an ellipse is, and is the ratio of the distance between the foci to the length of the major axis. Eccentricity will have a value between 0 and 1. The closer to 1 the eccentricity is, the closer the ellipse is to being a circle. The formula for eccentricity is $= \frac{c}{a}$.

Parabola: The set of all points in a plane that are equidistant from a fixed line, called the directrix, and a fixed point not on the line, called the focus.

Axis: The line perpendicular to the directrix that passes through the focus.

For parabolas that open up or down, the standard equation is $(x - h)^2 = 4c(y - k)$, where *h*, *c*, and *k* are coefficients. If *c* is positive, the parabola opens up. If *c* is negative, the parabola opens down. The vertex is the point (*h*, *k*). The directrix is the line having the equation $y = -c + k$, and the focus is the point $(h, c + k)$.

For parabolas that open left or right, the standard equation is $(y - k)^2 = 4c(x - h)$, where *k*, *c*, and *h* are coefficients. If *c* is positive, the parabola opens to the right. If *c* is negative, the parabola opens to the left. The vertex is the point (*h*, *k*). The directrix is the line having the equation $x = -c + h$, and the focus is the point $(c + h, k)$.

A hyperbola is the set of all points in a plane, whose distance from two fixed points, called foci, has a constant difference.

The standard equation of a horizontal hyperbola is $\frac{(x-h)^2}{a^2} - \frac{(y-k)^2}{b^2} = 1$, where *a*, *b*, *h*, and *k* are real numbers. The center is the point (*h*, *k*), the vertices are the points $(h + a, k)$ and $(h - a, k)$, and the foci are the points that every point on one of the parabolic curves is equidistant from and are found using the formulas $(h + c, k)$ and $(h - c, k)$, where $c^2 = a^2 + b^2$. The asymptotes are two lines the graph of the hyperbola approaches but never reaches, and are given by the equations $y = \left(\frac{b}{a}\right)(x - h) + k$ and $y = -\left(\frac{b}{a}\right)(x - h) + k$.

A vertical hyperbola is formed when a plane makes a vertical cut through two cones that are stacked vertex-to-vertex.

The standard equation of a vertical hyperbola is $\frac{(y-k)^2}{a^2} - \frac{(x-h)^2}{b^2} = 1$, where *a*, *b*, *k*, and *h* are real numbers. The center is the point (*h*, *k*), the vertices are the points $(h, k + a)$ and $(h, k - a)$, and the foci are the points that every point on one of the parabolic curves is equidistant from and are found using the formulas $(h, k + c)$ and $(h, k - c)$, where $c^2 = a^2 + b^2$. The asymptotes are two lines the graph of the hyperbola approaches but never reach, and are given by the equations $y = \left(\frac{a}{b}\right)(x - h) + k$ and $y = -\left(\frac{a}{b}\right)(x - h) + k$.

**Solids**

The surface area of a solid object is the area of all sides or exterior surfaces. For objects such as prisms and pyramids, a further distinction is made between base surface area (B) and lateral surface area (LA). For a prism, the total surface area (SA) is $SA = LA + 2B$. For a pyramid or cone, the total surface area is $SA = LA + B$.

The surface area of a sphere can be found by the formula $A = 4\pi r^2$, where *r* is the radius. The volume is given by the formula $V = \frac{4}{3}\pi r^3$, where *r* is the radius. Both quantities are generally given in terms of π.

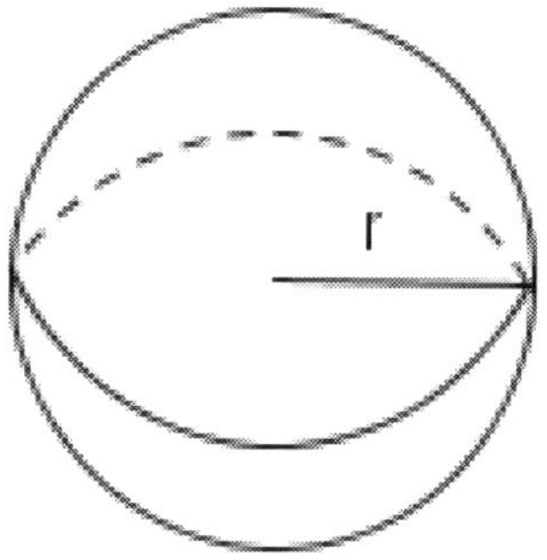

The volume of any prism is found by the formula $V = Bh$, where *B* is the area of the base, and *h* is the height (perpendicular distance between the bases). The surface area of any prism is the sum of the areas of both bases and all sides. It can be calculated as $SA = 2B + Ph$, where *P* is the perimeter of the base.

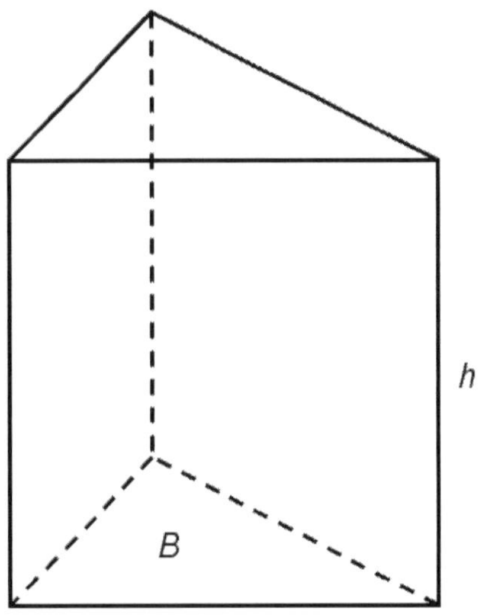


For a rectangular prism, the volume can be found by the formula $V = lwh$, where *V* is the volume, *l* is the length, *w* is the width, and *h* is the height. The surface area can be calculated as $SA = 2lw + 2hl + 2wh$ or $SA = 2(lw + hl + wh)$.

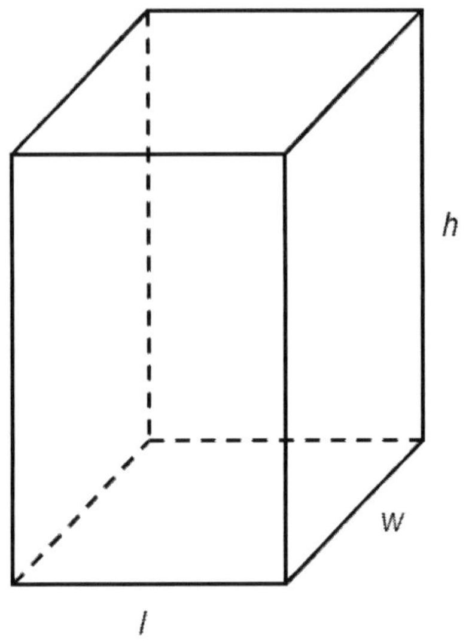


The volume of a cube can be found by the formula $V = s^3$, where *s* is the length of a side. The surface area of a cube is calculated as $SA = 6s^2$, where *SA* is the total surface area and *s* is the length of a side. These formulas are the same as the ones used for the volume and surface area of a rectangular prism, but simplified since all three quantities (length, width, and height) are the same.

The volume of a cylinder can be calculated by the formula $V = \pi r^2 h$, where $r$ is the radius, and $h$ is the height. The surface area of a cylinder can be found by the formula $SA = 2\pi r^2 + 2\pi rh$. The first term is the base area multiplied by two, and the second term is the perimeter of the base multiplied by the height.

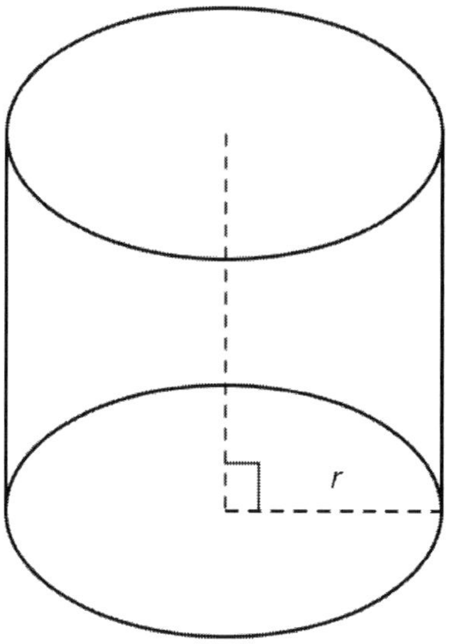


The volume of a pyramid is found by the formula $V = \frac{1}{3}Bh$, where $B$ is the area of the base, and $h$ is the height (perpendicular distance from the vertex to the base). Notice this formula is the same as $\frac{1}{3}$ times the volume of a prism. Like a prism, the base of a pyramid can be any shape. Finding the surface area of a pyramid is not as simple as the other shapes we've looked at thus far. If the pyramid is a right pyramid, meaning the base is a regular polygon and the vertex is directly over the center of that polygon, the surface area can be calculated as $SA = B + \frac{1}{2}Ph_s$, where $P$ is the perimeter of the base, and $h_s$ is the slant height (distance from the vertex to the midpoint of one side of the base). If the pyramid is irregular, the area of each triangle side must be calculated individually and then summed, along with the base.

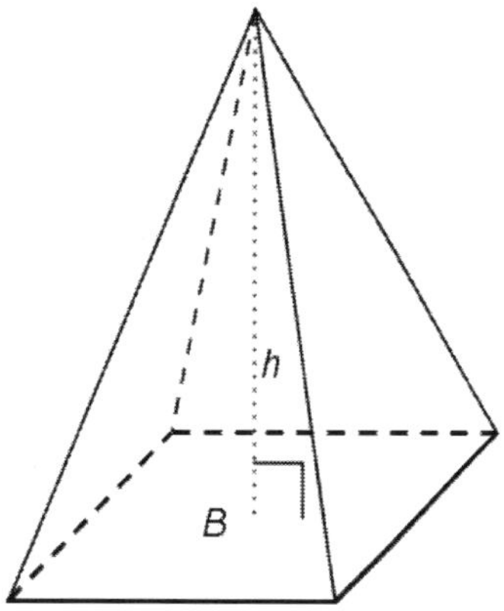

The volume of a cone is found by the formula $V = \frac{1}{3}\pi r^2 h$, where *r* is the radius, and *h* is the height. Notice this is the same as $\frac{1}{3}$ times the volume of a cylinder. The surface area can be calculated as $SA = \pi r^2 + \pi rs$, where s is the slant height. The slant height can be calculated using the Pythagorean Thereom to be $\sqrt{r^2 + h^2}$, so the surface area formula can also be written as $SA = \pi r^2 + \pi r\sqrt{r^2 + h^2}$.

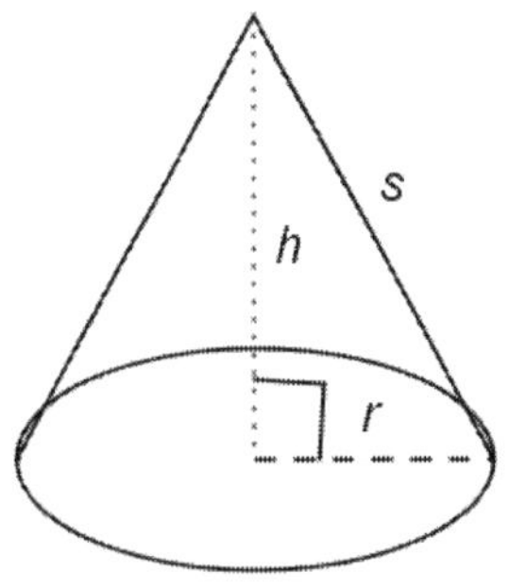

# *Practice Test*

## Reading

Directions: Each passage in the reading section is followed by several questions. Choose the best answer from the choices given.

*Questions 1 to 3 refer to the following passage*:

Alexander the Great died in Babylon at the age of 32 in 323 BC. He had been sick and febrile for two weeks prior to his death. Much speculation exists regarding his cause of death. Poisoning, assassination, and a number of infectious diseases have been posited. An incident mentioned by Plutarch may provide a significant clue. Shortly before his illness, as Alexander entered the city of Babylon, he was met by a flock of ravens. The birds behaved strangely, and many came to die at his feet. The strange behavior of these birds, taken as an ill omen at the time, is similar to the illness and death of birds observed in the United States in the weeks preceding the identification of the first human cases of the West Nile virus. This information suggests that Alexander the Great may have died of encephalitis caused by the West Nile virus.

1. The main purpose of this passage is to
   a. describe the symptoms of West Nile virus encephalitis.
   b. describe an incident involving birds and Alexander the Great.
   c. propose a cause for the death of Alexander the Great.
   d. connect Alexander the Great and Plutarch.

2. In the passage above, "posited" is synonymous with
   a. proposed
   b. implicated
   c. amplified
   d. infected

3. The author believes that the illness and death of birds observed in the United States indicated that the birds
   a. were an ill omen
   b. were ravens
   c. were mentioned by Plutarch
   d. were infected by the encephalitis virus

*Questions 4 to 7 refer to the following passage:*

The invalidation of the Ptolemaic model of the solar system is owed chiefly to Nicolaus Copernicus, a 15th century astronomer from Poland. An early Renaissance man, Copernicus studied a wide range of subjects encompassing mathematics, astronomy, medicine, and law. He studied at the University of Krakow, and, later at the University of Bologna. While in Italy, his investigations led him to question the widely held belief of the time that the Sun and planets revolved around the Earth.

In Copernicus' time, people believed that the Earth was motionless and fixed at the center of the universe. This model had originated with the Greek astronomer Ptolemy 1000 years earlier and was supported strongly by the Catholic Church. Copernicus, a church canon himself, challenged the Ptolemaic theory. In its place, he proposed a heliocentric or Sun-centered astronomical model. From his observations, made with the naked eye, Copernicus concluded that all the planets—including Earth—revolved around the Sun. He also measured the Earth's daily axial rotation and proposed this motion as the cause of the apparent movement of heavenly bodies. Working before the advent of the telescope, Copernicus could not prove his theories. He died in 1543.

4. Which of the following sentences best states the main premise of this passage?
   a. Copernicus was an astronomer who followed in the footsteps of Ptolemy.
   b. Copernicus's observations revolutionized astronomy in the 16th century.
   c. Copernicus concealed a heliocentric theory of astronomy.
   d. Copernicus was a bishop in the Catholic Church.

5. The passage implies that Copernicus could not prove his theories because
   a. they were wrong.
   b. they were opposed by the Catholic Church.
   c. he had no telescopes.
   d. he was too busy with his work in law and medicine.

6. In the passage above, the word "heliocentric" means
   a. with the naked eye
   b. a motionless Earth
   c. revolutionary
   d. with the sun at the center

7. This passage is best labeled as a
   a. cause and effect essay
   b. persuasive essay
   c. process analysis essay
   d. description essay

*Questions 8 – 11 refer to the following passage:*

Some wine aficionados prize the flavor of oak, usually imparted to the beverage through aging in wooden barrels. An alternative process, aging in metal casks with macerated wood chips, provides a stronger wood flavor in less time and therefore is less expensive. To test consumer preferences for wines processed in this manner, a survey of 618 people living in several East Coast cities was conducted early last year. Participants took a blind taste test of three samples of Oregon Pinot Noir. One sample was aged using macerated wood chips, one sample was aged under oak, and a third sample, the control, was aged in a metal tank. A questionnaire then asked subjects to rate the wines and then asked a variety of other questions aimed at categorizing their consumption habits.

Although a variety of factors influenced wine preference, the test exposed a pattern concerning a preference for strongly wood-flavored wines. A large proportion of those persons interviewed (45%) did not care for the tannic wines. However, a sizable minority of 25% especially liked them very much, and preferred the tannic wines to the other samples. Younger consumers particularly fell into this category. Connoisseurs reported greater appreciation for wines aged "under oak," or in normal oak barrels.

Many high quality wines are aged under oak today. Nonetheless, this process is time consuming; as a result, it makes wines more expensive. This survey demonstrated that price is very important in the buying decision, especially for people without extensive knowledge regarding wine. Many consumers are more concerned with price differences than with subtle differences in flavor. This trend defines a market segment that might be well-served by wines aged with wood chips.

8. The main purpose of this passage is to describe
   a. the process of aging wine with wood chips.
   b. consumer preferences in wines.
   c. the importance of price in wine marketing.
   d. a survey that tested consumer preferences.

9. The word "macerated" is closest in meaning to
   a. reduced
   b. liquefied
   c. persecuted
   d. facilitated

10. According to the passage, what percentage of respondents did not like oak-flavored wines?
   a. 75%
   b. 55%
   c. 45%
   d. 25%

11. Which of the following statements best explains the advantage of using wood chips to make wine?
   a. It is an inexpensive way of making wines that appeal to young people.
   b. It is an inexpensive way of making wines that appeal to connoisseurs.
   c. It is a faster way to make expensive wines.
   d. It makes wines that are indistinguishable from those produced by more expensive processes.

*Questions 12 – 14 refer to the following passage:*

The loss of barrier islands through erosion poses a serious challenge to many communities along the Atlantic and Gulf Coasts. Along with marshes and wetlands, these islands protect coastal towns from major storms. In the past seventy years, Louisiana alone has lost almost 2,000 square miles of coastal land to hurricanes and flooding. More than 100 square miles of wetlands protecting the city of New Orleans were wiped out by a single storm, Hurricane Katrina. Due to this exposure of coastal communities, recent hurricane seasons have proven the most expensive on record: annual losses since 2005 have been estimated in the hundreds of billions of dollars. This unfortunate trend is likely to continue, since meteorological research shows that the Atlantic basin is in an active storm period that could continue for decades.

12. Which of the following statements offers a supporting argument for the passage's claim that many coastal islands are eroding?
   a. Recent hurricane seasons have been expensive.
   b. The Atlantic Basin is entering an active period.
   c. Louisiana has lost 2,000 square miles of coastal land.
   d. Barrier islands are the first line of defense against coastal storms.

13. The passage describes recent hurricane seasons as the most expensive on record. Which of the following statements gives the implied reason for this increased expense?
   a. Hurricane Katrina was an extremely violent storm.
   b. Valuable buildings were destroyed in New Orleans.
   c. The Atlantic Basin is entering an active period.
   d. Destruction of barrier islands and coastal wetlands has left the mainland exposed.

14. Which of the following choices represents the best label for this passage?
   a. definition essay
   b. cause/effect essay
   c. comparison essay
   d. persuasive essay

*Questions 15 – 16 refer to the following passage:*

Intercity passenger rail is widely used in Europe and Japan. In the United States, it potentially could provide significant benefits to society by complementing other heavily used modes of transportation. Potential benefits include controlling increases in air and highway congestion, stemming pollution caused by aircraft and automobiles, reducing fuel consumption and energy dependency, and increasing passenger safety. Rail transport can compete in markets comprised of nearby cities as well as along routes that parallel heavily traveled highway or air corridors.

15. This passage is best described as one that
   a. advocates implementation of a passenger rail system.
   b. describes passenger rail systems.
   c. points out advantages and disadvantages of passenger rail systems.
   d. narrates a trip on a passenger rail system.

16. The author sees intercity passenger rail as
   a. a replacement for other forms of travel such as travel by air or highway.
   b. an alternative form of travel suited to all intercity routes in the United States.
   c. lacking any advantages over currently popular forms of travel.
   d. capable of augmenting currently available forms of travel in selected markets.

*Question 17 refers to the following passage:*

Absurdity is required for progress. It is absurd to try to change the world.

17. In this passage,
   a. the first sentence explains the second sentence.
   b. the second sentence explains the first sentence.
   c. neither sentence is a consequence of the other sentence.
   d. the two sentences comprise a circular argument.

*Questions 18 – 22 refer to the following passage:*

Magnesium is an important nutrient that supports immune system functioning and helps protect the body against cardiovascular diseases. Symptoms of magnesium deficiency rarely surface among populations in developed countries, but concern is growing that many people may not have sufficient body stores of this metal. Surveys show that most Americans do not receive a minimum daily requirement of magnesium in their diets.

Magnesium is absorbed from foods by the intestines, before the circulatory system transports it to the body's tissues. Less than one-half of ingested magnesium normally is taken up in this way. Health issues affecting the digestive tract may impair magnesium absorbance. For example, gastrointestinal disorders such as Crohn's disease can limit magnesium uptake. The kidneys normally limit urinary excretion of magnesium, a function that can help make up for low dietary intake. However, alcohol abuse and certain medications can affect this balance and thereby lead to magnesium depletion.

Symptoms of magnesium deficiency include vomiting, fatigue, and loss of appetite. More severe cases can include symptoms such as muscular cramps, seizures, and coronary abnormalities. Magnesium insufficiency also can affect the body's ability to absorb other cations, including calcium and potassium, and can lead to other health complications. Good sources of dietary magnesium include leafy green vegetables, potatoes, nuts, and seeds.

18. Which of the following statements is true?
   a. People with magnesium deficiency commonly exhibit fatigue and loss of appetite.
   b. People with magnesium deficiencies are often asymptomatic.
   c. Severe magnesium deficiency may lead to Crohn's disease.
   d. Magnesium is not absorbed by the digestive tract.

19. Which of the following labels best describes the previous passage?
   a. comparison essay
   b. definition essay
   c. cause and effect essay
   d. persuasive essay

20. Which of the following describes the intestine's normal absorption of magnesium?
   a. inefficient.
   b. very efficient except when disease is present.
   c. rarely observed among the populations of developing countries.
   d. enhanced by eating leafy green vegetables.

21. According to the passage, alcohol abuse can lead to which of the following problems?
    a. poor magnesium absorption.
    b. an impairment of kidney function.
    c. compromise of the immune system.
    d. gastrointestinal disorders.

22. The word "cation" is closest in meaning to:
    a. element
    b. nutrient similar to magnesium
    c. symptom of deficiency
    d. nutritional supplement

*Questions 23 – 24 refer to the following passage:*

Students may take classes in a wide variety of subjects for fun or self-improvement. Some classes provide students with training in useful life skills such as cooking or personal finance. Other classes provide instruction intended for recreational purposes, with topics such as photography, pottery, or painting. Classes may consist of large or small groups, or they may involve one-on-one instruction in subjects like singing or playing a musical instrument. Classes taught by self-enrichment teachers seldom lead to a degree, and attendance in these classes is voluntary. Although often taught in non-academic settings, these classes' topics may include academic subjects such as literature, foreign languages, and history. Despite their informal nature, these courses can provide students with useful work-related skills such as knowledge of computers or foreign languages; these skills make students attractive to potential employers.

23. Which of the following statements represents the central idea of this passage?
    a. Self-improvement classes teach work-related skills.
    b. Attendance is voluntary for self-improvement classes.
    c. Many different kinds of self-improvement classes are available.
    d. Cooking is one type of self-improvement classes.

24. Which of the following statements is true?
    a. All self-improvement classes offer training in recreational subject areas.
    b. Self-improvement classes usually are taught in non-academic settings.
    c. Some informal classes teach useful work-related skills.
    d. In order to learn a foreign language, a student must enroll in a formal, degree-granting program.

*Questions 25 and 26 refer to the following passage:*

The makeup she applied, although intended to display her pulchritude, instead revealed her narcissism.

25. In the context of this sentence, the word "pulchritude" means
    a. beauty
    b. dexterity
    c. skill
    d. sense of color

26. A synonym for the word "narcissism," as used in the text, is
    a. superiority
    b. respect
    c. conceitedness
    d. timidity

*Questions 27 – 30 refer to the following passage:*

The selection of trees for planting in urban areas poses severe challenges due to soil adversities and space restrictions both above and below ground. Restricted spaces, especially in "downtown" situations or in densely built neighborhoods, make selecting, planting, and managing trees in urban areas difficult. Urban sites pose adversities that severely constrain the palette of suitable trees. As a result, an urgent need exists to find tough, small species of trees for urban spaces. Dwarf forms of native species have not been utilized greatly, and some foreign species may prove to be appropriate.

27. Which of the following is NOT identified by the passage as a problem encountered when planting trees in urban sites?
   a. poor soil
   b. air pollution
   c. limited room for root development
   d. restricted space

28. In the context of this passage, the word "palette" means
   a. a board used by painters for mixing colors
   b. choice
   c. wooden platform
   d. repertoire

29. In the last sentence, which of the following statements does the author imply regarding dwarf forms of native species, which have not been greatly utilized?
   a. that they are too small
   b. that they are ill-suited to urban sites
   c. that they would do better in foreign locations
   d. that they would do well in urban sites

30. This passage is best described as a
   a. problem/solution essay
   b. cause/effect essay
   c. persuasive essay
   d. narration essay

*Questions 31 – 33 refer to the following passage:*

A new way to circumvent the cost and limitations of long distance telephone is called Voice over Internet Protocol, or VoIP. VoIP sends digital information over the internet to the person you are calling. The information may come from your phone or your computer, and may comprise both voice and video signal if you have a camera. Companies that specialize in such technology as well as some traditional phone companies offer VoIP services. Some services require that you call from a computer augmented by special software, a microphone, speakers, and a sound card. Other services allow you to call from any regular phone without special equipment.

31. The word "circumvent" is closest in meaning to
   a. reduce
   b. magnify
   c. elude
   d. camouflage

32. Which of the following is required to take advantage of VoIP services?
    a. a camera
    b. a telephone
    c. special software
    d. none of the above

33. The information in the passage best supports which of the following statements?
    a. Voice over Internet Protocol services are available in most telephone markets.
    b. Voice over Internet Protocol services digitally encode voice and visual information.
    c. Voice over Internet Protocol services provide higher quality signals than traditional telephone services.
    d. Voice over Internet Protocol services must be purchased from companies that specialize in the technology.

*Questions 34 – 37 refer to the following passage:*

The provision of this bill that prevents any nonprofit recipient of a housing grant from conducting voter registration is an outrageous, undemocratic amendment that imposes restrictions on promoting the most fundamental of our civil liberties, the right to vote. This provision forbids any nonprofits from even applying for a grant if they have encouraged voting in the recent past. Restricting the prerogatives of nonprofits in this way is a violation of the first amendment rights of these organizations. There is absolutely no justification for preventing the efforts of nonprofit organizations to encourage civic activities such as voting.

34. This passage is best described as a
    a. problem/solution essay
    b. cause/effect essay
    c. persuasive essay
    d. narration essay

35. The word "prerogative" is closest in meaning to
    a. privilege
    b. funding
    c. restriction
    d. ability

36. What is the author's tone?
    a. entertaining
    b. angry
    c. informative
    d. apologetic

37. What is the author's main argument against the provision?
    a. It will prevent voting.
    b. It is unconstitutional.
    c. It will prevent nonprofit organizations from receiving funding.
    d. It is unjustified.

*Questions 38 – 40 refer to the following passage:*

Women have made significant contributions to patent literature in fields as diverse as domestic technology and biomedicine. A woman was involved in the design of the first computer: Lady Ada Lovelace worked with George Babbage to build the "difference engine," a device that could add and subtract. More recently, Gertrude Elion won the 1988 Nobel Prize in Medicine for her invention of a leukemia treatment based on immunosuppressants. She holds numerous medical patents. In addition, women have served as leading members of teams developing surgical methods and all the current AIDS drugs.

38. The "difference engine" was
    a. domestic technology
    b. a device used in biomedicine
    c. a computer
    d. invented by Gertrude Elion

39. The structure of this paragraph is best described as
    a. Topic sentence and analysis
    b. Topic sentence and consequences
    c. Introductory sentence followed by causes and reasons
    d. Topic sentence followed by examples

40. The passage implies that
    a. women are more productive inventors than men
    b. many surgical methods are patented
    c. women's contributions to the patent literature have been underappreciated
    d. Gertrud Elion did not deserve the Nobel Prize

## English Language Skills

*For Questions 1 – 5, choose the underlined word or phrase that is unnecessary in the context of the passage.*

1. The company said it was unaware of any accidents or injuries that resulted from the problem. A spokesperson said the company was working on a fix for repairing the problem. Customers will be notified to bring their vehicle to a dealership for an inspection.
   a. or injuries
   b. said
   c. repairing
   d. to a dealership

2. A certain amount of advance planning is necessary in order to prevent situations like this one from arising. One should gather all interested parties before the event and have them come to a consensus regarding what activities will be needed.
   a. advance
   b. like this one
   c. interested
   d. activities

3. Coming upon her there, in her red satin dress, was an unexpected surprise. Jonathan was so pleased to see her that he almost dropped his packages, and an exclamation of pure joy escaped his lips.
   a. satin
   b. unexpected
   c. almost
   d. pure

4. Carter swung mightily at the third pitch and lofted a double to left field, over the head of the vegetarian shortstop.
   a. mightily
   b. to left field
   c. over the head
   d. vegetarian

5. Many flights were cancelled and travelers scrambled to find accommodation during the worst winter weather Spain had experienced since the blizzard of 2002, when all air travel in and out of the country then was halted for three days.
   a. to find
   b. weather
   c. blizzard
   d. then

*For Questions 6 – 10, choose the most appropriate word or phrase to complete the sentence.*

6. The tourists tried to make the best of things despite the ___________ weather.
   a. ugly
   b. inclement
   c. balmy
   d. insipid

7. The Ogallala Aquifer, which stretches from Texas to the Dakotas, is one of the major sources of water for the high plains, but it is rapidly being ___________ by drought.
   a. used
   b. contaminated
   c. depleted
   d. undermined

8. Evan felt that he was always being ______________ for things that were not his fault.
   a. castigated
   b. lauded
   c. interrogated
   d. rescinded

9. Amnesia, a _________ disorder in which a person loses long-term or short-term memories, can result from brain damage such as tumors.
   a. prerogative
   b. rational
   c. hidden
   d. cognitive

10. The cambium, a layer of _________ tissue between the bark and wood of trees, gives rise to new growth through cell division.
    a. redactive
    b. generative
    c. inactive
    d. reproductive

*For Questions 11 –20, choose the option corresponding to the word or phrase that expresses the meaning most fluently and logically. In each case, the first choice represents no change from the original text.*

11. What is irksome about Antoinette is that <u>she chooses to metal constantly</u> in the affairs of other people.
    a. she chooses to metal constantly
    b. she chooses to medal constantly
    c. she chooses to meddle constantly
    d. she mettles constantly

12. I intend <u>either to go on vacation in June or July</u>.
    a. either to go on vacation in June or July.
    b. either to go on vacation during June or July.
    c. to go on vacation in either June or in July.
    d. to go on vacation in either June or July.

13. Once he had determined the cause of the accident, the insurance investigator authorized payment of the claim.
    a. accident, the insurance investigator
    b. accident the insurance investigator
    c. accident; the insurance investigator
    d. accident: the insurance investigator

14. I would of forgot if you hadn't reminded me.
    a. would of forgot
    b. would have forgotten
    c. would of forgotten
    d. would have forgot

15. The bear finally came out of her lair, where she had hid all winter.
    a. she had hid
    b. she hides
    c. she hid
    d. she had hidden

16. I'm sorry. Neither Bob nor Juan are able to come to the phone right now.
    a. are able to come
    b. are going to able to come
    c. is able to come
    d. could come

17. The defendant was acquitted, which angered the victim's family.
    a. which angered
    b. angering
    c. which made angry
    d. this angered

18. Martha ran into a friend of her's at the mall.
    a. friend of her's
    b. friend
    c. friend of hers
    d. friends

19. More than anyone else in his class, Angelo prepared himself for the test.
    a. More than anyone else in his class
    b. More than anyone in his class
    c. More than anyone in class
    d. More than anybody in his class

20. Karen's car is faster than Louise's.
    a. is faster than Louise's.
    b. is faster than Louises car.
    c. is more fast than Louise's car.
    d. is fastest than Louise's.

*For Questions 21 - 35, each passage may contain an error of grammar or usage. Some sentences do not contain an error. If an error is present, it will be found in one of the underlined passages corresponding to the letters A-C. Select the letter corresponding to the part that must be corrected. If there is no error, select Choice D.*

21. This map of global economic development clearly demonstrates(A) that growth in the United States and Western Europe is(B) and will continue to lag behind the geographic sectors of Asia, Latin America, and significant portions(C) of Africa.
    a. A
    b. B
    c. C
    d. No error

22. It is unusual for the beginning of a formal investigation to be announced; (A) an investigation typically takes (B) many months to conclude (C).
    a. A
    b. B
    c. C
    d. No error

23. A recent major study showed that while (A) survival rates for babies born at 24 weeks have improved over (B) the last ten years, those of (C) younger infants have not.
    a. A
    b. B
    c. C
    d. No error

24. Emma was convinced, for some reason, (A) that she had been born to the wrong parents. Had some strange quirk of fate not intervened, (B) she should have been the Queen (C) of England.
    a. A
    b. B
    c. C
    d. No error

25. Some doubts existed about Emmanuel when he first was hired, (A) but he proved as resourceful, (B) if not more resourceful than, (C) the man he had replaced.
    a. A
    b. B
    c. C
    d. No error

26. I thought I did pretty good (A) on the math test, but my grade turned out to be well (B) below average for the class. In the end, I had to take the course over (C) during the summer.
    a. A
    b. B
    c. C
    d. No error

27. The two actresses flew (A) to Miami to film (B) the second season of the television series, which (C) will end with a reunion of the family.
    a. A
    b. B
    c. C
    d. No error

28. A special viewing (A) of the film is planned as a charity event. Mountain Entertainment produced the movie about a woman that (B) gave up her daughter to adoption because she could not afford to raise her (C). who?

a. A
b. B
c. C
d. No error

29. Germaine and me (A) are going to the game together. She (B) and I have been friends for several years now, and we often (C) go out together.

a. A.
b. B.
c. C
d. No error

30. Every morning out on (A) Keybrook Farm, Josh Cain, together (B) with three of his hands, milk (C) the cows before breakfast.

a. A
b. B
c. C
d. No error

31. Not certain (A) about what to do with his inheritance, (B) Rafael wanted to get a financial expert to advice (C) him.

a. A
b. B
c. C
d. No error

32. During their discussion, (A) the banker explained that each loan payment would comprise (B) two parts: one would be applied to the principle, (C) the other to the interest.

a. A
b. B
c. C
d. No error

33. I set (A) the newspaper down on the table, grab a glass of milk en route (B) to my room, and lie (C) down for a nap that usually lasts for an hour.

a. A
b. B
c. C
d. No error

34. Among (A) the many items being offered for sale during the charity auction are (B) a Cartier watch once worn by Charles DeGaulle, the French (C) president.

a. A
b. B
c. C
d. No error

35. Melanie called him on her cell phone (A) and said that she was stuck inside of (B) an elevator and almost certainly would be late for their meeting, he told me (C).

a. A
b. B
c. C
d. No error

*For Questions 36 – 40, please refer to the following passage, which contains a number of errors. Answer the questions by selecting the option that corrects an error in one of the underlined phrases. At most, one of the underlined phrases is an error. If none are erroneous, select Choice D, "No error".*

When I was seventeen, me and my brother would fish for mullet in the lake up by Aunt Lydia's house. We would get up early in the morning, and Aunt Lydia would make us a breakfast of oatmeal and eggs. It really got your motor firing. Then, we use to rummage around in the backyard for worms and bugs to use as bait. My brother Kenny was younger than me and he would get down on his belly in the mud and dig for them. When he had filled a pail, we would grab our fishing poles and would go down to the dock.

36. When I was seventeen, me and my brother would fish for mullet in the lake up by Aunt Lydia's house.
    a. At the age of seventeen,
    b. my brother and I
    c. by Aunt Lydia's house
    d. No error

37. We would get up early in the morning and Aunt Lydia would make us a breakfast of oatmeal and eggs. It really got your motor firing.
    a. We got up early in the morning on those days,
    b. made us
    c. Really, it got one's motor firing.
    d. No error

38. Then, we use to rummage around in the backyard for worms and bugs to use as bait.
    a. Then
    b. we used to rummage
    c. for worms and bugs, to use as bait
    d. No error

39. My brother Kenny was younger than me and he would get down on his belly in the mud and dig for them.
    a. Kenny is younger
    b. than I
    c. get prone
    d. No error

40. When he had filled a pail, we would grab our fishing poles and would go down to the dock.
    a. his pail was full
    b. we grabbed
    c. go down
    d. No error

## Mathematics

1. Which of the following numbers is the greatest?
   a. $10^3$
   b. 108.7
   c. $\sqrt{10{,}000}$
   d. $-1025$

2. Miguel buys a loaf of bread at the grocery store for $4.25. He also buys two bottles of soda at $2.15 each, a chocolate bar for $1.90, a bottle of shampoo for $5.25, and three magazines at $1.50 each. How much did he spend in all?
   a. $16.05
   b. $19.05
   c. $20.20
   d. $20.45

3. A charity organization is preparing a fundraising dinner. The goal is to raise $27,000. They must pay costs of $1,000 to rent the hall for the evening, plus $2,500 in wages for staff and $25.00 per plate of food served. If tickets to the dinner cost $150, how many tickets must the organization sell in order to reach their goal?
   a. 180
   b. 216
   c. 244
   d. 281

4. In the right triangle shown below, side AB is twice the length of side BC. What is the area of the triangle in $cm^2$?

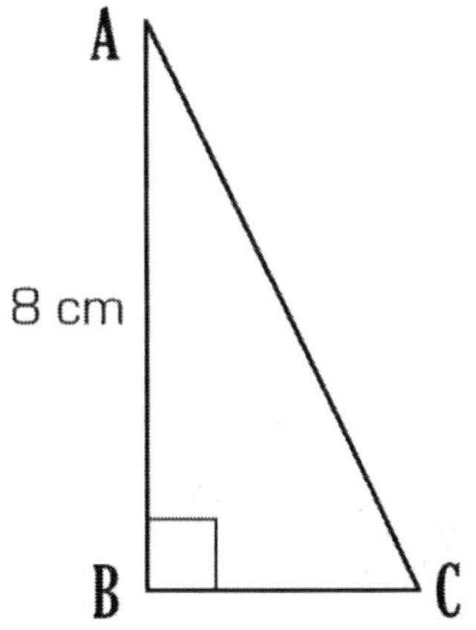


   a. 8
   b. 16
   c. 24
   d. 32

5. Cassandra must average at least 70 on three math tests to get a passing grade. Her scores on the first two tests were 64 and 80. What is the minimum score she must get on the third test in order to pass?
   a. 70
   b. 74
   c. 72
   d. 66

6. What is the least common denominator for the fractions $\frac{1}{15}$, $\frac{1}{21}$, and $\frac{1}{14}$?

a. 5
b. 210
c. 140
d. 91

7. The area of a circle is 8π. What is the length of the radius?

a. $2\sqrt{2}$
b. 4
c. 8
d. $3\sqrt{2}$

8. Which of the following equations might describe the function shown in the graph?

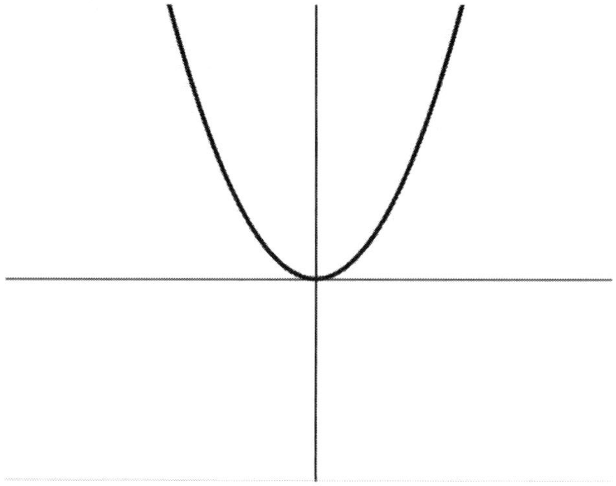

a. $y = -2x^2$
b. $y = 2x^2$
c. $y = 2x^2 + 7$
d. $y = 2x^2 - 4$

9. An airplane flies from New York to San Francisco, a distance of 2700 miles, at constant airspeed in 6.5 hours. The return flight, at the same airspeed, takes 6 hours. Determine the speed of the wind, assuming it to be constant.

a. 65 mph
b. 35 mph
c. 17.3 mph
d. 15.3 mph

10. Andrea runs 4 miles every day, but she wants to increase her distance in order to run a 26-mile marathon. She decides to add 2 miles each day to her distance until she achieves her goal. If she starts with 6 miles today, how many miles will she have run, in total, by the time she achieves her 26-mile goal?

a. 156
b. 162
c. 170
d. 176

11. The Quality Mushroom Company sells small mushrooms for \$5.95 per pound and large mushrooms for \$6.95 per pound. How many pounds of large mushrooms should be mixed with 2 pounds of small ones in order to create a mixture that sells for \$6.75 per pound?

a. 4
b. 6
c. 8
d. 10

12. In the figure below, two circles with radius of length R are tangential to one another. The line AB joins their centers. A second line, AC, extends from the center of one circle and is tangential to the other. What is the length of the line AC?

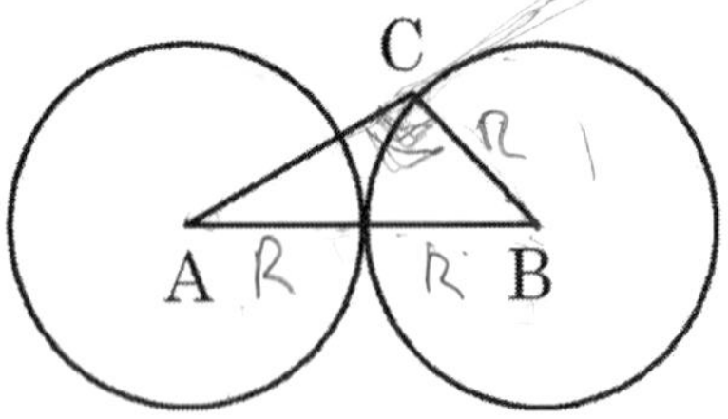


a. 3R
b. $2\sqrt{R}$
c. $R\sqrt{2}$
d. $R\sqrt{3}$

13. Which of the following represents an irrational number?

a. 1.7
b. $\sqrt{16}$
c. $\frac{1}{4}$
d. $\sqrt{12}$

14. Let *y* vary inversely as *x* and equal 12 when *x* = 4. What is the value of *x* when *y* = 18?

a. 6
b. $\frac{8}{3}$
c. $\frac{4}{3}$
d. $\frac{2}{9}$

15. Identify the median of the following data set: { 12, 14, 45, 9, 7, 16, 13, 4 }

a. 12
b. 12.5
c. 13
d. 13.5

16. The chart below shows the annual number of visitors to the Augusta Planetarium. Which year shows the greatest increase in visitors over the prior year?

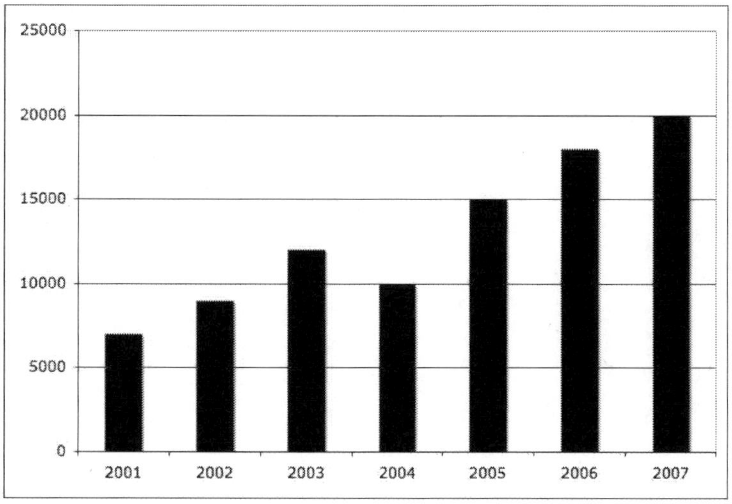


a. 2002
b. 2004
c. 2005
d. 2007

17. Jenny buys a lottery ticket. It has five digits. For each digit, there is an equal probability that any of the numbers 0 – 9 will be chosen. Jenny's number is 00573. What are the odds that she will win?

a. 100:1
b. 1000:1
c. 10,000:1
d. 100,000:1

18. Simplify the expression:

$$\frac{2+\frac{4}{y}}{\frac{y+2}{3}}$$

a. $\frac{y+2}{3}$
b. 3y
c. $\frac{6}{y}$
d. $\frac{y-2}{6}$

19. Regina goes to the ice cream store to get a cone with three scoops. There are nine flavors to choose from, and she wants to get three different flavors. How many different combinations of three flavors are possible?

a. 504
b. 84
c. 27
d. 16

20. The figure below shows two triangles that are ___________ .

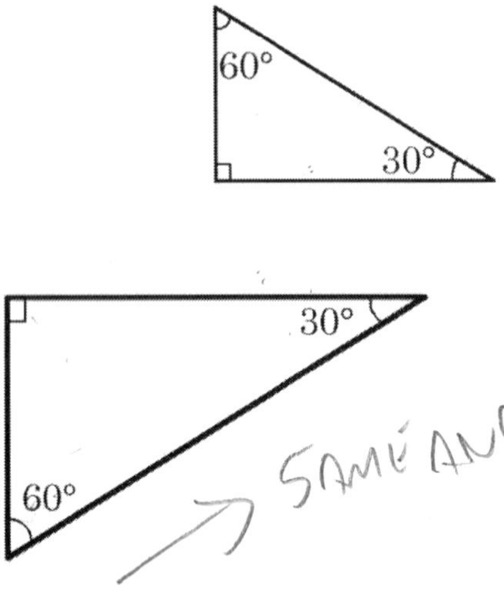


a. congruent
b. equilateral
c. similar
d. isosceles

21. An automobile manufacturer offers a rebate equivalent to 15% of the list price of a vehicle. If a new sedan normally sells for a list price of $30,000, what is the price that must be paid with the rebate?

a. $28,500
b. $27,500
c. $25,500
d. $23,500

22. A lumberyard charges $1 per cut to trim boards. Bob buys a 12-ft board and wants it cut into twelve 1-ft pieces. How much will he be charged for the cutting?

a. $12
b. $11
c. $13
d. $10

23. The sum of 14 and twice a number is 8. What is the number?

a. 3
b. – 4
c. – 6
d. – 3

24. The figure below shows a circle at center O intersected by a first line that forms a diameter AB and by a second line that forms a chord AC. If the perimeter of the circle is 720 m and the angle CAB between the two lines is 20°, what is the length of the arc segment BC?

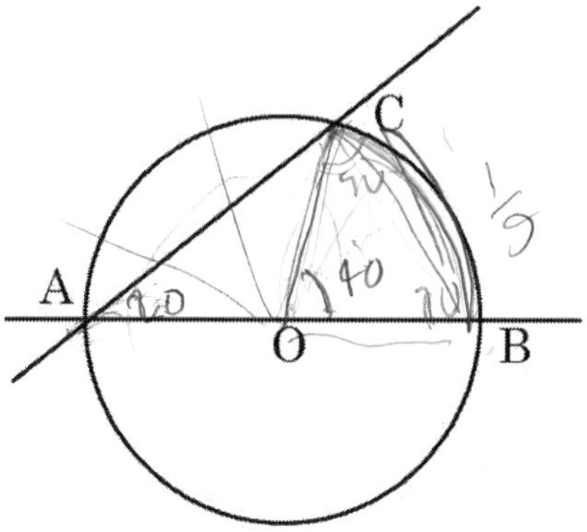


a. 120 m
b. 80 m
c. 75 m
d. 60 m

25. Find the intersection of the lines represented by the equations $y = -2x + 6$ and $y = 4x + 3$.
a. (0.5, 5)
b. (2, 5)
c. (2, -3)
d. (3, -2)

26. If May 7th falls on a Monday, which of the following dates will fall on a Wednesday?
a. May 21st
b. May 23rd
c. May 25th
d. April 31st

27. Bob and Ken are painting a room. If Bob paints the room alone, he can finish the job in 4 hours. If Ken paints it alone, he can finish the job in 6 hours. How long will it take them to paint it together?
a. 2 hours
b. 3 hours 15 minutes
c. 1 hour 48 minutes
d. 2 hours 24 minutes

28. In the figure below, a circle with radius $r$ is inscribed within a square. What is the area of the shaded region?

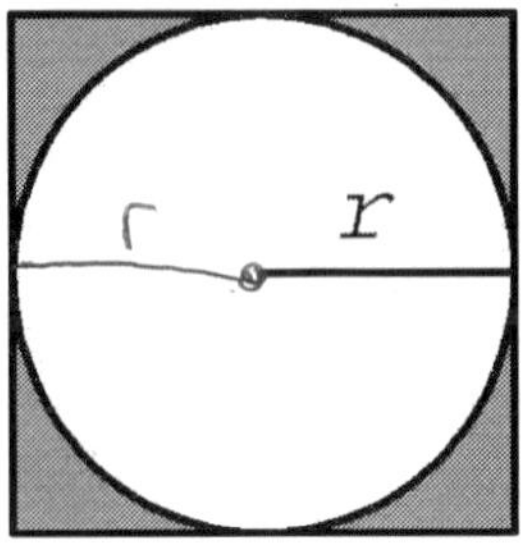


a. $4r - \pi$
b. $(4 - \pi)r^2$
c. $4r^2 - \pi$
d. $4r - \pi r^2$

29. What is the next term in the sequence 1, 3, 7, 13, 21, …?
a. 27
b. 29
c. 31
d. 32

30. Josephine invests a sum of money at 4% simple interest for a year. At the end of this time, she has earned $200 in interest. What was the original amount of money that she invested?
a. $5000
b. $4000
c. $6000
d. $6400

31. A line passes through the points (-1, 2) and (3, 8). What is the slope of the line?
a. $\frac{3}{5}$
b. $\frac{3}{2}$
c. $-\frac{2}{5}$
d. $\frac{6}{5}$

32. An irregular pentagon has three internal right angles and dimensions as shown in the figure below. What is the area in square feet?

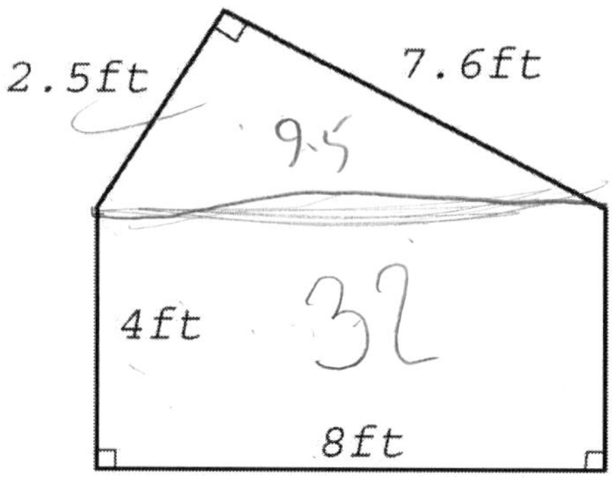


a. 41.5
b. 31.5
c. 46.5
d. 48.6

33. An oil drum containing 200 liters of oil falls to the bottom of a lake and begins leaking. All of the oil leaks out and forms a thin film, 1 micron ($10^{-6}$ m) thick, on the surface of the water. What is the area of the oil slick in $km^2$? (One liter is equivalent to 0.001 $m^3$)

a. 2
b. 0.2
c. 20
d. 25

34. If $a = 0.01$, find the value of $\frac{1}{a^2}$.

a. 0.001
b. 100
c. 1000
d. 10000

35. Solve for $x$ if $x^2 - 6x + 9 = 0$ and $x > 0$.

a. $\frac{1}{3}$
b. 3
c. –3
d. 2

36. Which of the following functions is graphed by the broken line in the figure?

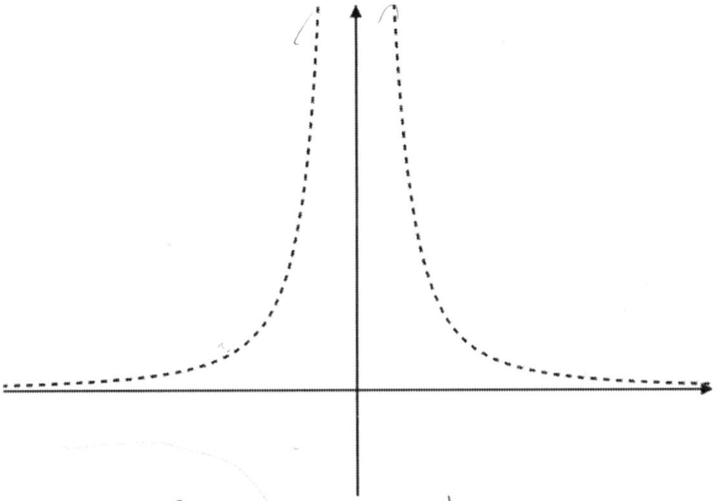

a. $f(x) = x^2$
b. $f(x) = \sqrt{x}$
c. $f(x) = \frac{1}{x}$
d. $f(x) = x^{-2}$

37. If $\sqrt{x} - 2 = 8$, determine the value of *x*.
a. 64
b. 66
c. 100
d. 144

38. A recipe for making 50 pancakes calls for 24 cups of flour. How many cups of flour are needed to make only 8 pancakes?
a. 3.84
b. 2.95
c. 4.41
d. 4.10

39. If *x* and *y* are both positive integers and $(11^x)^y = 121$, what is the arithmetic mean of *x* and *y*?
a. 2
b. 1.5
c. 11
d. 6

40. The figure below shows a square. If side AD = 10 and if AE = EB and BF = FC, what is the area of the shaded region?

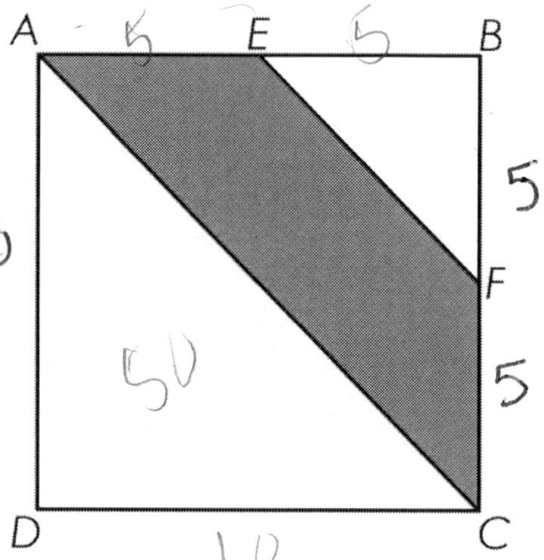


a. 37.5
b. 16.5
c. 24
d. 42.5

41. The sum of three consecutive integers is 36. What is the largest of the three integers?
a. 17
b. 14
c. 13
d. 12

42. A picture is to be printed onto a sheet of paper with dimensions of 8 ½ x 11 inches. A margin of 1 ½ inches is to be left on all sides of the picture. What is the area of the printed picture?
a. 42 in2
b. 44 in2
c. 46 in2
d. 48 in2

43. Let $f(x) = 3x + 4$ and $g(x) = 2x^2$. Which of the following expressions represents $f(g(x))$?
a. $2x^2 + 3x + 4$
b. $2(3x + 4)^2$
c. $6x^2 + 8$
d. $6x^2 + 4$

44. The figure shows two rectangles. Rectangle I is 50% longer than rectangle II. Rectangle II is 50% wider than rectangle I. What is the ratio of the area of rectangle I to the area of rectangle II?

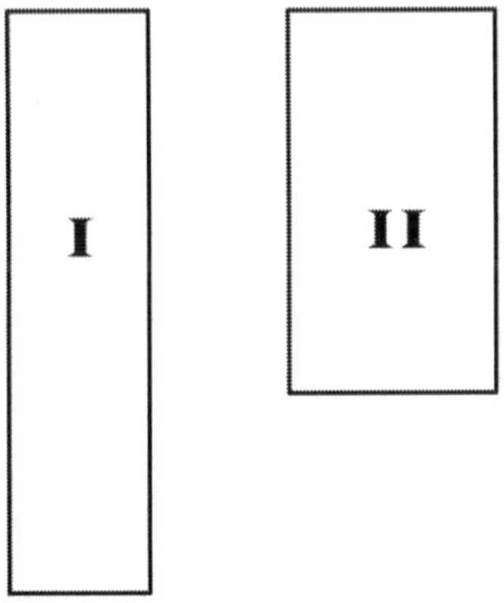


a. 1:1
b. 1:2
c. 1:1.5
d. 1:1.25

45. A number $q$ is chosen at random from the set { 2, 4, 6, 8 }. A second number, $r$, is chosen at random from the set { 2, 7, 16, 17 }. What is the probability that $\frac{q}{r}$ is a positive integer?

a. 50%
b. 33%
c. 25%
d. 12.5%

# *Answers and Explanations*

## Reading

1. C: Although the passage does describe some of the symptoms encephalitis caused by the West Nile virus as well as the incident in which the birds died at Alexander's feet, these descriptions are incidental to the paragraph's main purpose. The main idea of the paragraph is that Alexander may have died of encephalitis.

2. A: The third sentence, in which this word appears, reviews a number of possible, suggested, or proposed causes for Alexander's death. The author then recounts the incident of the ravens as evidence for a different cause of death.

3. D: The author's thesis holds that the birds contracted the encephalitis virus first and that it led to their death. The virus then spread to the human population, leading to the outbreak of West Nile encephalitis. The author suggests that this train of events occurred both in ancient Babylon and in the modern United States.

4. B: The passage describes how Copernicus made observations that contradicted the prevailing view of astronomy, held since the time of Ptolemy. The Ptolemaic theory asserted that the Sun and other planets revolved around the Earth. The passage states that Copernicus came to question the Ptolemaic theory, and that he challenged it. He did not conceal a heliocentric theory (Choice C), but rather propounded one.

5. C: The second paragraph in the passage states that Copernicus made his observations with the naked eye. The penultimate sentence states that he worked before the advent of the telescope and that he could not prove his theories. The paragraph implies that telescopes would have made this proof possible.

6. D: The third sentence of the second paragraph states that Copernicus put forward the principles of a "heliocentric or Sun-centered astronomy," in which the Sun was at the center of rotation of the orbiting planets.

7. D: The essay describes the history of Copernicus and his astronomical observations, telling the reader about his life and contrasting his astronomical observations to those previously made by the ancient Greeks. It does not seek to persuade or to promote a particular point of view. It does not describe or analyze a process or describe any cause-and-effect relationships.

8. D: Although the passage describes various methods of aging wine in the presence of oak as well as consumer price sensitivity, the passage's main purpose is to describe the results of a survey conducted in order to examine consumer preferences. The passage describes the number of people surveyed, the types of questions asked, and the results of the survey.

9. A: To macerate is to break into smaller parts, typically by steeping in a liquid. In this case, the process produces small wood chips with a large surface area that flavors the wine more efficiently than the interior surface of the barrels used traditionally.

10. C: The second paragraph states that 45% of those persons interviewed rejected tannic wines. Tannic wines are those flavored by tannins, components of oak bark. The meaning of the term can be inferred from the phrasing of the second paragraph, in which the 25% who strongly favored the wood-flavored wines are contrasted to those who categorically disliked the tannic wines.

11. A: The second paragraph states that young wine lovers, especially, fell into the 25% who preferred the wood-chip produced wines. The first paragraph states that the process is faster and therefore less expensive. Additionally, the last paragraph indicates that price sensitivity among consumers is an advantage for wines made with wood chips, from which one may infer that the process is less expensive.

12. C: The loss of coastal wetlands in Louisiana is an example of coastal island erosion caused by hurricanes, and so supports the statement. The other Choices are also statements that appear in the passage, but they do not provide direct support for the claim that many coastal islands are eroding.

13. D: The passage describes the loss of these coastal barrier lands to erosion. The fifth sentence then states, "the result is that recent hurricane seasons have been the most expensive on record." This establishes the cause-and-effect between barrier island erosion and monetary losses due to great storms.

14. B: The essay does not make comparisons or seek to define or persuade. Instead, this passage describes the role of coastal wetlands, gives examples of recent losses of these lands, and concludes these factors result in a substantial economic loss due to recent storms.

15. A: By pointing out only the benefits of a passenger rail system, the author attempts to make the case for the implementation of such a system in the United States. The author does not offer a description of the equipment or procedures used by such a system, but instead enumerates its advantages.

16. D: The author states that rail can complement other heavily used forms of transportation, including heavily traveled corridors between cities within close distances.

17. B: The logic of the passage holds that 1) trying to change the world is absurd; 2) progress changes the world; and therefore, 3) absurdity is required for progress.

18. B: The first paragraph indicates that symptoms of magnesium deficiency rarely are observed, but a concern exists that people may have insufficient stores of this nutrient.

19. C: The passage describes both the causes of magnesium deficiency (dietary shortage or poor uptake exacerbated by gastrointestinal disorders) and its results (reduced functioning of the immune system and lessened resistance to cardiovascular disease).

20. A: The second paragraph informs that less than one half of ingested magnesium is absorbed under normal circumstances.

21. B: According to the second paragraph, the kidneys usually limit magnesium excretion in the urine, but alcohol abuse and/or certain medications may affect this function. Impairment of this kidney function may lead to magnesium depletion. The passage does not state that magnesium uptake—a function of the intestines—is affected by alcohol.

22. B: The final paragraph indicates that magnesium deficiency can affect the absorption of "other cations," implying that magnesium itself is also a cation. The examples given, calcium and potassium, are also nutrients.

23. C: The passage explores the wide variety of self-improvement classes offered. As such, it touches upon the variety of content and subject matter, different venues in which the classes may be taught, and the range of enrollment sizes that may be encountered.

24. C: The passage points out that some of the subjects taught in informal courses may prove useful in the workplace and may make the student more desirable to potential employers. This includes topics such as computer science and foreign languages.

25. A: Pulchritude means "beauty," and in this case refers to the beauty of a person putting on makeup in order to make that beauty even more evident.

26. C: The word "narcissism" comes from the name of the Greek god Narcissus, who was so attractive that he enjoyed gazing at his reflection in a pond. It refers to excessive fascination with oneself, one's appearance, etc.

27. B: The first sentence identifies poor soil as a problem in the first sentence ("soil adversities"). The second sentence points to restricted space, both above and below ground (the latter restricting root development). Although air pollution also may affect the growth of urban trees, the passage does not mention this factor.

28. D: The word, derived from the board used by painters during the Renaissance, refers to the variety of techniques or materials available in any art. The third sentence of the passage informs us that this range is limited by the adverse conditions in urban sites. Note that the word refers to the range of available trees, and not to the choice made among them, so Choice B is incorrect.

29. D: Since space restriction is one of the major problems encountered in planting trees in urban sites, the author implies that dwarf trees–since they are small–would prove successful in this cramped environment.

30. A: The essay first poses a problem—namely, the difficulty of growing trees in urban environments due to poor soil and limited space. The author then suggests two solutions to this problem: dwarf trees, which are small and require limited space, and foreign species, which are less well known and may include some particularly hardy examples.

31. C: To "circumvent" means to get around an obstacle or problem or to find a way to avoid it. To "elude" has the same meaning. The problem in this case is one of high cost, and circumventing it leads to a reduction in that cost, as in Choice A. Nevertheless, Choice C is the closest in meaning.

32. D: Although certain circumstances might require each of the choices, the article makes a point of enumerating the variety of providers available and that different equipment configurations will work with different services. This includes computer-based and telephone-based services.

33. B: The second sentence defines VoIP as something that uses the internet to send digital information. The third sentence specifies that this information may comprise both voice and video signals. Although digital VoIP signals may be of higher quality than other technologies and may be available in most markets, the passage does not make these points.

34. C: The passage is an argument against a legislative proposal. Its purpose is to persuade legislators or voters to reject the proposal or the provision it discusses. The tone of the passage is contentious and opinionated. It does not attempt to present an opposing point of view or an analysis, as would befit cause/effect or problem/solution writing.

35. A: A prerogative is a right or privilege, in this case the right to conduct voter registration activities.

36. B: The author plainly is not attempting to entertain. The use of words such as "outrageous," "undemocratic," and "absolutely" imparts a strongly emotional tone to the passage, which can be described as antagonistic, irate, or angry.

37. B: In the third sentence, the author argues that the provision violates the first amendment of the Constitution. Although the passage also claims such a provision as unjustified, this claim offers not an argument so much as a rhetorical flourish.

38. C: The introductory phrase of the second sentence, "A woman was involved in the design of the first computer:" ends with a colon, indicating that an example will follow. Thus, the difference engine described in the following clause is an example of a computer. The difference engine is described further in the passage as a device that could add and subtract, which is the definition of a computer.

39. D: The first sentence introduces the topic, the contributions made to the patent literature by women. The remainder of the paragraph is dedicated to giving examples of these contributions, beginning with Lady Lovelace two centuries ago and continuing through present day contributions to biomedicine. The passage does not describe any causes or effects, so the passage cannot be considered an analysis.

40. B: The thrust of the paragraph asserts that women have registered many patents. The final sentence informs us that women have led teams that developed surgical methods. Although not stated explicitly, the paragraph implies that these methods have been patented.

## English Language Skills

1. C: The sentence states that the company is working on a fix for the problem. The word "fix" means "to repair." Since both words convey the same meaning, it follows that the latter word is not necessary.

2. A: The meaning of "planning" is "to develop a scheme or method in advance." Since the definition includes the concept of advanced timing, the use of the word "advance" is redundant.

3. B: A surprise is always unexpected, or it cannot be called a surprise. Since the word "surprise" already conveys the meaning of "unexpected," the latter word is redundant in this context.

4. D: All of the other underlined words add necessary detail to the description of a hit during a baseball game, but the fact that the shortstop may be a vegetarian is irrelevant to the rest of the depiction.

5. D: Since this final clause in the sentence begins with the word "when" ("when all air travel..."), the use of the conjunction "then" is redundant. Both words refer to the time of the blizzard of 2002. It is only necessary to refer to this once.

6. B: Inclement weather is rough, severe, or stormy weather. The context of the sentence suggests that the weather is bad, so tourists are forced to make the best of the situation. Balmy weather is pleasant and warm, so this choice does not appear appropriate. Weather seldom is described as "ugly," and Choice D, "insipid," does not make sense.

7. C: To deplete means to decrease significantly or to exhaust the abundance of a thing. The effect of drought is to decrease the abundance of water in the aquifer. This word is stronger than merely to use (Choice A): it means to diminish or to use up.

8. A: To castigate means to criticize severely, to rebuke. The use of the word "fault" in the sentence implies that Evan was chastised for detrimental events for which he bore no responsibility. As a result, "lauded," which means to praise, is not an appropriate choice.

9. D: Cognition is the ability of the brain to process information, and a cognitive disorder is one in which this ability is compromised. A loss of memory fits this definition. The disorder cannot be termed "rational," since this term means "realistic." Although the brain's rational functions may be impaired in amnesia, it is not common usage to refer to them as such.

10. B: The sentence describes how the cambium gives rise to new growth: this is the generation of new tissues. A generative tissue is one involved in growth or reproduction. Note that Choice D is incorrect because the tissue is involved in growth, not reproduction.

11. C: To "meddle" is to interfere in a situation without invitation. Metal is a noun meaning any one of a category of chemical elements. A medal is a decoration of honor. And "mettle," also a noun, indicates strength of character or fortitude.

12. D: In this case, the conjunction "either" applies to the choice between June and July, not to the possibility of going on vacation, as appears the case in the original. Choices C and D correct this. Paired conjunctions such as "either...or..." must be followed with the same structure (parallelism). Only Choice D maintains the same structure around the alternatives June and July.

13. A: The first portion of the sentence, preceded by the conjunction "once," is a dependent clause. The comma properly segregates the dependent clause, as in the original version.

14. B: To form the past perfect tense of the verb, use the auxiliary verb "to have" and the past participle of the verb. The past participle of "to forget" is "forgotten," so Choice B is correct.

15. D: From the context, we know that the bear had spent the entire winter hiding in her lair. As a result, the present tense (Choice B) and simple past tense (Choice C) are incorrect. To form the past perfect tense of the verb, use the auxiliary verb "to have" and the past participle of the verb. The past participle of "to hide" is "hidden," so Choice D is correct.

16. C: The subject of this sentence is either Bob or Juan, but not both. Two singular subjects connected by either/or or neither/nor require a singular verb. Since the singular form of the verb "to be" is "is," Choice C is correct.

17. B: In this sentence, there is no antecedent for the pronoun "which." It refers to the acquittal mentioned in the first clause, but the word "acquittal" does not appear. Choices C and D present the same problem.

18. B: The original is flawed because "her" is already a possessive pronoun, so that the addition of the possessive ending in "her's" is redundant. Choice C is also redundant, since the sentence already implies that the friend into whom she ran at the mall was her own. The statement made by Choice B is the most direct.

19. A: The original includes the necessary word "else" to make the comparison with anyone else in the class. Choices B-C are incomplete and illogical since Angelo himself is in the class: he could not prepare himself more than anyone *including* himself.

20. A: The comparative form of the adjective should be used in this comparison between two objects. The correct form of the comparative is "faster," not "more fast" as in Choice C. It is not necessary to repeat the modified noun, "car," which the sentence clearly implies.

21. B: This verb is an auxiliary to the verb "to lag" which follows; however, the form "is lag" is obviously incorrect. The sentence must be rephrased to accommodate the present and future tenses the author wishes to express. For example, "growth is lagging – and will continue to lag – the sectors…".

22. A: The semicolon is inappropriate here and should be replaced by a period, thereby dividing the text into separate sentences. Semicolons are used to separate two closely related independent clauses in situations where the second clause begins with a transitional adverb. No such adverb is present here.

23. C: The preceding pronoun "those" refers to the survival rates of infants, and the sentence contrasts the rates for 24-week-old births to those of younger births. Accepted usage requires parallel construction in this case, replacing the preposition "of" with "for" to match the one used earlier in the sentence.

24. C: In general, words that indicate titles are capitalized only when used as a proper name. Thus, "The queen of England is Queen Elizabeth."

25. B: The conjunction "as" is required after the word "resourceful" in order to make the sentence read smoothly. In dual comparisons such as this one, remove the intervening clause to test the sentence: "…he proved to be as resourceful as…"

26. A: Adjectives are words that modify nouns or pronouns. Adverbs modify verbs, adjectives, or other adverbs. The word "good" in this sentence modifies the meaning of the verb "did." It should be replaced by the corresponding adverb: "I did pretty *well* on the math test…"

27. D: There is no error in the sentence. The word "flew" is used correctly as the past tense of "to fly." "Film" may be used as a verb or as a noun. The conjunction "which" is correctly used to introduce a nonessential dependent clause. (Note: if this were an *essential* dependent clause, it would be necessary to use the conjunction "that.")

28. B: The pronoun "that" is used to refer to objects and things other than humans. In this sentence, it is used incorrectly to refer to "woman," and should be replaced by "who."

29. A: Pronouns must be used with the proper case. In this case, the pronoun is the subject of the verb and must be used in the subjective case, "I," and not in the objective case shown. For compound subjects (or objects), test the pronoun by removing the other subject: "me am going" obviously is wrong, whereas "I am going" is correct.

30. C: Subject and verb must agree. the subject of the verb here is Josh Cain and is singular, so the singular form of the verb, "milks" must be used. If the subject were transformed to a plural form, "Josh Cain and three of his hands...," the plural form would be correct.

31. C: *Advice* is a noun, meaning an opinion given to guide activity. The corresponding verb, meaning to give advice, is *advise*. Since Rafael wanted the financial expert to take action, that is, to give advice, the verb form is required.

32. C: The words "principle" and "principal" are often confused. The form used here, *principle*, means a fundamental law or a basic tenet of behavior. The form *principal*, which should be used here, means the amount borrowed on a loan (and may also mean the head of a school).

33. D: This sentence illustrates the correct use of a number of words that are often problematic. The verb "to set" means to put something in a place. It is often confused with "to sit', an intransitive verb meaning to be located or to be seated. "En route" is a French expression meaning "on the way." It frequently is misspelled as "in route." The verb "to lie" is intransitive and means to be in a recumbent position. It is often confused with the transitive verb "to lay," which means to put something down.

34. B: The subject of this sentence is the Cartier watch, which is singular (although it is to be found among many items). Therefore, the singular form of the verb, "is," is required.

35. B: The expression "inside of" is redundant, as is "outside of." It is sufficient to write "inside" or "outside." The clause "he told me" (Choice C), set off by a comma, is an appropriate way to convey an indirect quotation.

36. B: The underlined phrase is the subject of the verb, and the subjective case "I" must be used. For compound subjects (or objects) test the pronoun by removing the other subject: "me would fish" is obviously wrong, whereas "I would fish" is correct. In compound subjects, the first person pronoun is stated last.

37. D: Choice C is grammatically correct, but it is inconsistent with the informal tone of the remainder of the passage. Although "your" is a second person pronoun, it is commonly used to indicate an unspecified third person, as in this case.

38. B: This is a common misspelling. The phrase "used to" is a common, informal auxiliary used in place of "would" to indicate the past progressive. Another acceptable alternative, "we would rummage around," is best avoided here so as not to repeat the word "would" excessively.

39. B: The verb "to be" is implicit here, as "My brother Kenny was younger than *I was*." Thus, the pronoun is the subject of the verb, and the subjective case must be used. Choice A is incorrect because it involves a change of tense. Although Kenny is still younger than his brother, the passage is written in the past tense and, for consistency, this verb should be past tense as well.

40. C: The sentence, as written, is grammatically correct, but repetition of the auxiliary verb "would" renders it stylistically awkward. With Choice C, the auxiliary is implicit in front of the phrase "go down" (parallel construction) but is not actually repeated.

## Mathematics

1. A: In scientific notation, this is 10 raised to the 3rd power, or 1,000. Choice C, the square root of 10,000, equals 100. While the absolute value of Choice D is 1,025, it is a negative number, so that it is not as great as Choice A.

2. C: Add the numbers together, noting that there are two sodas and three magazines: \$4.25 + 2 × \$2.15 + \$1.90 + \$5.25 + 3 × \$1.50 = \$4.25 + \$4.30 + \$1.90 + \$5.25 + \$4.50 = \$20.20.

3. C: Translate the problem into an algebraic equation, and let *x* equal the number of tickets sold and therefore the number of plates of food that must be purchased. Then the desired profit will equal $27{,}000 = 150x - 25x - 1000 - 2500$. That is, the profit will equal the revenues per plate, minus the cost per plate and the fixed costs of the hall and staff. Simplifying this equation, $27{,}000 = x(150 - 25) - 3500$. Solving for *x* yields $x = \frac{30{,}500}{125} = 244$.

4. B: Note that the area of the triangle is one half the area of a rectangle of sides AB and BC. The formula for the area of a triangle reflects this: $Area = \frac{1}{2} base \times height$. Since AB is twice the length of BC, we have BC = 4 cm and the formula yields $Area = \frac{1}{2}(8 \times 4) = 16cm^2$.

5. D: To calculate the average grade, divide the sum of all the grades by the number of tests. This number must equal at least 70. That is, $\frac{Sum}{3} \geq 70$. Solving for the sum shows $Sum \geq 3(70)$, or 210. Since the first two scores, 64 and 80, add up to 144, the third score must be greater or equal to 210 – 144, or 66.

6. B: The least common denominator, or LCD, is equal to the least common multiple (LCM) of the denominators. To find this, factor the denominators completely: 15 = 3 × 5; 21 = 3 × 7; 14 = 2 × 7. The unique factors are 2, 3, 5, and 7. The product 2 × 3 × 5 × 7 = 210 is therefore the LCD. The three fractions are equivalent to $\frac{14}{210}$, $\frac{10}{210}$, and $\frac{15}{210}$.

7. A: The area of a circle is given by the formula $A = \pi r^2$, where *r* is equal to the radius. Since $8\pi = \pi r^2$, it follows that $r^2 = 8$ and that $r = \sqrt{8}$. Since 8 = 2 × 4, and $\sqrt{4} = 2$, it follows that $r = 2\sqrt{2}$.

8. B: All of the equations shown are quadratic functions, which graph as parabolas. Since the parabola shown in the figure has a minimum (that is, it opens upwards), the coefficient of the second-degree term must be positive. (The second degree term is the one that multiplies $x^2$). This rules out Choice A, since the term is negative. The parabola in the figure intercepts the origin of the Cartesian grid, passing through the point (0,0), so the constant term must be zero. This rules out Choices C and D.

9. C: Solve for both the wind speed *w* and the speed of the aircraft *s* by setting up a system of equations. On the eastward leg the wind accelerates the aircraft, so $\frac{2700}{6} = s + w = 450$. Conversely, on the westward leg, $\frac{2700}{6.5} = s - w = 415.4$. Subtracting the second equation from the first yields 2*w* = 34.6, so that *w* = 17.3 mph.

10. D: Determine the average distance run per day. If Andrea runs 6 miles on day 1 and adds two miles per day, she will reach her goal on day 11, since $\frac{26-6}{2} = 10$, and $10 + 1 = 11$. During these 11 days, the average distance she runs is $\frac{26+6}{2} = 16$ miles. So, her total distance is equal to 11 × 16 = 176 miles.

11. C: Let $x$ be the number of pounds of large mushrooms. The price for any quantity is $6.95x$. Two pounds of small mushrooms have a price of 2(5.95). For a quantity of the mixture, price equals $6.75(x + 2)$. This gives the equation $6.95x + 2(5.95) = 6.75(x + 2)$. To solve for $x$, use the distributive property to multiply the term on the right side, and gather the variables on the left: $0.2x = 13.5 - 11.9 = 1.6$, so that $x = \frac{1.6}{0.2} = 8$ pounds.

12. D: If $R$ is the radius, then AB has length $2R$. Segment CB is also a radius and has length $R$. Since AC is tangential to the circle centered at point B, it must be perpendicular to the radius at point C. Therefore, ABC is a right triangle and, from the Pythagorean theorem, $AC^2 + BC^2 = AB^2$. Substituting $R$ and rearranging yields $AC^2 = (2R)^2 - R^2 = 3R^2$. Solve for AC by taking the square root of both sides of this equation, which yields $AC = R\sqrt{3}$.

13. D: An irrational number is one that cannot be expressed as a simple fraction or as a ratio of integers. Since Choice A equals $\frac{17}{10}$, it is rational. Choice B, which equals 4, is also rational. However, Choice D is not, since $\sqrt{12} = \sqrt{3 \times 4} = 2\sqrt{3}$, and $\sqrt{3}$ is non-terminating, non-repeating decimal.

14. B: If $y$ varies inversely as $x$, then $y = \frac{k}{x}$, where $k$ is a constant. Given the initial values, it is possible to determine the constant by solving $k = xy = 4(12) = 48$. Now, if $y = 18$, the inverse relationship is $18 = \frac{48}{x}$. Solving this equation for $x$ yields $x = \frac{48}{18} = \frac{8}{3}$.

15. B: The median of a set is the middle number. First, arrange the set so that its members are in order: { 4, 9, 7, 12, 13, 14, 16, 45 }. For a set with an odd number of members, the median would simply be the centermost numeral. For a set such as this one, with an even number of members, the median is the average of the two centermost numbers. These are 12 and 13, so the median is 12.5.

16. C: Attendance in 2004 decreased from about 12,000 to 10,000 visitors. In 2005 it rebounded to 15,000 visitors, an increase of 5,000. This is the greatest year-to-year increase shown on the chart.

17. D: The odds that the chosen number will match Jenny's at any single digit is 10:1, since there are ten numerals from 0 – 9, each with equal probability of being chosen. The probability that the entire number will match is the product of those probabilities. Since there are five digits, that is 100,000:1.

18. C: First, find the least common denominator (LCD) for the numerator:

$$\frac{2+\frac{4}{y}}{\frac{y+2}{3}}=\frac{\frac{2y}{y}+\frac{4}{y}}{\frac{y+2}{3}}$$

Next, simplify the numerator:

$$\frac{\frac{2y}{y}+\frac{4}{y}}{\frac{y+2}{3}}=\frac{\frac{2y+4}{y}}{\frac{y+2}{3}}$$

Next, rewrite the fraction as the product of the numerator and the reciprocal of the denominator:

$$\frac{\frac{2y+4}{y}}{\frac{y+2}{3}}=\frac{2y+4}{y}\times\frac{3}{y+2}$$

Simplify by factoring:

$$\frac{2y+4}{y}\times\frac{3}{y+2}=\frac{2(y+2)}{y}\times\frac{3}{y+2}=\frac{2\times 3}{y}=\frac{6}{y}$$

19. B: This is an application of the fundamental counting principle, which states that if there are *x* ways to do one thing, *y* ways to do another, and *z* ways to do a third, then there are *xyz* ways of doing all three, if order is important, and $\frac{xyz}{3\times2\times1}$ ways if order is not important. Regina has a choice of nine flavors for her first scoop. Since no flavor can be used twice, she has a choice of 8 remaining flavors for her second scoop. Similarly, she may choose among 7 flavors for the third scoop. Multiplying 7, 8, and 9 yields 504. However, since the order in which she chooses the three flavors is not important, 504 must be divided by the product of 3, 2, and 1 to account for the different orders that are counted using the previous equation. Thus, the total number of combinations is $\frac{9\times8\times7}{3\times2\times1}=84$.

20. C: The triangles are similar because they have the same angles. Congruent triangles have the same angles and are of the same size. In an equilateral triangle, all three sides are the same length. Finally, in an isosceles triangle, two of the three sides are the same length.

21. C: Determine 15% of \$30,000 and subtract it from the original price. Since 15% of \$30,000 is $\frac{15}{100}\times \$30{,}000=\$4{,}500$, this yields \$30,000 – \$4,500 = \$25,500.

22. B: The first ten cuts will remove ten 1-ft pieces and leave the last two feet. An eleventh cut then cuts this last piece in half creating the final two 1-ft pieces.

23. D: Let *x* be the number in question. From the problem description, write the equation 14 + 2*x* = 8. Isolating the variable on one side of the equal sign yields $2x=8-14=-6$. Solving this equation for *x* yields $x=-\frac{6}{2}=-3$.

24. B: Imagine a line drawn from C to O. The angle COB is two times the measure of angle CAB, and is therefore equal to 40°. This can be calculated in two steps. Setting the sum of the angles in isosceles triangle ACO to 180°, one can determine that angle COA is 140°. Since COA and COB are supplementary, angle COB must equal 40°. Therefore angle COB subtends an arc segment equal to $\frac{40}{360}\times 720=80$ m.

25. A: At the point of intersection, the functions must be equal for the same value of *x*. To find this point, set the functions equal to one another and solve for *x*. The equality is expressed by $-2x + 6 = 4x + 3$. Solve for *x* by isolating the variable-containing terms on one side of the equal sign. This yields $6x = 3$, or $x = 0.5$. To find the corresponding value of *y*, substitute this *x*-value into either of the original equations. For example, $y = 4x + 3 = 4\left(\frac{1}{2}\right) + 3 = 2 + 3 = 5$. The point of intersection is (0.5, 5).

26. B: Since the seventh is a Monday, it follows that the 9th, two days later, will be a Wednesday. Subsequent Wednesdays will fall on 7 days, and multiples of 7 days, after the 9th, that is, 9 + *n*(7). Since 9 + 14 = 23, B is correct. None of the other choices equals 9 plus a multiple of 7. April 31st would be a correct answer also if April had 31 days, rather than 30.

27. D: Let Ken's rate of painting be the normal rate. That is, Ken gets 1 man-hour of painting done in an hour. Then the room requires 6 man-hours to be painted completely. Bob paints at a rate of $\frac{6}{4} = 1.5$ man-hours of work per hour, since he can paint the room in 4 hours. If they work together, the overall rate of work will be 1 + 1.5 = 2.5 man-hours per hour, and the total amount of time required to paint the room will be $\frac{6}{2.5} = 2.4$ hours. Since 0.4 hours = 24 minutes, this is 2 hours and 24 minutes.

28. B: Since the square is circumscribed, its side is twice the length of the radius, or 2*r*, and its area is $4r^2$. The area of the circle is given by $\pi r^2$. The shaded area is the difference between these two, or $4r^2 - \pi r^2 = (4 - \pi)r^2$.

29. C: Each term $T_n$ in the sequence is equal to the previous term plus the quantity 2(*n* – 1). For example, the third term equals 3 + 2(3 - 1) = 3 + 4 = 7. It follows that the 6th term will equal 21 + 2(6 – 1) = 21 + 10 = 31.

30. A: Since the interest rate is 4%, the amount paid after one year is *I* = 0.04 × *P*, where *P* is the amount of the original investment. Since *I* = $200, solving for *P* yields $P = \frac{\$200}{0.04} = \$5000$.

31. B: The slope of a straight line is the rate of change of the dependent variable (the *y* variable) with respect to the independent variable (the *x* variable). It often is described as the ratio of the *rise*, or change in *y*, to the *run*, or change in *x*. In this case, the *y* value increases from 2 to 8 (6 units) for a change in the *x* value from -1 to 3 (4 units). As a result, the slope is equal to the ratio $\frac{3}{2}$.

32. A: The pentagon may be considered the sum of a rectangle and a right triangle.

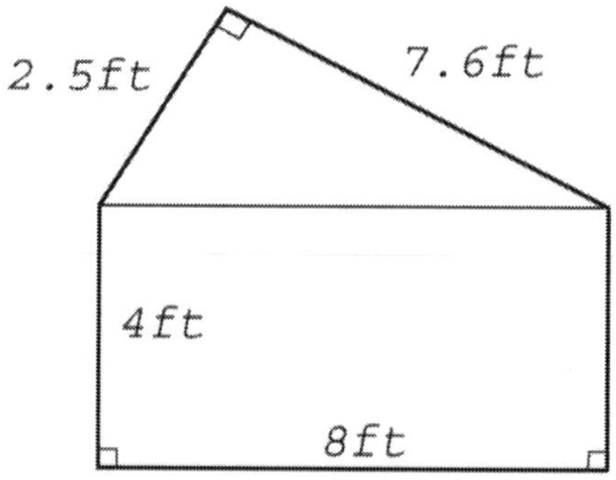


The area of a triangle is given by $A_T = \frac{1}{2}bh$, where *b* is the base and *h* the height. For a right triangle, one of the orthogonal sides may be taken as the height if the other is taken as the base. Thus, $A_T = \frac{1}{2}(7.6)(2.5) = 9.5\ ft^2$. The area of the rectangle is the product of its sides, $A_R = wl = 8 \times 4 = 32\ ft^2$. The area of the pentagon is the sum of these, $A_P = 32 + 9.5 = 41.5\ ft^2$.

33. B: The area of the oil slick is $A = \frac{V}{t}$, where *V* is the volume of oil and *t* is the thickness of the slick. Convert all units to meters for the calculation. This gives $A = \frac{200 \times 0.001}{10^{-6}} = \frac{0.2}{10^{-6}} = 2 \times 10^5$ m$^2$. To convert the answer to km$^2$, note that 1 km = $10^3$ meters, so that 1 km$^2$ = $10^3 \times 10^3 = 10^6$ m$^2$. The area of the slick is equal to $\frac{2 \times 10^5}{10^6} = 0.2$ km$^2$.

34. D: Since *a* = 0.01, the value of $\frac{1}{a}$ can be written as 100. Since $\frac{1}{a^2}$ is the same as $\left(\frac{1}{a}\right)^2$, the answer can be calculated as $\frac{1}{a^2} = 100^2 = 10{,}000$.

35. B: The equation can be factored to yield $(x - 3)^2 = 0$. This equation will be correct only if the expression within the parentheses equals zero. For *x* – 3 = 0 to be correct, we must have *x* = 3.

36. D: The function $f(x) = x^{-2}$ is equivalent to $f(x) = \frac{1}{x^2}$. It is always positive and is defined over the domain of all real numbers except *x* = 0. It approaches zero as *x* approaches positive or negative infinity, and it approaches infinity as *x* approaches zero. Choice A approaches infinity as *x* approaches infinity. Choice B is not defined for negative values of *x*. Choice C is negative for negative values of *x*.

37. C: Isolate the variable on one side of the equal sign by adding 2 to both sides of the equation. This yields $\sqrt{x} = 8 + 2 = 10$. Now, solve the equation by squaring both sides: $x = 10^2 = 100$.

38. A: Let *x* represent the required number of cups of flour and set up the proportion $\frac{x}{8} = \frac{24}{50}$. Solving this proportion for *x* yields $x = \frac{8(24)}{50} = \frac{192}{50} = 3.84$ cups of flour.

39. B: The expression $(11^x)^y$ is equivalent to $11^{xy}$, and 121 equals $11^2$. Therefore, we have $11^{xy} = 11^2$. If this equation is true, then $xy = 2$. Since *x* and *y* are both positive integers, their product can only be 2 if one of them equals 2 and the other equals 1. Their arithmetic mean then must be $\frac{2+1}{2} = \frac{3}{2} = 1.5$.

40. A: The area of the shaded region must be equal to the area of the square minus the areas of the two triangular areas ΔACD and ΔBEF. The area of a triangle is given by $A = \frac{1}{2}bh$, where *b* is the base and *h* is the height. Since ΔACD and ΔBEF are both right triangles, one of the orthogonal sides is the base and the other is the height. Further, since AE = EB and BF = FC, it follows that EB = BF = 5, this being one half the side AB. Thus, $A_{ADC} = \frac{1}{2}(10 \times 10) = 50$, and $A_{BEF} = \frac{1}{2}(5 \times 5) = 12.5$. The area of the square is the product of its two sides, or 10 x 10 = 100. Therefore, for the shaded region, *A* = 100 – 50 – 12.5 = 37.5.

41. C: Let *k* be the largest integer. Since they are consecutive and they add up to 36, we have the equation $+(k-1)+(k-2)=36$. Solving for *k*, we have $3k-3=36$, or $3k=39$, so $k=13$. The consecutive integers adding up to 36 are 11, 12, and 13.

42. B: The length of the paper is 11 inches. Subtracting the two margins, the length of the printed picture will be $11 - 1\frac{1}{2} - 1\frac{1}{2} = 8$ inches. Similarly, the width will be $8\frac{1}{2} - 1\frac{1}{2} - 1\frac{1}{2} = 5\frac{1}{2}$ inches. The area of the picture is the product of length and width, or $A = 8 \times 5.5 = 44$ square inches.

43. D: In the composite function $f(g(x))$, function $g(x)$ becomes the variable in function $f(x)$. Since $g(x) = 2x^2$, use this value in place of *x* in the equation for $f(x)$. $f(g(x)) = 3(2x^2) + 4 = 6x^2 + 4$

44. A: Let $L_1$ and $W_1$ be the length and width of rectangle I, and $L_2$ and $W_2$ the length and width of rectangle II. Then $L_1 = 1.5L_2$ and $W_1 = \frac{W_2}{1.5}$. The area of rectangle II is simply the product $L_2W_2$. The area of rectangle I is $L_1W_1 = 1.5L_2 \times \frac{W_2}{1.5} = L_2W_2$. That is, the two areas are the same.

45. C: The ratio $\frac{q}{r}$ can be a positive integer only if $q \geq r$, and if the division $\frac{q}{r}$ yields a whole number. The only value of set *r* that is less than or equal to any of the values in set *q* is the value 2, and there is 1 chance in 4 (25%) that it will be selected. If 2 is selected from set *r*, then any value selected from set *q* will yield a positive integer in the ratio $\frac{q}{r}$ (100%). Thus, the probability that $\frac{q}{r}$ is an integer is 25% x 100% = 25%.

53023824R00086

Made in the USA
Lexington, KY
18 June 2016